Exploring Scotland's Historic Landscapes

IAN and KATHLEEN WHYTE

Department of Geography
University of Lancaster

Drawings by

MOLLY HUTCHINGS

JOHN DONALD PUBLISHERS LTD
EDINBURGH

For James Whyte, 1911–1986
and Rebecca Mary Whyte, 1986–

ISBN 0 85976 166 5

Exclusive distribution in the United States of America and Canada by
Humanities Press Inc., Atlantic Highlands,
NJ 07716, USA.

Phototypeset by Print Origination, Merseyside
Printed in Great Britain by Bell & Bain Ltd., Glasgow

Contents

Introduction

The British landscape is one of the most varied in the world, incorporating a wide range of scenery. It has been utilised by man for numerous purposes from the beginnings of prehistory until the present day. Indeed, hardly any part of Britain is untouched by the influence of man, and even in the remotest areas you can find evidence of his activities. In many respects Scotland contains the most varied physical landscape of any part of Britain with remote, rugged mountains counterbalanced by fertile arable lowlands. The Scottish landscape is also rich in evidence of past human activities.

The Scottish Landscape

It is the richness and variety of the Scottish landscape which has caused us to write this book. We believe that with a little understanding of how landscapes have developed and a little time to look at them, tremendous pleasure can be derived from a walk or drive whether in the town or the countryside. On a day-to-day basis most of us travel around our home area without stopping to think about the features of its landscapes and how they came to be the way they are. In this book we have tried to encourage people to be more aware of the landscapes around them and of the elements of which they are composed. Although we focus on Scotland, a good deal of what we mention will have more general applicability within the British Isles. We hope that this book will help to encourage its readers to gain more pleasure from the Scottish landscape and to look more closely at other areas to which they may travel.

This book is not concerned with the development of Scotland's physical environment. It concentrates on how the natural landscape has been altered by man over the last few thousand years. Landscape history has only emerged as a distinct subject within the last 30 years or so, and most of the pioneer work has been done in England. Many aspects of the development of Scottish landscapes are poorly understood. There is considerable scope for enthusiastic people with observant eyes and questioning minds to discover many new things about the areas in which they live or which they visit on holiday.

Landscape Trails

This book consists of 18 trails which include a range of the landscape features which we feel to be important for understanding how the Scottish landscape has developed. Within such a limited space it is impossible to cover every part of Scotland or to include examples of every type of feature which you may come across. Inevitably, we have had to be selective. We have tried to emphasise those features which are more likely to be missed or misunderstood at the expense of more familiar elements: in our trail through the Old Town of Edinburgh, for example, we have omitted the big tourist attractions of the Castle and Holyrood Palace, which are impossible to miss and have been well written up elsewhere, in order to concentrate on the less obvious buildings which are nevertheless important in understanding how the town developed.

Each trail relates to a particular type of landscape feature or period. However, no trail is devoted exclusively to a single theme. Landscapes are not like that: they are, to use an oft-quoted expression, like a palimpsest, a parchment which has been written on, partially erased and re-used several times. All trails contain features from a variety of periods, and sometimes the prehistoric and the modern are juxtaposed. Some features which occur widely in Scotland and are more important for understanding the evolution of the present landscape appear in more than one trail: tower houses and planned estate villages for example. To avoid repetition we have described the detailed context of a particular feature only once and have cross-referenced from one trail to another where possible. We have tried to incorporate a reasonable geographical spread of trails, although we have concentrated more of them in areas which are more popular with tourists and more accessible. In addition, we have varied the length of the trails and the amount of energy which will be needed to complete them. Most of the trails are organised for people using cars but many include optional short walks.

We have tried to include in every trail some features which are well-known and impressive. Many places of this sort are open to

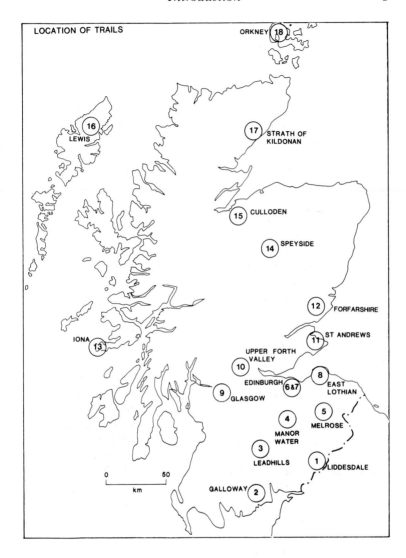

LOCATION OF TRAILS

ORKNEY (18)

(16) LEWIS

(17) STRATH OF KILDONAN

(15) CULLODEN

(14) SPEYSIDE

(12) FORFARSHIRE

IONA (13)

(11) ST ANDREWS

UPPER FORTH VALLEY
(10)

(8)

EDINBURGH (6&7)

(9) GLASGOW

EAST LOTHIAN

(5) MELROSE

(4) MANOR WATER

(3) LEADHILLS

(1) LIDDESDALE

0   50
km

GALLOWAY (2)

the public. In such cases we have attempted to provide a more general context within which you can interpret the details of particular sites. Where possible, we recommend that you also use the appropriate guidebooks to such sites: we have not tried to compete with them, but they are necessarily concerned with the details of the specific places they describe and do not always discuss them in a broader setting. We have also included features which are smaller, less obvious and less spectacular. These can often provide as much interest to someone who is keen to know how the landscape developed as the big tourist attractions and are more likely to be missed by a visitor who does not know the area. Some of the features are enigmatic and can be interpreted in different ways, as remains in the landscape do not in themselves always provide enough clues to their origin without supporting evidence from excavation or documentary sources.

We hope that even those who cannot cover the trails on the ground will enjoy reading them and studying the illustrations. As a general rule we recommend that you read through each trail before actually embarking upon it, so that you have an idea of what you are going to see. The appropriate sections can then be read at the stopping points.

Some General Points About Landscapes

As you travel round the countryside, whether following one of the trails or just generally, you might like to think about the following points in relation to the landscapes which you see:

1. How much of the character of the area is derived from the physical landscape; from the solid rocks or the superficial surface deposits? Is it hilly or flat? Are there interesting rock formations or unusual small-scale landforms?

2. To what extent does the appearance of the area reflect the activities of man? Does the shape of the land appear to have been altered; for example by drainage, reclamation or construction?

3. How many different periods can you find landscape evidence for? Dates on houses, bridges etc may help; other features such as ridge and furrow cultivation traces in fields, earthworks and prehistoric remains will be harder to pin down chronologically.

4. In what ways does the physical environment appear to have influenced man's activities; for example, lines of communication, the location of settlements and the type of land use?

Don't worry if you can't find many answers to start with. Landscapes are like crossword puzzles: the more time you spend studying them, the better you become at interpreting them. As you read through the trails and travel round, your knowledge will increase. Remember too that there are many elements in the landscape that no-one fully understands. Perhaps you will be the first to notice a particular feature, or perhaps your guess about the purpose of something will be the right one. Landscapes are often made more exciting by the presence of mysterious elements—a stone circle or an ancient cross—the real purpose of which is not known.

Some Practical Matters

Although a sketch map accompanies each trail, these have been designed to be used in conjunction with Ordnance Survey maps, especially the Landranger series at a scale of 1:50,000 (2cm = 1km) and the Pathfinder series at 1:25,000 (4cm = 1km). These are obtainable from good bookshops. The former series is suitable for exploring an area by car and is sufficiently detailed to be useful for walking. The latter series is better suited to exploring a smaller area in detail, particularly on foot, as it shows more antiquities and other landscape features such as field boundaries. Ordnance Survey maps are overlaid with the National Grid of 1 kilometre squares which allows you to pinpoint any spot precisely. We have given six-figure National Grid references to most of the places mentioned in the text to help you locate them. If you are not sure how to identify a place using this system, there are instructions on the Ordnance Survey maps.

The only way to really study historic landscapes is on foot, but most people who are exploring the Scottish countryside do so by car. Apart from the town trails, which are walks, all routes in this book are designed on the assumption that you are using a car, though most of them are short enough to be done easily in a day by bicycle. Many interesting landscape features are situated in remote and inaccessible locations but we appreciate that many families touring Scotland include young children or elderly people. Most of the features we have described are easily accessible from a metalled road or track, and we have only included a limited number of features which require longer walks to reach. The aim of each trail is to show you a selection of interesting things within a limited area in an itinerary which can be done comfortably in a day. If you do use Ordnance Survey maps, these will show you plenty of additional places to visit if you are spending some time in an area.

Where a trail involves a walk, we have made it clear how much distance and effort is involved. None of the trails requires you to walk over really rugged country, but for visiting many of the sites, even ones close to a road, we recommend that you wear stout waterproof footwear: walking boots or wellingtons for instance. Bearing in mind that the Scottish climate can be severe even at low levels, warm clothing and waterproofs, including waterproof trousers, are also essential.

A description of a particular feature in this book does not guarantee right of access. Many of the places which we describe are specifically open to the public: we have not given opening times because these can be altered without warning—you should check these locally. Other places are mostly adjacent to public roads. Where there is any doubt about access, you should ask permission before going off a public road. If you enter someone's land without permission, they are legally entitled to ask you to leave and you are required to comply. Remember the Country Code and, if you are going on to moorland, avoid the grouse-shooting season from August 12th to December 10th.

We would like to thank Claire Jarvis, of the Department of Geography, University of Lancaster, for drawing the maps.

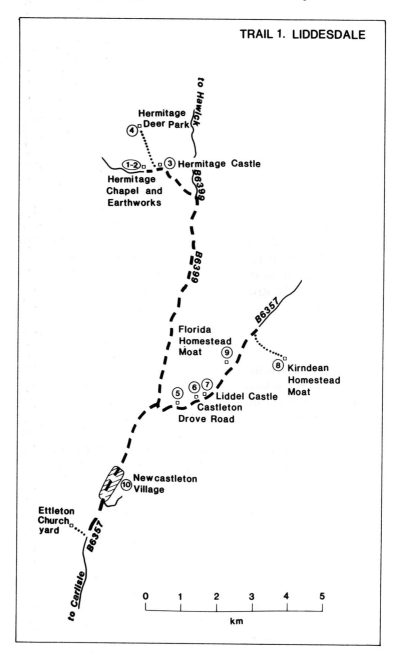

TRAIL 1. LIDDESDALE

ONE

Liddesdale: A Border Landscape

Ordnance Survey 1:50,000 sheet 79; 1:25,000 sheets NY 48, 49, 58, 59.

This trail involves a drive of about 20km with some optional walks.

Introduction

The line of the border between England and Scotland became fixed in more or less its present position in 1222 and did not alter significantly thereafter, though its course in one or two small areas was still in dispute in the 16th century. If you walk the line of the Border you will be struck by the lack of any landscape features which delineate it apart from modern fences. Often more striking are features such as old roads and trackways which cross the Border, linking the valleys on either side. This emphasises both that the Border was difficult to guard and patrol in the past and easy to penetrate, whether by smugglers in times of peace or raiders in times of war. The landscapes on either side of the Border are very similar, whether you are comparing the Berwickshire Merse with the Northumbrian plain or the hills at the head of Liddesdale with the Bewcastle Fells. The physical features are similar, and the differences in the human landscapes are often small in scale, stressing the links which existed between the peoples on either side of the Border in the past despite differences in nationality.

Yet in past centuries this was an area accustomed not only to periodic war but also to endemic small-scale raiding. The Borders were always the first area to be devastated by invading armies, but their inhabitants were liable to continual harassment even in times of so-called peace. In the period between the Wars of Independence in the 14th century and the Union of the Crowns in 1603 raiding became virtually a way of life on both sides of the Border, an occupation which fitted in quite conveniently with the slack periods of the agricultural year. Border warfare of this kind was not just a simple case of Scots versus English. The Border families

9

retained an almost clan-like structure down to the 16th century, and many families had branches on both sides of the frontier. There was often a good deal of co-operation across the Border and much internal feuding on either side, particularly in Scotland. Ties and allegiances formed a complex web which often ignored nationality. It was advantageous to the central governments of both countries to have a reserve of armed and trained inhabitants on the Border to counter any threats: the borderers produced the best light cavalry, but the price of this was continual lawlessness. The Scottish crown's control over its Border areas was intermittent and sometimes totally ineffective even as late as the 16th century. The mainly pastoral economy of much of the area meant that wealth, in the form of livestock, was in a highly mobile form, thus encouraging cattle raiding. It was only after James VI ascended the throne of England that an international problem was converted into a purely internal one, allowing co-ordinated measures to be taken on each side of the Border to stamp out raiding.

Of all the Border valleys, Liddesdale was the closest to England and the most remote from Edinburgh, the most vulnerable to attack but the best placed for raiding. The Border ballads, traditional songs which were collected and published by Sir Walter Scott and other antiquarians in the 18th and 19th centuries, have preserved a romantic image of border life in the 16th century, but in reality Liddesdale was a notorious den of thieves whose close links with many English families rendered their loyalty to the Scottish crown suspect. The visible expressions of this in the landscape were the numerous tower houses of the smaller landowners and the larger castles of the nobility. This trail looks at some of these and also other features relating to settlement in this area over the centuries.

1. Hermitage Chapel (493959)

The name 'Hermitage' derives from a monk of Kelso Abbey who settled as a hermit in this remote spot sometime in the 12th century. By about 1180 a small chapel had been built here which was later served by two monks from Kelso. Not surprisingly it became the chapel for the nearby castle. Its foundations are still visible by the stream some 400m upstream of Hermitage Castle, enclosed within a small cemetery. The chapel is a simple rectangular structure which may have been vaulted and is later than the one mentioned in 1180; some of its architectural features suggest a 14th-century date. Between the river and the boundary of the burial ground there is a green mound. Tradition, and the Ordnance Survey, mark this as the grave of the Cout (colt) of Kielder—in reality Sir Richard Knout, Sheriff of Northumberland in the later 13th century. He was an adversary of Lord Soulis and was supposedly killed in a fight at this spot. When his attackers found that they could not pierce his armour they drove him into the river and held him under with their lances until he drowned.

2. Hermitage Chapel; Earthworks (493959)

The chapel is surrounded by a series of earthworks whose interpretation provides some problems. The burial ground overlies and is enclosed by a squarish earthwork of earlier date. It consists of a bank on all four sides with an outer ditch on three sides, the fourth being protected by the stream. Beyond the ditch is a further bank with a second ditch outside it on the northern and western sides. Further upstream there is a larger rectangular enclosure marked by a bank on three sides with the river forming the fourth. There are some indistinct mounds inside it which may be the foundations of buildings. Beyond the two sets of earthworks, a hollowed roadway bounded by parallel banks approaches the chapel and then turns west along the outside of the enclosures to cross the stream further upstream.

What were these earthworks designed for? Without excavation it is impossible to be certain, but there are various possibilities. One is that this was the original Hermitage Castle, first mentioned in 1244. On this interpretation the squarish earthwork would have been some kind of motte and the rectangular enclosure the remains of the bailey. However, compared to other earth and timber castles of comparable importance, such as the Mote of Urr (Trail 2), the defences here are insubstantial and unimpressive. A second possibility would explain the earthworks as a homestead moat, ditches and banks surrounding a fairly modest hall or farmstead rather than a major castle, dating perhaps from the 14th century. You will see a clearer, less ambiguous example of a homestead moat later in this trail.

3. Hermitage Castle (497961)

Hermitage is one of the best-preserved medieval castles in Scotland and probably one of the most distinctive in appearance. Its stark, uncompromising outline, together with its remote setting, combine to give it a powerful atmosphere of menace, which is best appreciated on a dull winter's day. It is no surprise to learn that one of its owners, Lord Soulis, was reputed to have been a warlock and was supposedly boiled in oil by his enemies!

Hermitage Castle

At first sight the castle does not appear to stand in a particularly good defensive position. The river protects it on one side, however, and two small tributaries on the others create areas of marshy ground which would have made a close approach difficult. The castle stands within earthworks which may well be older but which were altered, probably in the 16th century, to accommodate artillery. A broad ditch surrounds the castle on three sides. To the north there is a rectangular courtyard enclosed by a rampart and ditch. To the west of the castle an angular earthwork seems to have been a ravelin, a projecting bastion for cannon, while at the north-east corner of the inner enclosure there are signs of another gun platform.

There was a castle on this site in the 13th century, the earliest occupiers being the de Soulis family. During the Wars of Independence and thereafter the castle changed hands between Scottish and English forces several times. It was then held by the Earls of Douglas and later the Earls of Bothwell. In 1540 the castle was taken into crown control as part of the Lordship of Liddesdale. It was probably at this time that the artillery fortifications around the castle were made and the gun loops inserted in the castle walls. The Earls of Bothwell still had the use of Hermitage, though, and it was here that Mary Queen of Scots visited Bothwell in 1566 after he had been wounded while trying to arrest someone in his capacity as Warden of the Scottish Middle March. For much of the 16th century Hermitage was garrisoned under the direction of an officer known as the Keeper of Liddesdale. The Scottish and English Borders were each divided into three Marches which were under the control of wardens appointed by their respective monarchs. Liddesdale, falling within the Middle March but more closely linked geographically with the West March, was so troublesome that this special officer was appointed to keep an eye on its inhabitants. The castle later passed into the hands of the Scotts of Buccleuch; one of the Dukes of Buccleuch restored it extensively in the early 19th century.

The earliest record of a castle at Hermitage is in the 13th century. Nothing remains of this except, possibly, the remodelled earthworks. The earliest part of the present castle is right at the core, a rectangular block with two wings and a central court. The plan is very much an English one resembling many contemporary fortified manor houses south of the Border, and it is likely that it was built during the mid-14th century when it was in the hands of the Dacre family. This building seems to have been severely damaged during the Border wars of Richard II. In the later 14th century the Douglases built a rectangular tower house around the surviving stonework with a short wing at the south-west corner. Towards the end of the 14th century the tower was massively extended in a novel way by the addition of large towers at three of the corners of the original castle, and a fourth, particularly huge one at the south-west corner.

As at Threave (Trail 2) the wall head of the castle was pierced with holes for timbers which supported a wooden gallery or hoarding which projected from the walls as an extra defence. This was later abandoned in favour of a stone parapet. On two sides of the castle, instead of running the parapet into the recesses between the towers, a novel idea has been used. This was to bridge the gaps between the towers by arches at the tops of the walls. The masonery of the arches carried the parapet across the gaps between the towers. These arches, and the recesses behind them, form the most distinctive feature of the castle. The parapet at the top of the walls, and the crow-stepped gables on the eastern tower are 19th-century restorations which give the castle a misleading air of homogeneity in its design.

The next site involves an optional walk of about 2km. If you do not wish to do the walk continue the trail at No. 5.

4. Hermitage Deer Park (494969)

The 1:25,000 Ordnance Survey map has the slopes of Hermitage Hill, to the north of the castle, marked with the words 'deer park'. Hunting was a major pastime for medieval monarchs and landowners who reserved large areas of woodland and upland country solely for this activity. In these hunting forests settlement and cultivation were generally forbidden and even the grazing of livestock was restricted to preserve the game. At one time large areas of Scotland were reserved as royal hunting forests or as game preserves for private landowners. The term 'forest' was a legal one and, like the 19th-century deer forests of the Highlands, did not necessarily imply that the land was wooded. As population grew and the margins of settlement expanded during the medieval period, there was growing pressure to open up these forests to colonists. Nevertheless, some of them survived until quite a late date; one of the last, Ettrick Forest, covering much of the sheriffdom of Selkirk, was only granted out to settlers during the 16th century. As the hunting forests were progressively diminished it became necessary to construct special deer parks in which the game could be protected. These were small in comparison with the forests but could nevertheless cover quite large areas. The one at Hermitage was of this kind. Deer parks were usually enclosed by a substantial boundary, sometimes a ditch and paling, in other cases a stone wall. Occasionally traces of these survive into the modern landscape. If you feel like some exercise after visiting the castle, a climb of about 130m up Hermitage Hill (about 20-30 minutes) will, apart from opening up a fine view of the valley and the castle below, bring you to a stone dyke crossing the hillside from east to west at a height of about 350m between 486973 and 495972, a distance of over 1km. This wall, which is known as the White Dyke from the limestone blocks of which it is made, formed the boundary of the deer park which was attached to the castle. Parts of it are nearly 2m high and 1.5m thick, but in other places the stones have been tumbled into a rough heap. Where the wall is intact you can see that it is very crudely made of large stones. This is a characteristic of early boundary walls, differentiating them from the more carefully made and narrower stone walls of the 18th and 19th centuries.

5. Castleton: A Main Drove Road (499896)

In this area you can find many traces of old roads. They are especially noticeable where they climb out of the valleys on to the ridges, forming slanting terraces along the hillsides. Some of these roads were purely local, often being used to bring down peat to farmsteads in the valleys. Other roads were main through routes carrying traffic from one dale to another and across the Border. Roads like these were worn rather than constructed. They often followed the ridges where the going was drier and easier: in locations like these they are often faint and difficult to follow today because traffic could spread out over a wide area leaving comparatively little trace on the ground. Such roads become more conspicuous where they were forced to narrow in to negotiate some obstacle like a steep hillside or the crossing of a stream. In such situations the concentration of traffic often produced series of hollow ways which can still be seen today. From the late 17th century the trade in livestock, especially cattle, from Scotland to England became very important. A large proportion of the cattle came from the Highlands. They were sold to English buyers at the great cattle trysts of Crieff and Falkirk and were then driven south to England, many of them as far as London. The main drove road from Falkirk came down the Hermitage Water and across Nine Stane Rig to reach the Liddel Water near Castleton. On the north side of the road at 499896, immediately past a cottage with a plantation of young firs behind, you can see a wide gap bounded by fences: this is the line of the drove road. Drove roads were often fenced in to prevent the cattle from straying on to private grazing and arable land. Opposite this, on the south bank of the Liddel, you can see a number of hollow ways climbing up from the river, marking where the drove road crossed the stream.

6. Castleton (509898)

The large parish of Castleton takes its name from the settlement which grew up adjacent to Liddel Castle (see below), the castle-toun. A major fortress like Liddel Castle was a natural focus for settlement and Castleton is a common Scottish place name. As with Urr and Buittle (Trail 2), the early importance of this settlement may have waned with the abandonment of the castle.

Castleton cross

Now only a single farm is left. Nothing remains even of the medieval parish church which once stood here, but while abandoned churches were frequently robbed of their stone, their burial grounds were often more persistent landscape features, and the one for Castleton survives at 509898. At 511898, in a muddy field a short way off the road, there is an old base for a stone cross (the shaft is a modern one). In 1672 the Duke of Buccleuch obtained permission from the Scottish Parliament to hold a weekly market and three annual fairs at Castleton, and the cross may mark the site used for these activities. Around the cross you can see the remains of old boundaries, some of them turf (feal) dykes, which seem to pre-date the modern ones. In the later 18th century the main focus of settlement within the parish became the new estate village planned by the Duke of Buccleuch (see below). Without great originality it was named Newcastleton.

7. Liddel Castle (510900)

Unlike Hermitage, which is unusually well preserved, only the earthworks remain of this earlier but equally important site. Even so, these are impressive enough. The castle stands on a terrace with an unexpectedly steep bluff falling to the River Liddel. On the northern and eastern sides the ground drops into a tributary valley. The more open south side has been defended by two massive ditches with a rampart between them. The entrance to the castle seems to have been on the west side, right above the slope falling to the river. There are no surviving buildings. The castle was probably built as the centre or 'caput' of an estate granted to an Anglo-Norman incomer, Ranulph de Soules, who came from David I's English lands in Northamptonshire. The castle seems to have gone out of use by the 14th century, being replaced by the earliest castle at Hermitage as the main fortress of the de Soulis family. On the far side of the Liddel Water the fields sloping down to the valley floor have good examples of ridge and furrow ploughing (Trail 5).

The next site requires an uphill walk of just over 1.5km across open moorland and will take about 30 minutes to reach, starting from a track on the east side of the road near Florida farm (519908). If you do not wish to do this walk, continue the trail at No. 9.

8. Kirndean: Homestead Moat (532909)

On the hillside above Kirndean there is a small, square earthwork about 30m across inside. It consists of a bank up to 5m wide and 0.5m high with signs of an entrance on the west side. This plan is typical of a type of site known as a homestead moat or moated site. They are very common in parts of England where several thousand are known. They occur in Ireland too and are also known from southern Scotland, although they have yet to be studied in detail. The earthworks, which would presumably have been topped by a palisade, normally surrounded a large farmstead or manor house, providing a simple yet effective defence against small parties of raiders or wild animals, particularly if the moat was filled with water. In England they are associated with the late medieval colonisation of thinly-settled woodland areas and are thought to date from the 14th and 15th centuries. In Scotland, if their date is comparable, they may reflect a form of defence used by smaller landowners before tower houses became general. You will see that the area around the moat has been cultivated—these traces of ridge and furrow ploughing are later than the moat and may well date from the Napoleonic Wars when much marginal land was ploughed up under the stimulus of high cereal prices (Trail 5).

9. Florida: Homestead Moat (517908)

If you do not wish to walk up to the moat above Kirndean, a less well-preserved but more accessible one is visible beside the Liddel Water north of the farm of Florida at 517908. Half of the square moat has been eroded away by the river, but the remainder of the site is very similar to the one above Kirndean.

10. Newcastleton (4887)

Newcastleton is an example of a planned estate village (Trail 2), the largest and most ambitious on the Scottish Borders. It was established by the third Duke of Buccleuch in 1793 as a weaving centre. Its plan has a main street with a central square and two smaller ones at either end. A minor street runs along the river roughly parallel to the main street with cross streets between. As with most other Scottish planned villages, the cottages are mainly

Newcastleton: planned estate village

single storey, designed in this case for weavers and having large front
windows providing light for the looms. The wide main street gives
Newcastleton an air of spaciousness, but the way in which the
buildings give right on to the pavement without any front gardens
makes the atmosphere of the village rather dour. This layout is
typical of Scottish estate villages and was often resorted to because
landowners feared that if the cottagers (who were often smallholders as well) had any space in front of their homes they would use it
as a site for their dunghills, ruining the appearance of the community. Because of the presence of the river on one side of the village
and steeply rising ground on the other the rectangular plots of land
which were granted to settlers in the new community were laid out
down the valley to the south of the village, and on the slopes there
you can see the remains of the pattern of strip holdings.

11. Ettleton Churchyard and Millholm Cross (472863 & 476861)

*About 1km south of Newcastleton on the main road you will see a
signpost on your right pointing up a steep, metalled road to*

Ettleton Churchyard. Although the track is narrow, there is plenty of parking at the churchyard which stands on a shelf above the valley floor. The view from the churchyard over Liddesdale is a fine one. As was the case with Castleton, there are now no traces of the old church of Ettleton: only the burial ground, which is still in use, remains. Old Scottish churchyards can tell you a good deal about the character of the local community in the past (Trail 3). Although Ettleton does not have some of the impressively carved 17th and early 18th-century tombstones which some Scottish churchyards have, you will nevertheless find some attractive sculptured stones, especially in the lower part. In the centre of the churchyard, within a railed-off enclosure, are fragments of older grave slabs and a cross shaft dating from the 13th and 14th

Tombstone, Ettleton churchyard

centuries: although the stones are weathered, can you make out any of the motifs?

In the corner of a field at the junction of the main road and the track to the churchyard stands the Millholm Cross. There is just room to park a car at the bottom of the track; you can reach the cross through a small gate in the field. Crosses were erected for a variety of purposes in the past: as the symbolic centre of a church-yard or monastery, as boundary and route markers, as the symbol of market rights (see above), and also to commemorate individuals. Little is known about Millholm Cross except that it is thought to commemorate one of the lairds of Mangerton: the remains of Mangerton Tower stand beside the old railway line a short distance to the east. The cross stands nearly 3m high and has a modern top. The shaft bears an incised sword as well as two sets of initials.

Mangerton Tower stands at 480854 and can be reached by walking along the old railway line. The Ordnance Survey marks the sites of at least 20 tower houses in Castleton parish, highlight-ing the density of small fortified houses in this former frontier zone. In view of this it may seem surprising that there are no good surviving examples of tower houses in the area. This is a reflection of the damage done by English raids in the 16th century and also of the usefulness of the towers as sources of stone for the building of later farmsteads. It is worth remembering that these smaller towers (whose general features are described in Trail 10) were the homes of smaller landowners who were primarily farmers when they were not engaged in raiding. The sites of many of the towers have continued in use as farms to the present day. Only the lowest storey of Mangerton Tower remains to show that it was a simple rectan-gular structure. It belonged to a branch of the Armstrong family, one of the most notorious groups of thieves and raiders on the Border, and was burnt at least twice during the 16th century before its final destruction in 1601 on the eve of the union of the Scottish and English crowns.

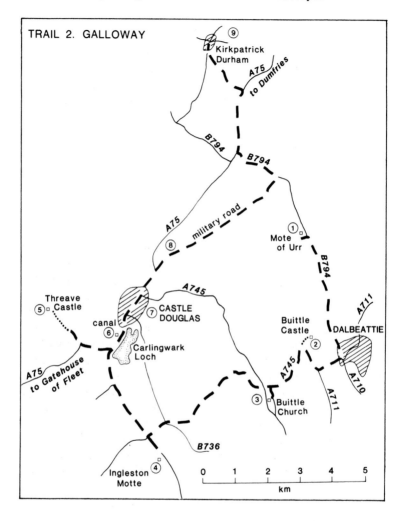

TWO

Galloway: Norman Castles and the Frontiers of Feudal Settlement

Ordnance Survey 1:50,000 sheet 84: 1:25,000 sheets NX 75, 76, 77, 85, 86.

This trail involves a drive of about 45km with some short walks.

Introduction

In other trails we mention the importance of the penetration of Anglo-Norman ideas into Scotland between the late 11th and 13th centuries with the active encouragement of the Scottish Kings. We emphasise the important contribution to the Scottish landscape of the introduction of continental monastic orders (Trail 5) and the planned trading settlement or burgh (Trail 11). But these new influences were not merely a movement of ideas: they also involved the immigration of new settlers and the introduction of a new structure of landholding, the feudal system. Between the 11th and late 13th centuries Scotland was a land of opportunity for the younger sons of Norman families who had little hope of inheriting land at home, whether this was in Northern France or England, and who were willing to move to a more remote and backward country if there was the promise of a large estate. Some families whose main estates were in Normandy thus came to have cadet branches in both England and Scotland, and many individuals held land on both sides of the Border. With relations between Scotland and England generally amicable before the outbreak of the Wars of Independence at the end of the 13th century, this did not cause great difficulties, but thereafter such families had to choose which monarch they owed allegiance to. Some families who chose to come to Scotland in this way did far better than their stay-at-home relatives. The de Brus family and the Fitz-Alans (who became hereditary stewards of Scotland and later established the Stuart dynasty) are outstanding examples.

The authority of Scottish kings in the 12th century over what was still in many respects a tribal society was often ill-defined and disputed. This explains why they were so keen to encourage Anglo-Norman knights to come to Scotland because, by granting them lands on their royal estates, or other lands which had fallen vacant or been forfeited, they could consolidate their own power base and extend their influence into areas of Scotland, such as Galloway and the West Highlands, which were not yet securely tied to the Crown. The feudal tenures by which land was granted to the incomers had the mutual obligations of lord and vassal clearly set out by written charters. The most important of these was the provision of military service to the Crown, providing a reserve of skilled knights which was far better than relying on mercenaries or foreign support, which Scottish kings had been forced to do on several previous occasions. The incomers in turn were only prepared to settle if they received a secure title to their lands. The needs of both lord and vassal were met by feudal tenures under which incoming families held their estates in perpetuity in return for providing military support to the king.

The Anglo-Norman settlement in Scotland was neither a military conquest nor a large-scale colonisation of empty lands. It was a gradual infiltration which nevertheless affected most parts of southern and eastern Scotland to the Moray Firth and beyond. The incomers either supplanted existing landholders or in some cases married into their families. They often brought dependents and retainers, but the native population was not displaced on a large scale. In areas like the Lothians the territory granted to these opportunist knights was usually small: a village and its surrounding lands, a unit which often became a parish in later times, was normal. In other parts of Scotland, where the land was less fertile or less densely settled, much larger blocks of territory were granted, like the gift of Annandale, some 200,000 acres, to the de Brus family. In areas which were firmly under the control of the Crown the changes in landholding were peaceful. In other areas, such as Galloway, where royal influence was limited, the granting of feudal estates had the aspect of a frontier policy designed to surround, control and eventually to penetrate rebellious regions.

In the 12th century Galloway was still an independent lordship, almost at times an independent kingdom. One of its rulers, Fergus, was actually styled 'king' of Galloway in some documents. In 1160

Malcolm IV, King of Scots, mounted a major expedition to subdue the area. Fergus abdicated and Galloway was pacified, and divided between his two sons. In the wake of this campaign came the first grants of land to the new feudal retainers. The area remained a frontier zone for some time. In 1174 and again in 1185 there were uprisings by the native Galwegians who attacked and burnt many of the new castles built by the immigrants, and who may also have built mottes of their own in imitation. Charter evidence for this period is scanty, so that we can only directly relate a few of Galloway's earth and timber castles to specific Anglo-Norman families. Thus we cannot be sure which of the mottes that survive today were built by natives or immigrants. The conflict between Galwegian and Norman ended in the 13th century, partly for dynastic reasons as the line of the Lords of Galloway ended in three women who all married Anglo-Norman nobles.

The settlers introduced the motte and bailey castle as the indispensable means of protecting each new-won estate. Mottes are particularly common in certain parts of Scotland, notably Ayrshire, the Clyde valley, Menteith, Aberdeenshire and, of course, Galloway. Galloway is dotted with the remains of them: over a third of all the mottes which have been discovered in Scotland are in this region. Mottes are virtually absent in areas like the Lothians. Here they may have been replaced by more substantial stone castles at an early date, or in a more peaceful area they may not have been necessary at all. In Galloway, a less prosperous region, stone castles replaced earth and timber ones more slowly and, due to changes in landownership which altered the size of estates and the locations of their main defensive centres, many mottes survived intact, without being obliterated by later structures.

On this trail you will see some of these early castles, and also examples of the later stone ones which replaced them. Galloway remained a relatively remote and distinctive region within Scotland down to the 17th century, but growing contact with the outside world, particularly the cattle trade with England, brought increasing prosperity. Enclosure in the 18th and 19th centuries produced the neat landscape of small regular fields which survives today, and as well as looking at various medieval castles we shall also be examining elements relating to later landscape changes.

1. The Mote of Urr (815647)

*Park by the roadside at Netheryett (818647) just south of
Haugh of Urr. There is a footbridge across the river to the
motte.*

The origins of the motte and bailey castle are not entirely clear:
some of its elements may have come direct from Normandy, while
others may have originated in the diverse homelands of William I's
motley band of followers. In late Anglo-Saxon England fortifications belonging to individual landholders were uncommon: the
accent was on communal defence. The idea of personal castles, as
well as their actual design and construction techniques, was thus
novel. In Scotland, personal fortifications were probably more
common: many stone forts on duns from Iron Age times appear to
have continued in use into the medieval period. Nevertheless, the
design of the new castles was distinctive and is easy to identify in
the landscape. While each individual motte was a one-off response
to local requirements and conditions, they all tended to share the
same standard features.

The motte was a circular flat-topped earthen mound like an
inverted pudding basin. It was either completely artificial or was
shaped around an existing landform or outcrop of rock. The flat
top of the motte was defended by a timber palisade, and within this
there was usually a timber tower. The bottom of the motte was
surrounded by a broad ditch crossed by a wooden drawbridge. The
area on top of the motte was generally too limited to serve all the
needs of the garrison, so extra accommodation, stabling and
storehouses were provided below in the bailey. This oval or
rectangular levelled area was defended by its own ditch and timber
palisade. The motte was separated from the bailey which could be
abandoned if necessary in time of attack.

The Mote of Urr is the most impressive of the Galloway mottes.
It stands on low-lying ground by the River Urr and would once
have had the additional protection of marshy ground which would
have hindered the approach of attacking forces. It looks particularly imposing if you approach it down the valley from Bridge of Urr.
The motte itself rises some 10m above the level of the bailey and is
surrounded by a broad ditch. Excavation has suggested that the
surface slope of the motte was plastered with a thick layer of clay to

Mote of Urr; the motte is on the left, and the ditch separating it from the bailey is on the right

stabilise the soil and to make it more slippery for attackers trying to scale the mound. Mottes were often placed at one end of the bailey so that they shared the same outer ditch. Here, however, the motte is wholly within the bailey so that two separate lines of defence existed. The bailey is an exceptionally large one: over 5 acres. The ditch surrounding the bailey is some 15m wide and 3m deep. You can see the remains of an entrance with a causeway crossing the ditch on the west side. The impressive size of the motte reflects the status of its builder, William de Berkeley. Berkeley came to Scotland from the small Somerset village of Berkley in the following of another feudal lord. He eventually rose to be the king's chamberlain from c1171 to c1190, and was a successful and wealthy man. The Mote of Urr was the administrative and defensive centre of his estate, the visible expression of his feudal rights and the place where his courts were held. Excavation has indicated that the motte was destroyed by fire on one occasion and then rebuilt. It remained in use into the 14th century but not necessarily in its original role. Some faint terraces are visible on the south slope of the motte. It has been suggested that these may have been part of the lost burgh of Urr. The settlement was referred to in a charter in

1262 and, however small, was apparently a going concern with resident burgesses. Nothing more is heard of it thereafter: presumably it declined when the castle itself went out of use.

Follow the A710 south past Dalbeattie and turn right on to the A711. At the junction with the A745 turn right. After half a kilometre a narrow metalled road drops down towards the river on your right. There is little room for parking but there is limited space at the farm of Buittle Place. The castle lies between the farm and the river.

2. Buittle Castle (819616)

Motte and bailey castles were built quickly to provide immediate protection for their owners and dependents. Earth and timber were not ideal materials for fortification in the long term, because the timber rotted and was vulnerable to fire. Consequently, earth and timber castles were often rebuilt in stone from the 12th century onwards although, as we have seen at Urr, some mottes remained in use with little modification as late as the 14th century. Where the stone castle was built on the same site as its predecessor the motte was often largely obliterated. Buittle Castle is a good example of this although it is in a badly ruined condition. The stone castle appears to date from the late 13th century. It was probably built by John Balliol before 1269 and marks the first stage in the evolution of the stone castle in Scotland. The ruins are overgrown so that it is difficult to gain a clear impression of the castle's layout. The site is quite a strong one, being defended by the river with a trench and rampart on the landward side. The castle appears to have consisted of a curtain wall with at least five round towers, an early type of plan for a stone castle. The entrance seems to have been on the west side where there are signs of the foundations of a drawbridge with flanking towers. The site still has traces of its earlier character, though. The small plateau on which the castle stands may be the remains of the motte while the larger enclosure to the west and north of the castle appears to have been the bailey. The castle was probably a residence of the Lords of Galloway and was the home of Lady Devorgilla, one of the heiresses to the Lordship of Galloway, who married John Balliol, an Anglo-Norman knight. Their son, also called John Balliol, became King of Scots for three brief years before abdicating in 1296. The castle was garrisoned by English forces during the Wars of Independence, and when it was recaptured by Robert Bruce in 1312 or 1313, he had it destroyed as part of his policy of denying the English potential holding points: the castle was never rebuilt.

Just below the castle, beside the river, you may be able to see the remains of a bridge which carried an 18th-century coaching road. The road ran along the southern edge of the bailey and then cut through the gap between the bailey and the castle. Dominating the farmstead of Buittle Place, beside the castle, is a later tower house which is still inhabited. The tower dates from the 16th century and is on an L-plan; you can see the turnpike staircase in the angle of the two wings. In classic tower-house fashion (see below) the main

Tower house, Place of Buittle

entrance is on the first floor and there is a separate doorway into the former ground-floor storage area.

Like Urr, Buittle is also the site of a failed medieval burgh. In 1325 Sir James Douglas obtained a charter from Robert I authorising the foundation of a burgh of barony. No trace of this exists and it is unlikely that it ever got beyond the planning stage. As with the settlement at Urr, the abandonment of the castle is likely to have killed off the project.

3. Buittle Church (808599)

The remains of the old church at Buittle are a good example of a simple medieval Scottish parish kirk. There was a church on this

Old parish church, Buittle

site in 1275, when it was granted by Lady Devorgilla of Buittle
Castle to the abbey of Sweetheart, which she had founded in
memory of her husband, John Balliol. The ruined church may
well date from the 13th century: it consists of a plain rectangular
chancel which is unusual in being wider than the nave. There are
three lancet windows in the east wall, the middle one interrupted
by the insertion of a later rectangular doorway. In the south wall a
round-headed doorway has been blocked up. The modern church
beside it dates from 1819 and there are some interesting, if weathered, sculptured tombstones on the south side of the old church.

4. Ingleston Motte (774579)

This motte is much smaller than the one at Urr and is less well
preserved. It does not appear to have been surrounded by a ditch
and there is no indication of a bailey, though this could easily have
been ploughed out over the centuries: alternatively there may only
have been a wooden palisade round the bailey, without a ditch. The
motte seems to have been shaped around a rocky outcrop to reduce
the effort required in constructing an entirely artificial mound.
The place name of the adjacent farm, Ingleston, means, literally,
'the settlement of the English': originally there must have been a
settlement of retainers here, brought in by the castle's first lord.
This place name occurs elsewhere in Galloway in immediate
association with a motte.

5. Threave Castle (739623)

The road to Threave Castle leads off the A75, to the right,
about 2km south of Castle Douglas, and is clearly signposted.
Park in the visitors' car park at Kelton Mains. From there a
good path leads down to the River Dee (about 1km). Access to
the castle is by ferry boat; ring the bell to attract the attention
of the custodian.

Threave Castle, which dates from the 14th century, is perhaps the
most impressive example of an early tower house in Scotland. The
ancestry of the tower house can be traced back to the wooden towers
which topped the mottes, and to the stone keeps which replaced
them. Tower houses were simplified versions of keeps in which the

tower itself was the main defence with only light outworks rather than the massive curtain walls of the larger baronial castles. They were cheap to build, durable, and effective as a defence against all but a very well equipped force. They contain all the elements of a medieval hall in miniature, and another way of looking at them is to consider them as a hall, with its private apartments at one end and storage facilities at the other, telescoped and stood on end for easier defence. Tower houses were the standard late-medieval defence of all but the greatest landowners and are extremely common in Scotland, although they were also built in Ireland and there are a few examples in northern England. There were at least 150 of them in Galloway alone, so that they can be seen in this area as the late-medieval equivalent of the smaller mottes.

The simplest tower houses consisted of a single square or rectangular block of three or four storeys. The ground floor was a storage area into which livestock might be driven for protection if necessary. This room was generally roofed by a stone vault, and the only direct communication with the upper floors was by a small trapdoor or 'murder hole'. This made it more difficult to burn the tower. The rooms above were reached by a first-floor entrance, via an outside staircase or sometimes a ladder which could be drawn up. The first floor was generally a hall, with private apartments above and a parapet walk on the roof. The upper rooms were reached by a spiral or 'turnpike' staircase which twisted to the right. This meant that any attackers trying to force their way upwards had their sword arms trapped against the well of the staircase while the defenders had room to swing their weapons— always provided that both attackers and defenders were right-handed! Larger towers had more sophisticated plans such as L shapes with the staircase in the angle between the two blocks. Towers rarely stood in isolation. Like the wooden towers on top of mottes, they were very short of space internally and usually had ranges of outbuildings which have rarely survived. The outbuildings were often surrounded by a defensive perimeter wall or barmkin. Tower houses were first built in the late 13th and early 14th centuries, but they continued in use, with new ones being constructed, into the 17th century.

Threave is probably the only late-medieval castle in Galloway which has a wider regional significance rather than a purely local function. Rectangular in plan, it was built by Archibald the Grim, third Earl of Douglas, between 1369 and 1390. It has long been suspected that there may have been an earlier fortification on the site—perhaps a Norman motte—but if so, then all trace of it has been removed by later building operations. Douglas had been granted the Lordship of Galloway in 1369 and he made Threave his principal residence. The island site was ideally adapted for defence, but the tower itself was built very strongly. The curtain wall or barmkin surrounding the tower is a feature of considerable interest. It is later in date than the castle and consists of a strong wall on the north and east sides which may originally have stood to a height of 2.6m with a parapet on top and walkway behind. In front of it is a massive rock-cut ditch which, when flooded, had the castle standing on an island within an island. The wall linked three circular towers, only one of which survives in good condition today. An entrance in the centre of the east wall was surmounted by a gatehouse 8m high. The curtain wall is pierced with arrow slits, while the towers had gun loops on the two lowest floors; dumbell-shaped ones of unusual design at the bottom and ones with a more usual inverted keyhole shape above. On the side facing the river there was a less imposing stone wall enclosing a small rock-cut harbour which allowed boats to provision the castle. The western side of the castle was not overlooked by high ground on either bank and was only defended by a turf wall.

Threave Castle

The wall around the castle, particularly on the north and east sides. was evidently designed as an outer defence against attack by artillery. It has provided historians and archaeologists with a puzzle in terms of its date. Some have claimed that it dates from the late 1440s, before the siege of 1455 when James II took steps to curb the power of the Douglas family which was proving a threat to the throne. The castle held out successfully for over three months and was eventually taken by bribery rather than force. If the curtain wall dates from this time, then it is the earliest surviving artillery fortification in Scotland and one of the earliest in Europe. On the other hand, secure dating is only available for the lower west wall, and evidence that the walls on the northern and eastern sides were contemporary has not been completely convincing. Other historians would prefer to date the wall to the early 16th century and have suggested that references to work on a new artillery house at the castle before 1455 related to some hurriedly-constructed earthwork which was later replaced by the surviving wall. Incidentally, the persistent local story that the great cannon Mons Meg, now on display at Edinburgh Castle, was forged by a local blacksmith for use in the siege of 1455 has been shown to have no foundation. Documents show that the gun was cast in Mons in 1449 and was given to James II by the Duke of Burgundy in 1457.

The tower itself rises some 25 metres, with its own internal well. Just below the top of the wall you can see a row of holes. These were for beams which supported a timber gallery projecting outwards, allowing missiles to be dropped on any attackers who reached the base of the wall. The entrance, which is above ground level, leads into a kitchen, a feature which is often missing in smaller towers due to lack of space. In such situations the kitchen was housed in an outbuilding.

6. The Carlingwark Canal (761614)

With its rugged topography and lack of large-scale industry Galloway may seem an unlikely area in which to find canals, which are often thought of as having been built primarily to move coal and manufactured goods. Yet much of the traffic on a number of British canals in the late 18th and early 19th centuries was in agricultural produce. The idea of building canals to serve rural districts was often mooted by local landowners, though many such schemes were over-optimistic and impractical. At least one Scottish canal, in Aberdeenshire, was built principally to serve agriculture; and here, between Carlingwark Loch and the River Dee, are the remains of another one which was never completed. The channel which is now called Carlingwark Lane, running from the loch at 761614, may seem on first appearance to be merely a ditch draining the marshy ground south-west of Castle Douglas. It was cut in 1765 for Sir Alexander Gordon of Culvennan to lower the level of the loch and allow marl to be extracted from its bed for use as an agricultural fertiliser. The channel, which was up to 5m wide and over 1m deep, allowed marl to be brought by boat to the River Dee and from there upstream to Loch Ken to supply the farmers around the shores of the loch, the boats returning with cargoes of timber. To improve navigation on the Dee another shorter section of canal with a lock was cut near Culvennan between 736635 and 734644, but all that is visible today is a marshy hollow.

Following the success of this modest engineering venture, plans were made to extend the canal from Carlingwark Loch to Orchardstown Bay on the Solway, and to further improve its upper section on the Dee, creating a 26 mile-long waterway, with the further possibility of extending it into south Ayrshire to allow coal and lime to be brought in. Grain and building stone were to be sent down the canal to the Solway. Like so many of these canal schemes, estimates of the likely traffic and revenues were wildly over-optimistic. It was probably fortunate for the would-be investors that they were unable to interest sufficient people in backing the scheme to allow it to go ahead. The silted-up channel of Carlingwark Lane survives to show what might have been.

7. Castle Douglas (7662)

This settlement was originally a small hamlet on the military road through Galloway (see below). In 1789 it was bought by William Douglas, merchant and landowner, who laid it out as a planned estate village on a large scale. Over 300 such estate villages were built in Scotland during the later 18th and early 19th centuries, from Galloway to Caithness. Many were designed to diversify employment on their estates, acting as centres for industry: often textiles but also sometimes fishing, quarrying and other activities. They also acted as local market centres and often embellished the approaches to an estate mansion. At a period when agriculture was being reorganised and improved, they accommodated many local people who had been displaced from farming. These estate villages were often laid out on a regular pattern, the smaller ones with a single straight main street, the larger ones like Castle Douglas on a grid plan. Landowners often provided the money for public buildings like a church or school, and sometimes financed industrial development. The amount of control which they exerted over the development of the settlement varied. Some proprietors laid down strict regulations about the design of buildings, so that their villages appear very unified in their design; others gave more scope to individual developers to design their own properties.

William Douglas was a local boy made good: from a poor farming background he rose from being a peddlar to become one of Glasgow's richest merchants, making a large fortune in the trans-Atlantic trade, with some privateering too. Like many successful merchants, he bought his way into the landed gentry, gradually building up an estate in the neighbourhood of his original home. He bought the lands on which Castle Douglas stands from Sir Alexander Gordon of Culvennan. The extraction of marl and the cutting of the Carlingwark Canal had led to the growth of the original hamlet, and it was only lack of funds which prevented Gordon from developing a planned settlement there himself. Douglas did manage to lay out a village of generous proportions; a main street, King Street, is flanked by Queen Street and Cotton Street and is intersected at right angles to form a grid layout. The open areas of parkland at either end of the modern settlement were originally common grazing for the villagers' livestock. Douglas named the settlement after himself, a common practice among village developers at this time. In 1792 he had Castle Douglas created a burgh, which was an unusual step, giving the settlement a large measure of self-government, though he retained some overall control. While some estate villages remained small, like Kirkpatrick Durham (see below), Castle Douglas was one of the few which developed into a sizeable town. It functioned as a textile-manufacturing and market centre at first, but the coming of the railway in the late 1850s also made it a holiday centre.

To get to the next feature, the Military Road, turn right off the A75 about 1km north of Castle Douglas.

8. The Military Road (772635)

In Scotland military roads are usually associated with the Highlands (Trail 14), but an important one was built through Galloway from Gretna Green to Stranraer and Portpatrick to facilitate the movement of troops to and from Ireland. The first survey for the road was carried out in 1757, and construction by groups of soldiers took place in 1763-4. Much of the work involved the upgrading of existing stretches of road by providing a proper surface, widening the carriageway and cutting drainage ditches at the sides, but some totally new stretches and many bridges were built. Most of the line of the road is still in use today, sometimes to A-class standard. However, a long section from Castle Douglas to Haugh of Urr and on to the outskirts of Dumfries has survived as a back road which, apart from its modern surface, preserves much of the character of the 18th-century road. If you are returning eastwards you can continue on this road beyond Haugh of Urr, or otherwise return to the A75 from Haugh of Urr and continue north along it until you reach a minor road on your left signposted for Kirkpatrick Durham.

9. Kirkpatrick Durham (7870)

This is another Galloway planned village, on a more modest scale than Castle Douglas. Kirkpatrick Durham was developed by the parish minister, the Rev. Dr. David Lamont, who inherited land and became an enthusiastic agricultural improver. The village consists of a single main street with a cross street near its west end. The building plots run off at right angles behind the cottages, giving a geometrical appearance to the settlement which is characteristic of planned villages. The settlement has not changed greatly since Lamont's day. Most of the cottages are modest single-storey ones, formerly weavers' cottages, some with dormers, but near the crossroads there are some two-storey houses, some of them former inns.

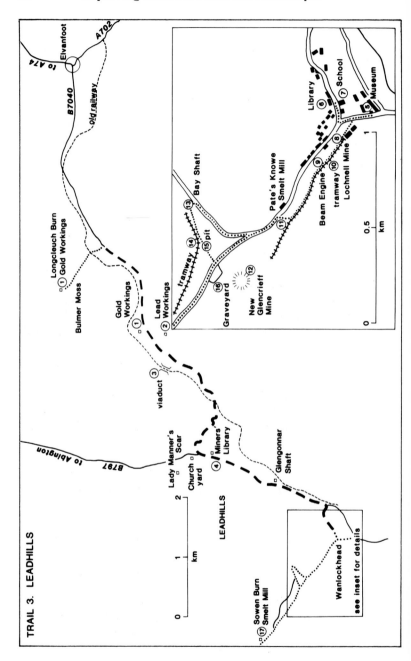

TRAIL 3. LEADHILLS

THREE

Leadhills and Wanlockhead: Mining in the Uplands

Ordnance Survey 1:50,000 sheet 78; 1:25,000 sheets NS 81, 91.

This trail involves a drive of about 12km with some optional short walks.

Introduction

Driving through the upper part of Clydesdale on the A74, the country seems isolated and thoroughly rural with scattered farmsteads and cottages and only occasional hamlets. It can be a surprise to leave the main road and come upon the two large villages of Leadhills and Wanlockhead on either side of the watershed between the Clyde and the Nith at altitudes of over 400m. These were mining, not agricultural settlements, though. Lead has been mined in this area from at least the 13th century until the 1950s, and there are many remains here of landscape features relating to mining activity. Although it has left fewer visible traces, it was gold which first made this area famous in the 16th century. Silver, too, could be refined from the lead ore. The mineral wealth of this area made it Scotland's premier non-ferrous mining area and caused one 19th-century writer to call the district 'God's Treasure House in Scotland'.

The most attractive approach to Leadhills from Edinburgh or Glasgow is from Elvanfoot, just off the A74, up the valley of the Elvan Water.

1. Elvan Water: Alluvial Gold Workings (907164)

Although the monks of Newbattle Abbey were mining lead in this area during the 13th century, it was the discovery of gold in the 16th century that really put it on the map. The Scottish crown was perennially short of bullion and during the 16th and early 17th centuries leased out the mineral rights on Crawford Moor, as the area was then called, to various mining and prospecting experts.

In the 1540s the Scottish coins known as 'Bonnet Pieces' were produced from Leadhills gold. Gold from this area also went into the Scottish regalia. Because of a lack of native skills in prospecting and mining, the Scottish crown encouraged various foreign experts, including Dutch, Germans, French, Flemish and English, to try their luck in the area. The most famous prospector was an Englishman, Bevis Bulmer, a flamboyant character, who undertook the large-scale development of the gold workings in this area during the 1590s. He employed up to 300 men during the summer in washing the gravels of the streams for gold.

One of the sites which he worked was at the head of the Longcleuch Burn which joins the Elvan Water at 922169. If you walk up the shallow valley for about 1km above the old railway embankment you can find the remains of the excavations of his workers at 912178. The 1:25,000 Ordnance Survey map marks the site with the intriguing inscription 'Gold formerly wrought here', and the hillside above, Bulmer Moss, still bears Bulmer's name.

A little further up the main valley of the Elvan Water you can see the remains of opencast gold workings close to the roadside on your right at 907164. The ground is hummocky and pitted with hollows where the gold-bearing gravels have been excavated. Despite attacks from robbers, substantial quantities of gold were produced from this area. In one year gold valued at £100,000 Sterling is claimed to have been recovered. Most of the gold was alluvial and came from the river gravels, but Bulmer and one or two other prospectors claimed to have mined it direct from veins of quartz. Although stray lumps of gold-bearing quartz have been found in the area, none of these gold mines have been located in recent times. Gold prospecting was in later centuries a sideline for lead miners in this area, and gold can still be recovered from the tributaries of the Elvan Water and Shortcleuch using a traditional gold pan or a sluice box. Permission from the estate should be obtained before trying your luck as a prospector: you can enquire about this at the tourist information centre in Leadhills.

2. Lead Working: Glen Ea's Hill (905150-907156)

High on the hillside on the opposite side of the valley from the gold workings you can see a long, straight scar running down the slope. This has been caused by mining for lead. Scars like this were sometimes produced by a process called 'hushing', which was an attempt to clear away the subsoil and expose the bedrock right down a hillside in order to search for veins of lead. This was done by channelling surface water into a small reservoir as high on the hillside as possible and then bursting the dam. The resulting flood washed away the subsoil, and if the process was repeated often enough a gully was cut down to the bedrock. Alternatively, the miners may merely have been following a vein which lay close to the surface. Although the main lead-bearing veins are situated around the villages of Leadhills and Wanlockhead, there are a number of thin veins like this one on the edges of the mining field, and these have often been explored in the past by trial workings.

3. The Leadhills and Wanlockhead Light Railway (901159)

On your drive up the Elvan valley you will have noticed the track of an old railway line, below you to the left as you leave Elvanfoot and then above you to the right. This is the line of the Leadhills and Wanlockhead Light Railway which was completed to Leadhills in 1901 and to Wanlockhead in 1902. Before this, ore and

Viaduct, Leadhills and Wanlockhead Light Railway

smelted lead was carried by cart to Biggar and then on to Leith. The building of the Caledonian Railway's line through the Clyde valley in 1848 and the South Western Railway Company's line through Nithsdale in 1850 greatly reduced the cost and difficulty of shipping out the lead, but this branch line allowed sidings to be brought straight to the mines themselves. The line was closed in 1938 after the mines had been abandoned, but at 901159 you can see a fine eight-arch viaduct built on a curve with brick piers and concrete arches.

The hillsides in this area are mainly covered in heather moor. The area is still shot over for grouse, and you can see lines of grouse butts on some of the hillsides. The heather is burnt over periodically to increase the number of grouse that the area can support. Grouse like to feed on the tender shoots of young heather but also appreciate the long, woody heather as cover from predators. The heather is burnt in small areas as a result, giving a patchwork appearance to the hills. The burning has to be carefully controlled: when done properly the heather roots, which are resistant to burning, soon recover but if the heat is too intense, then all the vegetation may be killed off and the soil may be eroded.

This is sheep-farming country, but hill sheep farming is not as profitable an occupation as it once was. This is evident in the landscape by the tumbled condition of many of the stone walls. It is no longer economical to repair them due to the high cost of labour: barbed wire fencing is much cheaper and is often used alongside a crumbling dyke.

Drive into Leadhills and park your car in the centre of the village. There is a car park next to the school, just beyond the Miners' Library, on the left hand side as you drive up the main street.

4. Leadhills Village (8815)

Much of the village consists of rows of single-storey miners' cottages, built of local rubble, with dormer windows. They date from the 19th century when the Hopetoun family, who owned the mining field on this side of the watershed, sunk a lot of capital into improving the village. The cottages have been built in a series of short rows, most of them running north-south, but without a regular plan so that the village has a complicated network of minor roads and trackways which you may like to explore.

The Miners' Library was founded in 1741 by the poet Allan Ramsay. Ramsay, the son of a Leadhills mine manager, was born in the village in 1686. At the age of 15 he was apprenticed to an Edinburgh wigmaker. He later became a bookseller and achieved fame as a literary figure and collector of traditional songs. As a result of the existence of the Miners' Library and the one founded a few years later in Wanlockhead the lead miners, despite their isolation and hard working conditions, were unusually well read for their day. The library now functions as a tourist information centre. Inside are exhibits relating to the history of lead mining in the area as well as a collection of the original records of some of the mining companies who operated at Leadhills.

The Co-op store in the village is a descendant of the shop run by the mining company in the 19th century. Although company shops were eventually banned because of the way some unscrupulous owners used them to exploit their workers, an exception was made in the case of Leadhills whose remoteness made it difficult for miners' families to obtain the provisions which they needed.

In the centre of the village you can see the bell, on top of wooden scaffolding, which was rung to warn the community of an accident in the mines.

The churchyard at the north end of the village contains many tombstones recording the fate of men who were killed underground. Many of the workers in the lead smelters also died young, poisoned by the lead fumes. The women who washed and picked the ore had a safer job and often lived much longer. There is also the grave of John Taylor who, according to his tombstone, lived to the age of 137. From the north-east side of the churchyard you can see the remains of old clearance banks of stone forming rectangles within the area of improved grazing (888154). These probably mark the boundaries of smallholdings worked part-time by miners to supplement their wages, a practice which was common in other upland mining areas in Britain.

Walk out on to the hillside above the village to the west using one of the many grassy tracks. From here you have a good view of its setting. The village is too high for most crops, though potatoes and hay can be grown and even, in the past, some oats. As in other remote lead-mining areas, the miners were encouraged to reclaim land themselves and cultivate it to help with provisioning the community. At one time some 600 acres were improved, but much of this was let go during the 19th century when communications with the outside world improved. But you can still see the area of improved pasture around the village, extending to some 300 acres, and contrasting sharply with the unimproved moorland beyond. There are some traces of cultivation ridges (Trail 5), showing that this area was formerly under crop. Part of the improved land beyond the opposite side of the village has been converted into a nine-hole golf course, one of the highest in Britain.

From here you can see most of the area of the mining field. The lands of Leadhills, including the mining area, were owned at the beginning of the 17th century by Thomas Foulis, an Edinburgh goldsmith. On his death in about 1611 he was succeeded by Robert Foulis, probably his brother, in the lands of Leadhills and by his brother David in the neighbouring lands of Glendorch. When Robert died in 1633 he was succeeded by his two daughters, Ann and Elizabeth. When Elizabeth died in 1637 Ann became heiress to the mining field. She was still a minor, however, and her lands were seized by her uncle, David Foulis. She took her case to the Court of Session and chose John Hope, an Edinburgh advocate, to defend her. John Hope won the case and he also won the heart of Ann Foulis. On their marriage he took over management of the lead mines which had only been worked sporadically, and he developed them on a much larger scale than previously, so that by the later 17th century lead from Leadhills was a major Scottish export. The profits of the mines made a major contribution to the prosperity of the Hope family who became Earls of Hopetoun, and towards the building of Hopetoun House near Queensferry. Although the Hopetoun estates worked part of the mining field themselves, at times they leased most of it out to various companies who paid them a royalty on every ton of lead smelted. Most of the remains of mining activity which you can see around the village relate to the most intensive phase of activity from the later 18th into the 19th century. Beyond the village to the north is a great gash in the hillside, Lady Manner's Scar (882159). This marks the location of the Susanna Vein, the most productive ore vein in the area, which has been worked by horizontal adits and opencast mining. Most of the mining activity was on a smaller scale, and on the hillside above Leadhills you can see numerous small dumps marking shallow shafts and some opencast workings. The most important shaft in the area lies below you to the south of the village (882139). The Glengonnar Shaft was in use until the 20th century, and the railway line runs into sidings close by. The smelting of the lead was done further down the valley beyond Lady Manner's Scar at 887177. This remote site was chosen so that the community would not be affected by the poisonous lead fumes from the smelter. The chimney of the smelt mill stood until the 1960s when it was dismantled for safety reasons.

Due to the hilly topography of the area many of the veins could be reached by horizontal levels or adits driven into the hillsides, but drainage was a problem. The mining field is drained by a main level called Gripps level which runs from the foot of the Glengonnar shaft and reaches the surface about two miles down the Glengonnar valley. It was driven in the 1790s, and although mines were worked below this level, they could only be drained by constant pumping, and have been flooded since the mines were abandoned.

Return to your car and follow the main road south from Leadhills towards Wanlockhead. At the summit of the pass between the two settlements the road and railway run side by side. The railway line crosses the pass in a cutting through solid rock (880134). This was the highest railway summit in Britain at an altitude of 457m.

Park your car at the museum in Wanlockhead village. This part of the trail involves a walk of 3.5km through Wanlockhead with an optional extra walk of 2.5km to the smelt mill at Sowen Burn.

The lead mines at Wanlockhead were developed a little later than those at Leadhills. The watershed between the two villages marks the boundary between the Hopetoun estates and those of the Duke of Queensberry. There are no underground connexions between the two parts of the mining field, although at one time an ambitious scheme was proposed to solve the drainage problems of the mines once and for all by driving a new drainage level, lower than any existing ones, for seven miles to come out on the other side of the Lowther Hills at Enterkinfoot, and link through from Wanlockhead to Leadhills. As with Leadhills, the Queensberry estates leased the mining rights to a succession of companies at various times, but for some periods during the 19th century they worked the mines themselves.

The village is more scattered than Leadhills but has a similar character with rows of miners' cottages dating from the 19th and early 20th centuries and one or two larger buildings. Much of the tidy appearance of the village, as with Leadhills, is due to investment by the respective landowners and the mining companies in the 19th century when, with higher wages being offered in other less remote mining areas, they had to improve facilities in order to retain their workforce. You can pick out the more substantial house belonging to the former mine manager.

Turn right down the side road through the village.

5. The Museum (973128)

In the centre of the village one of the two-roomed miners' cottages has been converted into a museum with displays relating to the history of lead mining in the area. This is the start of a lead-mining trail which has been laid out by the Wanlockhead Museum Trust.

6. The Miners' Library (876131)

Following the success of the library established by Allan Ramsay at Leadhills, the inhabitants of Wanlockhead set up a subscription library of their own in 1756. It was originally housed in a cottage provided by one of the mining companies, but in 1788 the first proper library was built. This was replaced in 1850 by the present building. It has been constructed along similar lines to the miners' cottages but with the entrance in one end allowing three windows to be built in for better lighting. The building still houses the library and archive material relating to the activities of mining companies in the area.

7. The School (873129)

There was a school at Wanlockhead in the 18th century, but the oldest part of the present building dates from the 1850s and was financed by the Duke of Buccleuch, who also paid the salary of the schoolmaster. The school was enlarged in the early part of this century when there were over 100 pupils. With the closure of the mines in the 1930s the population of the village dropped from around 1000 to about 200. The school was finally closed in 1977, the children being transferred to Leadhills. It is still used as a village hall.

8. The Lochnell Mine (872130)

On the left-hand side of the road a horizontal adit leads into the Lochnell mine which runs under Wanlock Dod, the hill above the village. The mine was worked during the 18th and 19th centuries, and part of the workings were kept open after this as they provided access to other mines which were still operating. The level can be entered with guides from the museum and explored for a short distance.

9. The Beam Engine (872131)

Two major problems of mining at Leadhills and Wanlockhead were draining the mines and providing power for the drainage machinery. Horse gins were still used for pumping in the 19th century but they were not as effective as steam engines. Coal for the steam engines had to be imported, and was expensive, so that every

Water bucket pumping engine and site of horse gin, Wanlockhead

effort was made to use water power for the pumping machinery where possible. This engine, which stands beside the concrete capping of a shaft above the Straitsteps mine, was a water-bucket pumping engine, the only surviving example in Scotland. It dates from the last quarter of the 19th century, showing how in remote locations like this water power could remain competitive with steam (Trail 10). The beam was raised and lowered by the action of water pouring into a bucket which hung from one end of the beam. The weight of the full bucket pulled the beam down, and when the bucket reached ground level it emptied automatically, causing the beam to rise once more. The bucket was filled from a cistern on the hillside above and water for the cistern was collected by a lade running round the hillside. The mechanism was extremely simple and needed little attention or maintenance. While the beam engine pumped water from the mine, the ore was raised by a horse gin, with a circular walkway, nearby.

10. The Old Tramway (871130)

On the opposite side of the valley a raised embankment marks the line of an old mine tramway. Although the mining field was not served by a railway until 1902, the need to move large quantities of material between the mines, crushing sheds and smelters led to the building of many short tramways, with the wagons drawn by horses. The indicator plinth shows a view of the area in 1775 with waterwheel-powered pumps in action on the site of the Straitsteps Mine. Notice the lade bringing water to these wheels. The location of the mining field on a watershed made it difficult to obtain enough water to drive water wheels. In this case a lade collected water from the Mennock valley to the south and brought it over the watershed to the mine.

11. Pate's Knowe Smelt Mill (868132)

This was the main site for smelting lead at Wanlockhead during the late 18th and early 19th centuries. The ore was washed and crushed here using water power. Excavations in the 1970s revealed the outlines of the mill and two hearths built from cast-iron bricks. The design of the hearths had become obsolete by the 1840s when operations were transferred to the smelt mill at Sowen Burn, a mile further down the valley.

Pate's Knowe smelt mill with New Glencrieff mine in background

12. The New Glencrieff Mine (865135)

This was the last mine to be worked in the area, during the late 1950s, and the surviving buildings date from this time. Although much of the spoil from the mine has been removed from the site, a large hill of it still dominates the valley floor.

13. Whyte's Cleuch and the Bay Mine (868137)

Follow the track up the tributary valley of Whyte's Cleuch. The site of the Bay Mine was also excavated in the 1970s, revealing a variety of features. Among the earliest were a row of massive stone blocks, the base for the cylinder of a steam engine built by William Symington in 1790. Early Newcomen steam engines were not used at Leadhills or Wanlockhead because they required too much coal. Even the later more efficient steam engines were only used when lead prices were high enough to warrant the cost of importing coal. After the 1830s, with a slump in prices, the use of steam engines was abandoned and water power came into its own again. The stone pillar on the other side of the concrete cap of the shaft was part of a water-powered pumping engine which was built in the 1840s. Water to drive the engine was obtained from lades constructed round the hillside above. The problem with engines of this type was that their water supply might fail in a dry summer or a cold winter, so the steam winding engine which brought out the ore from the mine was also used to work the pumps. The brick foundations of the engine house can also be seen.

14. Mine Tramway (866137)

On the level area beside the Bay Shaft stood an ore-crushing plant and sidings for another tramway. The tramway ran along the hillside down to the smelt mill at Sowen Burn. The wagons ran down the gradient to the smelt mill under gravity and were hauled back empty by horses.

15. Waterwheel Pit (866135)

Halfway between the Bay Mine and the main road down the valley you can see the remains of a stone waterwheel pit for another water-powered pumping engine. It dates from the late 19th century and was an auxilliary pumping engine designed to help with pumping water from the Bay Shaft after heavy rain. A small reservoir was built in the hillside behind the mine to provide a head of water for the 9m diameter wheel.

16. Graveyard (865136)

The isolated graveyard contains, like its counterpart in Leadhills, tombstones relating to miners who died in accidents underground.

If time and energy permit you can extend the walk for another 2km down the valley of the Wanlock Water to the smelt mill at Sowen Burn.

17. Smelt Mill, Sowen Burn (855144)

This is the best-preserved smelt-mill site in the area. The effects of poisonous lead fumes on the surrounding vegetation are remarkable. The vegetation has been killed off and the bare hillside has been eroded into gullies like miniature 'badlands' topography.

Smelt mill, Sowen Burn

The landscapes of many parts of Central Scotland have been influenced by the effects of mining, not only for coal but also for ironstone and oil shale. Landscape features relating to pre-20th century mining activity in such areas have often been removed for safety reasons and due to destruction by large-scale modern industry. It is often in more remote areas that traces of early mining survive best, and in such localities it was often non-ferrous metals that were being sought. Although the Leadhills-Wanlockhead area is the largest of such mining fields, other interesting examples can be visited such as Strontian in Argyllshire. A set of gold workings with channels for washing the gravels can be seen on the Glengaber Burn near St Mary's Loch (215237). Although little is known about them, they are probably roughly contemporary with Bevis Bulmer's workings on the Longcleuch. Places where lead has been mined or at least prospected for can often be identified on the map from 'Lead' elements in place names.

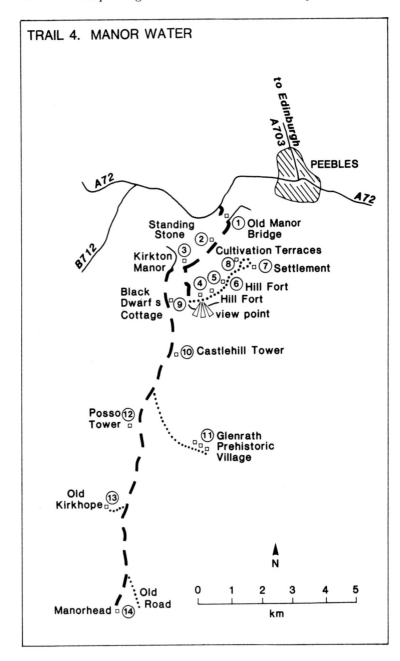

TRAIL 4. MANOR WATER

FOUR

Manor Water: Landscape and Settlement in a Border Valley

Ordnance Survey 1:50,000 sheet 73: 1:25,000 sheets NT 02/12, 03/13, 23/33.

This trail involves a drive of 20km with a number of optional short walks.

Introduction

The steep-sided valley of the Manor Water is over 15km long but although it is so close to Peebles it is quiet and unfrequented, partly because it has no through road. Manor Water has no nationally famous historical sites but nevertheless there are a lot of interesting landscape features to see. There are abundant remains of settlement from later prehistoric times ranging from large hillforts to small homesteads. On this trail you can walk through the fields, enclosures and hut foundations of an extensive prehistoric village. There are also interesting remains from later times. Unlike many parts of the Borders, Manor Water was split into several small estates in late-medieval times: it is possible to study the remains of the tower houses which belonged to each landowner, and half a dozen are clearly visible. While these towers may not be as dramatic as some of the famous castles and fortified houses of the Borders, the bonus here is that several of their sites have been completely abandoned, so the associated outbuildings, enclosures and gardens are clearly visible as well as the towers themselves.

1. Old Manor Bridge (231394)

Until the bridge over the Tweed at 229395 was built in the late 19th century, the road from Manor Water to Peebles lay over the shoulder of Cademuir Hill on the south side of the river. Manor Water was spanned by a bridge with a single wide arch which was built in 1702, as an inscription on the bridge indicates. It was built at a period when very little money, either from local or national

Old Manor Bridge

sources, was directed into road construction and maintenance. Bridges were the only part of the communications system which attracted finance, and even then often not enough. Bridges were frequently built using funds donated by generous proprietors or from money raised by public subscriptions. In this case the money came from the vacant stipend of the parish of Manor. The Earl of March, who had the patronage of the kirk at Manor (the right to appoint the minister), took the opportunity of diverting the minister's stipend, at a time when a new church was under construction and there was no resident minister, into a useful public work: the bridge was the result.

2. Standing Stone (228387)

Built into a wall on the north side of the road is a prehistoric standing stone some 2m high. The stone has been moved from its original location which, according to a late 18th-century map, was in the middle of the field to the north-west. Small landscape features like stones. whether inscribed or otherwise, have often been moved in the past and are not necessarily in their original locations. The reasons for this are frequently obscure: sometimes it was the whim of a landowner. Later in the trail you will see another example of a stone which has been moved at least twice over distances of several kilometres.

Standing stone built into wall, Kirkton Manor

3. Kirkton Manor (219379)

The parish church of Manor dates from the late 19th century. It replaced an earlier church which was completed in 1702. This one in turn had superseded one or more previous churches going back to early medieval times. Although, as we will see later, there may have been a chapel at the southern end of the valley there is no indication that the parish church was ever located anywhere else. This has been the focal point of the community living in the valley for many centuries.

Over most of Scotland, apart from the south-eastern lowlands, villages were not a normal feature of the settlement pattern in medieval times (Trail 8). Partly because better-quality arable land was often scattered in discontinuous patches, settlement was usually dispersed in small units, sometimes isolated steadings and cottages and often in small hamlet clusters or 'ferm touns' in which a group of tenant farmers worked together in co-operation.

Sometimes, however, the possession of a non-agricultural function gave one of these ferm touns some extra local importance and a distinctive name. A township situated close to a landowner's residence might become known as the Castle-toun or one with a water mill the Mill-toun. Castleton and Milton are common place names today. The settlement which clustered around the parish church was frequently known as the Kirk-toun and was often the most important meeting place for the inhabitants of a large parish. A good deal of business was transacted outside the kirk after services on Sunday, while the kirktoun often possessed other services like the smithy and the ale-house, and was the location for a weekly market and annual fairs. Many kirktouns were developed as estate villages during the 18th and 19th centuries. Kirkton Manor has, however, preserved its character as a hamlet: small but still the largest settlement in the valley. Immediately behind the Post Office you can see the old smithy. Before the later 18th century Scottish farmers mostly used oxen for ploughing but they kept horses and ponies for other farm work and for transport. On many estates tenants were bound by the proprietor to use a particular smithy and might have to help bring in coal for the smithy's forge. This example dates from the late 18th or early 19th century and was later enlarged to give a building with a forge at one end and a shoeing floor at the other. If you walk to the back of the churchyard and look over the wall you will see Kirkton Mill, still with its wheel in place although the mill lade below is overgrown. The mill, like the smithy, was a normal feature of rural kirktouns.

From Kirkton Manor follow the side road to your left past Milton (the site of the former estate mill) round the slopes of Cademuir Hill. Stop near an old quarry at 218369. The walk over Cademuir Hill to see various prehistoric features is about 5km. If you do not wish to take this section of the trail, continue the itinerary at No.9. Although the initial climb is a stiff one (about 20-30 minutes), the ground flattens out into a gentle ridge giving easy walking and fine views over Manor Water and the surrounding hills. Stop for a rest after the first 120m of steeper slopes and look at the valley below you.

4. Manor Water: Field Patterns

If you look down into the valley you can see the contrast between the neat pattern of small, squareish fields on the valley floor and the unenclosed rough pasture above. The regular character of the enclosures in the valley shows that they are fairly recent in origin. They date mainly from the 1820s when the Laird of Barns, who owned the lower part of the valley, sank a lot of money into improving his estate. He replaced the old open arable lands by enclosed fields and drained the waterside hay-meadows. Most of the fields in the valley are used today for improved grazing but periodically some of them are ploughed up for turnips, oats or a crop of hay. Before the 18th century, when communications with the lowlands were still difficult, every farmer on Manor Water grew some grain—oats and barley—for the direct needs of his household in baking and brewing. Much of the valley floor land which would have been ideal for wintering livestock was used up in this way and this restricted the number of animals which could be kept. Once communications had been improved it was possible to reduce the amount of land under cultivation and to grow fodder crops like turnips for the animals. This allowed more animals to be wintered, and the farms were able to concentrate on commercial livestock rearing to a much greater degree than before.

5. Hill Fort (224370)

Cademuir Hill has a number of prehistoric sites on its slopes. The first one that you come to, if you follow the ridge eastwards, is a hillfort on a low rocky summit along the ridge. It is defended by a massive stone wall up to 6m thick consisting of a core of rubble between two faces of walling. Some of the facing stones can be seen but the wall, which has been robbed for stone at a later date, has slumped down to form a litter of stone around the slopes of the hill. The entrance to the fort lies on the south-west side via a lower terrace which is bordered by a stone wall.

Perhaps the most interesting aspect of this fort lies on the far side where, to the north-east of the main rampart, there is a gully some 3m deep and 35m across. On the far side of this you can see sets of upright stones stuck in place on the slopes of the gully. This feature is known as a 'chevaux de frise'. It was designed to slow down and break up the formation of a group of attackers coming at the fort along the ridge. There are about 100 stones in place but there may originally have been many more. They would not have been visible to charging attackers until they came over the crest of the slope above the gully. This kind of defence is not widespread in western Europe, being confined to central Spain and a few examples in Scotland, Wales and Ireland. There may have been some linkage between Britain and the Spanish examples, but another possibility is that this type of defence was common in other parts of Europe but that it was usually constructed from wooden stakes set in the ground which would have left no trace on the surface at the present day. There is a similar feature at another fort in this area at Dreva (126353). The date of the fort is uncertain—it may have been occupied during the Iron Age or possibly even after the Roman withdrawal.

6. Hill Fort (230375)

If you follow the ridge eastwards to its summit you come to the remains of a much larger fort, enclosing an area of about six acres. This is the biggest fort in this area and although it is not comparable with a major tribal capital like the fort on Eildon Hill North (Trail 5), it must have dominated an extensive area with many smaller settlements. Like the previous fort it was defended by a thick stone wall which has tumbled down to form a band of debris on the hillside. You can make out the positions of the inner and outer facing stones of the wall in some places. The fort was also defended on most sides by an outer rampart some 10m beyond the main one. This rampart does not seem to have been finished. There are no traces of a rampart on the south-east side where it has probably fallen down the slope. The entrances were on the east and south-west sides. Inside the fort you may be able to make out the remains of platforms cut into the slope to support timber huts. Over 30 have been identified and there is room for many more. The evidence indicates that this fort, like the one at Eildon Hill, was abandoned when the Romans arrived.

7. Fort and Settlements, The Wham (235379)

If you continue along the ridge with the boundary wall on your right, just after you pass the lowest point there is a small hillock with the remains of a series of features. First there is a hill fort with a stone wall 4m thick running round the summit and an outer rampart, similar in character to the previous two, and traces of an outer rampart some 12m beyond. Partly overlying the fort, and doubtless using much of the stone from it, is a later settlement enclosed by an irregularly-shaped stone wall some 2m thick with a central dividing wall of similar thickness. Inside this you can see where the ground has been levelled to provide platforms for four huts. To the west and south of the settlement are the remains of four rounded and four rectangular enclosures. They are clearly later than the fort as they overlie the ramparts in places, but it is not possible to say whether they are contemporary with the stone-walled settlement or later. Subsequent occupation on this site is shown by traces of the foundations of a rectangular house in one of the southern enclosures. This may be the one marked on a map of 1775. The settlement with its timber houses is similar to a number of others in the Manor Water area; they may date from around the time of the Roman invasion of Scotland.

8. Cultivation Terraces (234388)

From this settlement drop down the north face of the ridge a short way to a series of terraces on the hillside. These show up best on a clear day when the angle of the sun is low—especially in winter. Flights of terraces like these are common in the upper part of the Tweed valley and its tributaries. They are thought to have been used for cultivation but surprisingly little is known about their origin. Although they are particularly frequent in this area, they occur widely in south-east Scotland. They are rare elsewhere in Scotland, although they do occur in one or two places north of the Forth. Similar terraces are widespread in England from the Pennines to the chalk downlands of the south.

That these terraces were designed for cultivation is shown at some sites by their gradually changing into ridge and furrow plough marks (Trail 5) on more gently sloping ground. In such cases they are thought to have been the result of ploughing in fixed strips across a slope. Under such circumstances the soil tended to be removed from the upper part of the strip, accumulating at the downslope edge and gradually forming a terrace feature. Else-

where the overall steepness of the slope makes such almost accidental origins unlikely and it is probable that the terraces have been
deliberately constructed to create level surfaces for cultivation,
sometimes with retaining walls of stones cleared from the flat areas
of the terraces.

The date of these features is a puzzle. In general, their association
with strip cultivation has suggested that they represent a specialised type of open-field cultivation, a system of agriculture which is
believed to have developed only during later Anglo-Saxon times.
Certainly at places like Glenrath (see below) such terraces overlie,
and are clearly later than, 'Celtic' field systems of small square
plots which are thought to date from Roman or even post-Roman
times. If a late Dark Age origin is suggested for the earliest of these
features, then their marked concentration in the hilly areas of
south-eastern Scotland could fit in with the Anglian occupation of
this area (Trail 8), though some of these terraces may have been
created much later and may have remained in use as recently as the
17th century. Their relative rarity in the Lothians and Berwickshire could be explained by the lack of steeper slopes in these areas
and the obliteration of such features by later cultivation. They may
only have survived in areas which were little cultivated in later
times. There are indications that large areas of these terraces may
have been destroyed by later human activities so that the distribution of those which survive may not necessarily be representative.

Cultivation terraces occur elsewhere in Manor Water: on the
slopes of Woodhouse Hill (212375) and above Glenternie (208366).
In all cases where they occur they are situated close to the remains
of Iron Age forts and homesteads, and this might lead one to
suppose that they were associated with these settlements. This may
be a dangerous assumption though. It is likely that both types of
landscape feature have been preserved in these areas due to lack of
later intensive land use and have been removed on the lower slopes
due to subsequent cultivation.

*Return along the ridge and walk back to your car. Drive back
to the main road up the valley.*

*For those who have not included the walk up Cademuir Hill,
continue the trail here.*

9. The Black Dwarf's Cottage (211370)

Beside the road, just beyond Woodhouse farm, is a single-storey cottage dating from the early 19th century. Its front faces eastwards and can be seen by walking a short way down a side track. The north end of the cottage has a normal appearance but at the south end of the building you can see a very small window and an unusually low door little more than 1m high. Above the door is the date 1802 with the initials 'DR'. They stand for David Ritchie, a

Black Dwarf's Cottage

cripple with severely deformed legs who, after a meeting with Sir Walter Scott, provided the writer with the model for the Black Dwarf in the novel of the same name. Ritchie was a local 'character' and the cottage, with the entrance and windows adjusted to his height, was provided for him by Sir James Naesmyth of Posso who owned this part of the Manor valley, an example of the paternalism which many Scottish landowners showed to the inhabitants of their estates.

10. Castlehill Tower House (214355)

At one time there were at least eight tower houses along Manor Water and its tributaries. Some of them survive as mere earthwork sites (see below). Others, like the ones at Manorhead and Hallyards, have become incorporated into later buildings. None has survived intact. The layout of tower houses has been described in Trail 2, but those on Manor Water were built for lairds with moderate estates and for their larger tenants rather than by powerful and wealthy landowners. Their towers were correspondingly smaller and more modest than large baronial ones like Threave Castle, but they were more typical of the fortified houses which proliferated throughout Scotland into the 17th century.

Tower house, Castlehill

Castlehill tower stands on a rocky hillock overlooking the valley. An approach to the tower has been cut through solid rock on the north-east side and there are traces of a wall or barmkin enclosing the top of the hill. It is likely that there were outbuildings associated with the tower but these have vanished. The tower is thought to have been built in the later 15th century and still stands to the level of the second storey on the west side. At the bottom of the wall you can see a square hole which was originally the chute into which the tower's garderobes or toilets discharged. Upstanding rocky sites like this may have been ideal for defence but, without a supply of running water, they provided problems for waste disposal! The ground floor of the tower has a double stone vault and would have been used mainly for storage. The entrance was on the ground floor, leading to a staircase in the angle of the wall which gave access to the upper floors. Originally there may have been at least four storeys.

11. Glenrath: Prehistoric Village and Field System (213328–228323)

This site involves a walk, there and back, of about 6km along a level track. Leave your car on the main road near Hallmanor Cottage (207343) and follow the track through the farmstead of Glenrath and into the side valley of Glenrath Hope. If you do not want to include the walk, continue the trail at no. 12.

It is not often in Scotland that you can walk through an entire prehistoric landscape with the remains of huts, fields, boundary walls and other features. You can do this in the steep-sided, flat-bottomed valley of Glenrath: the walk itself is an attractive and easy one. About half a kilometre beyond the farm of Glenrath the track passes a small plantation of conifers on each side and runs under the steep slopes of Greenside Craig. The remains of the ancient settlement are scattered along the valley floor to the east of this point over an area of 35 acres on the left of the track. The most extensive remains occur where the valley floor opens out beyond Greenside Craigs, as far as the cottage at Glenrathope.

The remains consist of a series of circular stone huts with surrounding enclosures. Such huts occur elsewhere in the Manor Valley and overlie both the hillforts and the settlements with the platforms for timber huts. This probably places them in the Roman or post-Roman period. In Glenrath the remains mostly lie close to the foot of the hillside slopes a little way from the track. The field systems extend from these huts towards the track. They consist of stone boundary banks running downslope across the valley floor with horizontal breaks of slope or 'lynchets' running at right angles between them. The lynchets have been produced by prolonged cultivation accumulating soil on the upslope side of the boundary between the fields and removing it at the downslope side. Some of these breaks of slope have the remains of stone dykes on top. The stone boundary walls and the lynchets at right angles to them form a pattern of small square fields which are characteristic of late prehistoric field systems. In the middle of some of the fields are piles of stones of varying size resulting from the clearance of stones from the cultivated land. On either side of a small plantation at 222326 you can see some more prominent terraces. These are cultivation terraces similar to the ones on Cademuir Hill and they appear to be later in date than the small square plots of the earlier field system.

This field system with its associated settlements does not have many close parallels in Scotland, but similar sites have been identified in northern England where they are thought to date from the Romano-British period or a little later. It is possible that the remains in Glenrath were once more widespread and extended down into the main valley, but have been obliterated by later cultivation and stone robbing. The chance survival of this area of fields so low down in the valley shows how intensively the landscape was exploited in later prehistoric times. Clearly there was dense settlement and extensive cultivation in the valleys and prehistoric man was not confined to the higher hillslopes where the woodland cover was thinner and the soils more easily worked. The remains of the settlements which we can see today on Cademuir Hill and the other slopes above the valley may have formed only a proportion of those which once existed and may not be totally representative.

12. Posso: Tower House and Outbuildings (200322)

It is a mistake to imagine that late-medieval tower houses stood grim and isolated in the landscape. The space within a tower was often very restricted, necessitating outbuildings for storage and servants' accommodation, while most of them were also attached to working farms with their barns and byres. Where towers are adjacent to or incorporated into later farms these outbuildings have usually disappeared. At Posso, however, the entire site has been abandoned and you can get a good impression of the setting of a 16th-17th century tower house. The tower is the first building which you will notice. It stands to second-floor level on the west side but is lower elsewhere. The ground plan of only about 9 × 7m did not provide a great deal of room, and this probably led to the construction of the attached outbuildings which you can see. On the south side of the tower are the remains of a separate rectangular building, while to the east is a much larger range, parts of which are still quite well preserved. To the south of the tower and its attendant buildings are a series of earthworks which are probably the remains of a garden and orchard. These are laid out in a series of terraces, and on one of the widest you can see the remains of a squareish platform surrounded by a ditch and bank. Almost certainly these are the remains of an ornamental pond.

13. Old Kirkhope: Chapel Site and Other Remains (194307)

This is a complicated site whose interpretation poses some interesting problems. Leave your car at 199309. Follow the track up the side valley which leaves the main road on the right just beyond Langhaugh at 199309. After about half a kilometre you will see a small enclosure above you to your right. Inside this, on a stone base, is a hollowed-out block of rock known locally as the 'font stone'. In fact, although the hollow has been enlarged to make it look more like a font, the block of stone is the base for a stone cross. It is known to have been moved to this site in 1874. Previously it stood further down the main valley at a point where the lands of Glack, Hallyards and Caverhill met. It seems unlikely, however, that a stone cross would have been erected for such a purely secular purpose. It is probable that the cross had been moved from an even earlier location, the most likely place being within the churchyard at Kirkton Manor. The demolition of the cross and the removal of its base may have occurred after the Reformation.

Why was the cross base moved to this remote site? The enclosure also contains a cross erected in 1873 for Sir James Naesmyth of Posso and a memorial to the Burnet of Barns family. This concentration of monuments related to the tradition that this was the site of a chapel in earlier times. At one time open-air services were even held here and the 'font stone' was removed to this spot because it was believed at the time that this was where it had originally come from. Along with the persistent tradition of a chapel here there was

Stone cross base and later monuments, Kirkhope

a belief that this had been the original site of the parish church. It seems quite likely that a chapel may have been built in medieval times to serve the inhabitants of the remote upper part of the valley who would otherwise have had a long walk to the parish kirk, but there are no indications in surviving historical records that this was ever the location of the main church for the parish. The place name 'Kirkhope' nevertheless points to the existence of a former ecclesiastical site. More tangible evidence of the importance of this site as a religious focus at an even earlier date can be seen if you walk about 200m west-north-west of the enclosure. Here there is a circular setting of stones and within it a concrete replica of an early Christian grave marker: the original is now in the museum at Peebles. The stone has incribed on it a cross, the name 'Coninie' and another word which has been partly lost, and is thought to date from the 6th century.

But where was the medieval chapel? The local people point to a series of foundations and grassy mounds immediately adjacent to the enclosure. Just beyond its south-west corner is a mound covering the remains of a rectangular building. Immediately below the cross base and other monuments is a rectangular enclosure divided in two with the remains of a small rectangular building in one half. On the hillside above are a number of artificial platforms and terraces, while the remains of an old road run below the enclosure with the foundations.

Although the site has not been excavated, the Royal Commission on Ancient Monuments, who have examined the surface remains, do not consider that either building resembles a chapel. Instead they have suggested that the rectangular structure to the south-west of the memorials is the remains of a small tower house (though the rectangular plan might suggest a more modest stone bastle, or fortified farmhouse). The terraces would have been gardens, forming an assemblage similar to that at Posso on a smaller scale. It is quite possible that the remains of a chapel do exist, but if the identification of the visible remains is correct, then the chapel has probably been robbed to its foundations to provide stone for the tower.

14. Manorhead: Old Road (199286)

Just under 1 km/from Manorhead farm an old track leads off from the left-hand side of the modern road, crosses the stream and then climbs steadily up the eastern side of the valley, which is much less steep than the western side. The road contours around the slopes of Redsike Head above Bitch Craig and then crosses the watershed to drop down into the valley of the Meggat Water. The road can be seen clearly as a terrace on the hillside. If you have time it is worth walking at least the first stretch of it to examine it in detail. The road appears to have been at least partially constructed rather than just worn. It is quite carefully graded for wheeled vehicles, with traces of rough metalling in places and drainage ditches on the upslope side to carry off floodwater. There are indications that this track was used as a cart road well into the 19th century but the route itself is far older. It may also have been used for droving cattle south to England in the 18th century, although the main drove road out of Manor Water is thought to have run up Glenrath (see above) and across the hills to the Douglas Burn. There is a dense network of abandoned roads in this area, some running from valley to valley, others following the watersheds. Most of them were used into the early 19th century and were abandoned with the construction of the first improved turnpikes through the main valleys. An even older route, the 'Thieves' Road', follows the crest of the hills on the west side of the head of Manor Water.

The modern road up Manor Water ends at Manorhead, a sheep farm in a classic valley-head site surrounded by steep hillslopes. The farmstead incorporates the lower storey of an earlier tower house, the highest in the valley, probably dating from the 16th century. The only clue to this is the rough character of the stonework at the base of the walls.

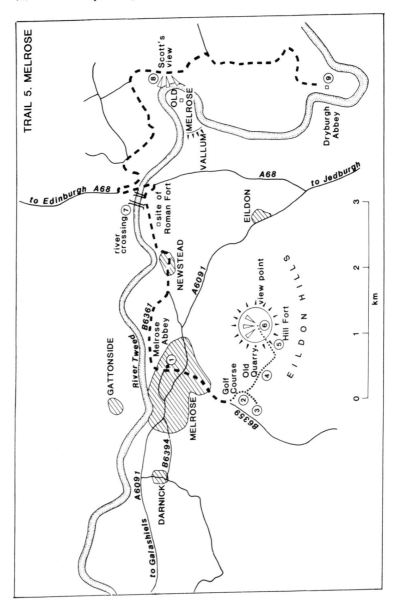

TRAIL 5. MELROSE

FIVE

The Central Tweed Valley: Medieval Abbeys in the Landscape

Ordnance Survey 1:50,000 sheet 73: 1:25,000 sheet NT 43/53.

This trail involves a drive of 15km and includes an optional walk to the summit of Eildon Hill. Stout footwear and waterproofs are recommended for this.

Introduction

The central part of the Tweed valley where hill and lowland merge has been a meeting place of routeways and an important focus of settlement at various periods. The prominent landmark of the Eildon Hills was an ideal location for a large hillfort in Iron Age times, the 'oppidum' or capital of a tribe known to the Romans as the Selgovae. After the Romans had subdued them and emptied the hillfort, they established their own headquarters at the foot of the hill, a base which was the key centre in the Roman occupation of southern Scotland. In post-Roman times the promontory of land surrounded by the Tweed to the east of the fort became the site of an early-Christian monastery. During the 12th century the Cistercians established Melrose Abbey 3km away, a monastery which was to become one of the wealthiest in Scotland.

The degree to which the original landscape from these periods of occupation has survived varies a lot. Although the Romans may have partly demolished its ramparts, the fort on Eildon Hill was so high up that it has not been disturbed very much, and the foundations of many of its huts can still be traced. On the other hand, cultivation and stone robbing have removed all surface traces of the Roman fort and the Celtic monastery. Melrose and Dryburgh Abbeys, despite the damage wrought by English armies and Scottish reformers, remain two of the finest ecclesiastical monuments in Scotland.

There is a car park immediately outside Melrose Abbey.

1. Melrose Abbey (549343)

By the 11th century Celtic monasticism was in decline (Trail 13). This was due partly to the eclipse of the Celtic church after the Synod of Whitby in 663 which favoured the church of Rome as the model for Christianity in Britain and, more dramatically, as the result of Viking raids on coastal monasteries like Iona and Lindisfarne. Into this vacuum the descendants of King Malcolm Canmore introduced monastic orders which had originated on the Continent and which had become widely established in England following the Norman Conquest. The abbey was one of the major innovations, along with the burgh and the motte and bailey castle, which reflected in the landscape of 12th-century Scotland the penetration of Anglo-Norman influences.

Most of the West European monastic orders went through a cycle in which they were founded under a strict set of rules which gradually became more relaxed as the abbeys and priories belonging to the order were granted more and more land, becoming wealthier and more worldly. New orders were then founded by people who had become dissatisfied with the slackness of the existing ones, and these then gradually followed the same course. Between the establishment of Melrose Abbey and its 15th-century rebuilding the Cistercian rule became more relaxed, and you can see this process reflected in the architecture of the abbey church with the contrast between the simple design of the 12th-century stonework and the flamboyance of the 15th-century rebuilding.

David I favoured the new, stricter rule of the Cistercians rather than that of the older-established Benedictines of whom they were an offshoot, and in 1136 he granted land at Melrose for the foundation of a new Cistercian house. A group of monks was sent from Rievaulx in Yorkshire to establish the community which was sufficiently successful to start founding daughter houses of its own after a few years.

Early Celtic monasteries had possessed relatively little land. They had been ascetic, simple communities. David I and his successors, and the more powerful feudal barons following their example, made huge grants of land to the new abbeys. The initial grant to Melrose included over 5000 acres and was supplemented by later donations. These grants included good-quality arable land along the Tweed, but in addition the monks of Melrose acquired grazing rights on over 17,000 acres of upland waste and pasture, which was held as royal hunting forest, between the Leader and Gala Waters, as well as pastures in the Cheviots and Teviotdale. The rule of the Cistercians required that they should seek out places of solitude for their abbeys. It is difficult to believe that there was not a pre-existing population along the Tweed when the monks arrived, but the lay people on the lands granted to the abbey are likely to have been moved or re-organised to suit the Cistercian system of estate management. The monks who officiated in the abbey formed only a small part of the organisation of a Cistercian estate. The monastic lands were cultivated by groups of lay brothers who had no ecclesiastical duties and who lived and worked together in communal farms called 'granges'. This word often survives as a modern place name in the vicinity of medieval abbeys: for example, at Drygrange on the Leader Water just above its junction with the Tweed. Most of the Melrose granges were probably established on existing farms, adopting their names without adding the 'grange' element.

The lowland granges were arable farms but the real wealth of Melrose and other Border abbeys lay in their upland pastures which extended north into the Lammermuirs and south into the Cheviots. The Cistercians were active colonisers and developed these areas as huge sheep ranges. Melrose eventually had a flock of around 12,500 sheep, the largest of any of the Border abbeys, and wool was a major revenue earner for the monks.

Instead of looking at the abbey as an isolated set of buildings, try to imagine it as the nucleus of a medieval big-business corporation with extensive lands and far-flung trading interests. It required a broad base of granges and sheep farms to maintain the abbey at the apex of the pyramid and to finance extensions and rebuilding. The Cistercians had a reputation as efficient farmers and estate managers. The abbey also derived income from appropriating the revenue of various parish kirks. The right to appoint the incumbent of a parish had usually belonged to the descendants of the landowner who had established the church. Many pious proprietors, however, had granted those rights to nearby religious houses which often installed threadbare, poorly-trained curates and creamed off much of the income for the abbey itself.

The ruins of the abbey are, despite damage, still impressive. Monasteries were laid out on a fairly standard plan which varied

Melrose Abbey

only in detail between one abbey and another. The convention was for the cloister to be located on the south side of the abbey church with the main buildings of the monastery grouped around the other three sides. In this way the bulk of the church sheltered the cloister from northerly winds and did not block out the sunlight. The east range was generally the dormitory, the south range the refectory, and the west side usually consisted of storehouses. There was often an outer courtyard to the west with guest houses, barns and stables. The abbot frequently had a separate house, and the infirmary too was normally detached from the main group of buildings. Most abbey churches had similar plans to cathedrals. Cistercian abbeys differed from those of other orders in that on the west side of the cloister accommodation was usually provided for visiting lay brothers. The abbey churches of Cistercian houses were not open to the local community, and instead of the nave which would have held the lay congregation in a cathedral church there were two choirs, one for the monks, the other for the lay brothers.

At Melrose the cloister is on the north side of the church rather than the south, probably due to drainage difficulties. The cloister is smaller than at Rievaulx, the mother house, but it is nevertheless quite large by Scottish standards. The buildings around the cloister are represented by foundations only, but enough remains for you to appreciate their layout with the aid of the notices or the guide book. The monastic buildings date mainly from the 12th century, but the only portion of the church from this period is at the western end where the stonework is typical of the rather severe early Cistercian style. Most of the abbey church dates from the 15th century: the abbey was burnt three times by English troops during the 14th century, and after the last devastating attack in 1385 a major rebuilding of the church was undertaken. It was reconstructed in a highly ornate, exuberant Perpendicular style with elaborate windows and a wealth of sculpture. The huge window at the east end of the church is particularly fine. It seems to have been constructed under the direction of a master mason from Yorkshire, but some of the other work from this period has been attributed to French masons. The church was badly damaged by the English again in 1544 and many of the statues were probably defaced at the Reformation. Part of the nave continued to be used as the parish church until the 19th century.

Commendator's house, Melrose Abbey

The detached house to the north of the abbey appears originally to have been the abbot's dwelling. It was remodelled around 1590 as a house for the lay commendator who had taken charge of the abbey and its lands after the Reformation.

The River Tweed, which runs half a kilometer away from the abbey, was an obvious source of water for drinking and drainage purposes. On the north side of the abbey you can see the canal that the monks constructed, over 2km long, leading past the abbey and rejoining the river lower down. On its way the water powered the abbey's corn mill and flushed out its sewers. A similar canal had been built at Rievaulx where the first Melrose monks had originated.

The abbey buildings were situated in the centre of a monastic precinct of 40 acres which was bounded by a stone wall; the concept was similar to the smaller precinct at St. Andrews (Trail 11) or the vallum at Iona (Trail 13). No traces of this wall now remain. The main gateway to the abbey was from the south with a gatehouse and a free-standing cross in front. The cross was probably located fairly close to the present market cross of Melrose which is later, dating from the 16th century with a modern base.

If you would like to do all, or part, of the optional walk follow the B359 out of Melrose to the south. If you do not wish to do the walk take the B361 signposted for Newstead out of Melrose to the north and continue the trail at No. 7.

2. The Eildon Hills: Cultivation Traces (544330)

It is possible to climb the Eildon Hills from various directions. The main route leads off from the B6359 just south of the market place of Melrose (548338). A more interesting route, which is shorter and less of a climb, starts from further south on the B6359 at the golf course (543333). Access to the golf course is permitted for walkers but take care to keep to the boundary fence because of the danger of flying golf balls. Follow the line of the fence past the clubhouse towards the hills. Once you reach the top of a low ridge you will see a stile crossing the fence which separates the golf course from the rough grazing beyond, and a footbridge over the stream. Before you reach the stile look at the fairway of the golf course on the slope facing the hills. It is divided into a series of strips which take the form of low ridges separated by hollows. These are cultivation ridges, often called 'ridge and furrow', and were produced by ploughing. Before undersoil drainage became widespread in the mid-19th century, the normal way of draining a heavy soil was to plough it into a series of parallel ridges. Water drained from these into the furrows and then downslope into larger field drains. The ridge was produced by ploughing a strip of land so that the furrow slice always fell towards the centre and away from the edges. Historians have debated to what extent early ridge and furrow was produced accidentally as a result of ploughing the scattered strips of land into which medieval open fields were divided or whether ridge and furrow was created deliberately to facilitate drainage. At a later date agricultural treatises leave no doubt that the ridges were designed for drainage.

The ridge and furrow here is very straight and regular: each ridge is about 5m wide. This is the hallmark of later cultivation, often from as recently as the Napoleonic Wars when a good deal of marginal land was ploughed up because grain prices were high. Ridge and furrow which is less regular and curves noticeably is usually older, sometimes medieval. The curves were due to the difficulty of turning a medieval ploughteam of eight or more oxen yoked in pairs: the ploughman tended to start edging his team round into a turn before he reached the end of the strip.

You can also find traces of ridge and furrow on the slopes of Eildon Hill beyond the golf course. Golf courses are good places to look for traces of old field systems or other landscape elements because the short-cut grass of the fairways allows many features to show up which would be invisible under other types of land use: but first make sure that you have a right of access and beware of golf balls!

3. Melrose Golf Course: An Old Trackway (544329)

Melrose golf course also preserves traces of old trackways. If, before crossing the stile, you follow the edge of the golf course south-west towards the cottage in the trees, just beyond it you can see a trackway, marked by a continuous hollow, running from the plantation on your right, across the golf course, and disappearing under the modern road to the cottage. Where it cuts through the low ridge at the plantation, the road takes the form of a hollow way over 1m deep. Trackways like these are even harder to date than ridge and furrow. The cultivation ridges seem to run across the trackway, suggesting that it is older, but whether it dates from the 18th century or medieval times is impossible to say merely by looking at the surface features. This is a good example of a road which was worn by use rather than deliberately constructed, and throughout Scotland, particularly among the hills of the Southern Uplands, you can find examples of these running up from the cultivated valleys on to the moorland above (Trails 2 & 4). In this case the tracks can be traced across the rifle range beyond the golf course (do not follow them!), but they fade out on the higher ground.

4. Eildon Hills: Bourjo Quarry (548327)

As you follow the footpath from the golf course towards the pass between the two summits you come to the remains of an old quarry at an altitude of just over 240m. This is thought to have been the source of most of the stone used in the 15th-century rebuilding of Melrose Abbey. It is possible that some of the stone for the original abbey may have been robbed from the Roman fort (see below). Much of it was obtained from quarries at Dingleton and Harley-burn, now on the outskirts of Melrose. You can still make out traces of the quarry face and waste heaps at this site which is known by the curious name of Bourjo. There are also signs of a road running downhill from the quarry by which the stone was brought to the abbey. Sledges are more likely to have been used than carts for transporting such a heavy commodity on a steep slope, but at least it was a downhill run!

5. Eildon Hill North: Iron Age Hillfort (5532)

The ramparts on Eildon Hill North can be seen from a long way off. The fort was a counterpart of Traprain Law (Trail 8), a major capital or 'oppidum', in this case of a tribe known as the Selgovae. The fort was about the same size as the one at Traprain and underwent a similar evolution, expanding from a small defensive perimeter around the summit in a series of extensions to its final circuit of over 1.5km. The ramparts of the last phase, which are the most clearly visible ones, consisted of three concentric lines of defences, but in many places they appear as terraces rather than as upstanding features. These terraces may have been deliberately cut into the hillside to provide level foundations on which the ramparts were raised. The ramparts may have been eroded, or possibly deliberately levelled, although in places they still remain clear. Within the defences of the fort you can find the remains of hut platforms scooped into the hillside. Nearly 300 have been identified and more have been destroyed on the south side of the hill by later cultivation and a plantation. If even a proportion of these hut sites were occupied at any one time, then the fort may have had a permanent population in excess of 1000.

Bearing in mind that the fort was the capital of an extensive territory, you might wonder whether there are any other features in the landscape which relate to it. There are several smaller forts in the area which are likely to have been contemporary with the oppidum, but more intriguing is an earthwork which has come to be known by the misleading name of the 'Military Road'. It consists of two ditches and two banks and appears to be a defensive earthwork rather than a mere boundary marker. It has been traced for over 6km and has undoubtedly been obliterated by cultivation in other places. It may have run from the Tweed south-east to the Ale Water, linking up three smaller outpost forts in its course. For most of its course it runs over relatively inaccessible moorland but it can be seen on the slopes of Cauldshiels Hill (516316) and Faughill Moor to the south-east. It is thought that it was part of an unfinished defensive perimeter, a kind of outer defence for the fort, though whether against the Romans or a neighbouring tribe is not clear.

Unlike Traprain, where occupation continued throughout the Roman period, the fort on Eildon Hill North was abandoned when the Romans arrived. The damaged condition of the ramparts may be due to deliberate demolition by them. It has been inferred from this that the Selgovae offered active resistance to the Romans and had to be put down, while the Votadini, further north, were less aggressive and entered into a treaty which allowed them to keep possession of their capital. The lack of Roman forts in East Lothian certainly suggests that the Romans did not consider this area to be a threat. In the central Tweed valley, by contrast, having ousted the Selgovae from their oppidum, the Romans established a base at the foot of the hill which became the key centre of their operations in southern Scotland.

On the very summit of the hill you can find traces of a circular ditch, enclosing an area with a diameter of about 11m. This has proved to be the remains of a drainage ditch surrounding a Roman signal station. The signal tower itself was of timber and commanded a wide view of the countryside. From the top messages could be related to and from the Roman fort below.

6. The View from Eildon Hill North

From the top of Eildon Hill on a clear day you can get a good impression of the settlement pattern around Melrose. The former monastic granges of Darnick, Gattonside, Newstead and Eildon appear as large clusters, almost villages. They were originally large monastic farms, over 1000 acres in some cases. From the late 13th and early 14th centuries onwards the Cistercians began to reorganise their estates by leasing their granges out to ordinary tenants rather than cultivating them by lay brothers. The tenants received shares in the townships, and in order to give each one a fair mixture of good and poorer land their holdings were fragmented into large numbers of strips and parcels. Because the granges had been so large, clusters of tenanted farms grew up on them. In the decades before the Reformation, when the church was being squeezed hard for money by the Scottish crown, the sitting tenants were given the opportunity to obtain secure possession of their lands by converting their ordinary leases into feu-ferme, a tenure which involved a substantial down payment in cash and an annual feu duty thereafter, but which allowed the occupant to hold the land in perpetuity and pass it to his heirs. Most of the tenants in these townships became small proprietors in this way but their scattered shareholdings were fossilised into a complex pattern of fragmented ownership. Only during the 18th century were these small landowners able to use earlier legislation passed by the Scottish Parliament to divide out their property so that everyone had his land in a compact block. Although much amalgmation of property has taken place since then to create a smaller number of large, modern farms, the distinctive settlement pattern of the former monastic tenants remains.

To the east of Newstead, on the low plateau north of the old railway line, is the site of the Roman fort of Newstead. Nothing is visible now of this important Roman base. Given that the direct influence of the Romans north of the defensive line which became Hadrian's Wall was intermittent and brief compared with their occupation of southern Britain, it is not surprising that they have left relatively little trace in the modern Scottish landscape. Their occupation of Scotland was a purely military one without the towns and villas of the Romanised south. Roman remains have often survived best in marginal areas where the ground has not been disturbed much since: for example the site of the signal station.

The Romans generally built their forts on low ground, trusting to the quality of their defences and the superior discipline of their troops rather than to the inaccessibility of the site. As a result these forts have often been obliterated by later cultivation and settlement. Newstead is a classic example of this, for despite the massive character of its defences, revealed by excavation, nothing is visible on the surface. Excavation has shown that there were four successive forts on the same site, the last one having a stone wall 2m thick backed by a 12m-wide clay rampart with ditches in front. The stone was presumably robbed by later builders and the rampart eventually levelled by weather and cultivation.

Return to your car, drive back to Melrose and take the B6361 through Newstead. If you have missed out the walk, continue the trail here.

7. The Crossing of the Tweed (574347)

The Tweed was not an easy river to bridge in the past, being wide and liable to flood. At one time there was no bridge between Peebles and Berwick. The flood plain of the river is wide between Melrose and Newstead but lower down, near its confluence with the Leader Water, it narrows between hillsides which provide firm foundations for a bridge. The Roman road, Dere Street, the Romans' main eastern route through Scotland from the Cheviots to the Firth of Forth, may have crossed the Tweed near here though the exact point is uncertain. The same crossing place has been used at a later date for the road bridge, built between 1776 and 1780, and the delicate-looking railway viaduct with 19 arches which was built by the Berwickshire Railway Company in 1865, as well as by the modern road bridge.

Railway viaduct and modern road bridge, Leaderfoot

Cross the Tweed by the modern road bridge and turn right just beyond it on to a minor road. Follow the signposts for Dryburgh Abbey.

8. Scott's View (594343)

The high point of the road which runs above the cliffs of the river on the slopes of Bemerside Hill is known as 'Scott's View' as it was supposedly the famous writer's favourite vantage point. From here you certainly get a fine panorama over the Eildon Hills. Look below you, however, to the promontory of land which is almost cut off by the river. The map marks this site as 'Old Melrose', hinting at some kind of occupation pre-dating the abbey. This was, in fact, an ecclesiastical site far older than the Cistercian monastery. It has been suggested that a church on this site was the centre of a very early Christian diocese in the 6th century, founded from Carlisle where Christianity continued to survive after the Roman withdrawal. During the 7th century it came under the influence of Celtic monasticism. St. Aidan, a monk from Iona and later bishop of Lindisfarne, founded a monastery here in the mid-7th century. It was here that St. Cuthbert, one of the most influential religious figures of his day, lived as a novice and a monk before he moved to Lindisfarne. The monastery at Melrose was destroyed in 859 by Kenneth, King of Scots, but some kind of religious life continued. In the 11th century a chapel, dedicated to St. Cuthbert, was built here. It is not clear why, when David I granted the lands of Melrose to the Cistercians, they chose to establish their abbey on a different site further upstream. Perhaps there was more room in the area that they chose compared with the restricted peninsula of Old Melrose. No surface remains of the Celtic monastery or the later chapel survive, but at 585340 an earthwork, consisting of a bank up to 4m wide and 1m high, runs up from the river on a line which, if continued, would cut off the neck of the promontory. The rest of the bank seems to have been destroyed by cultivation and the planting of trees but it is thought to be the vallum, or boundary wall, of the 7th-century monastery.

9. Dryburgh Abbey (591317)

At Dryburgh you can see the remains of another of the Border abbeys. It has many general features which are similar to Melrose but also some interesting differences in detail. The abbey was

Dryburgh Abbey

founded in 1150 by Hugh Morville, the Constable of David I, showing how the pious monarch's example was imitated by his followers. The site was granted to the Premonstratensian canons, an order which had been founded in 1120 with the aim of introducing a more ascetic spirit into the rule of the Augustinian canons, just as the Cistercians had attempted to reform the Benedictine rule. The abbey did not receive as large a grant of land as Melrose, as it was not a royal foundation, and it was never as important or as wealthy. It suffered a similar fate at the hands of English armies in the 14th century and again in the 16th, but in this case it was the church which suffered particularly, and more remains of the cloister and monastic buildings. The nave of the church, which

15th-century arch, Dryburgh Abbey

was rebuilt in the 15th century like the one at Melrose, survives only at foundation level for the most part but the west end has a fine entrance with a rounded arch. Superficially this might seem Norman but the rounded arch was re-introduced in some late-medieval Scottish churches and this one dates from the 15th-century rebuilding. The transepts and chancel of the church, dating from the late 12th and early 13th centuries, are better preserved and their simple, well-proportioned style contrasts with the ornate and elaborate later church at Melrose. Enough of the buildings around the cloister have survived to give a good impression of how the canons must have lived. The east range is particularly well preserved with a dormitory above and a library, parlour, and chapter house (the administrative centre of the abbey) below. The cloister is laid out to the south of the church on the classic model, with a refectory on the south side and some cellars on the west. There is likely to have been an infirmary and abbot's house to the east of the cloister but these have not survived. South of the cloister you can see the deep artificial channel which led off from the Tweed to provide water. You may wish to spend some time walking round the site and absorbing the peaceful atmosphere of the place.

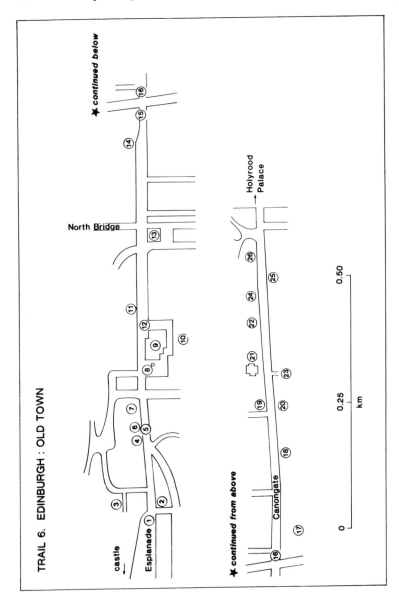

TRAIL 6. EDINBURGH : OLD TOWN

SIX

Edinburgh: The Old Town

Ordnance Survey 1:50,000 sheet 66; 1:25,000 sheet NT 27.

A walking trail of 1.5km.

Introduction

The city of Edinburgh is familiar to Scotsmen and visitors alike. Its major monuments—the Castle, Holyrood Palace, the crown spire of St. Giles—are world famous and instantly recognisable. Yet the way in which individual buildings fit into the modern townscape of the city, and the manner in which that townscape has evolved through time, are often less well appreciated. A study of these elements in the development of Edinburgh can tell us a good deal about how people lived in the city in the past and how their lives and activities shaped the town around them. Although, as you would expect with a capital, certain functions and activities were unique to the city, a study of the townscape of Edinburgh can also provide many insights into the ways in which Scotland's other large towns have evolved. To consider all the interesting features of a city with such a long and varied history would require a separate book. Inevitably, we have had to be highly selective, but the two trails that follow, covering the Royal Mile and the New Town, are designed to help you to understand the essential features of the medieval town and the dramatic way in which it changed during the 17th, 18th and early 19th centuries. Edinburgh Castle and Holyrood Palace are so well known and have been described so often that we have omitted them in order to focus on less well-known features of the townscape, but if you have time you may wish to include a tour of these at the beginning and end of the trail. Guide books to both are widely available in Edinburgh.

1. The Castle Esplanade

From the Castle Esplanade you get a good impression of the site of the old town. The volcanic plug on which the Castle sits provides an ideal defensive site with easy access only from the east. There was probably a fortification of some sort here in prehistoric times, but the Dark-Age fortress and the early-medieval royal castle provided the original focus which attracted a trading settlement. The steep faces of the Castle Rock have been cut by ice sheets coming from the west. The rock protected a tail of softer sedimentary rocks in its lee forming a long ridge descending gradually from the Castle to Holyrood Palace. On either side of this 'crag and tail' feature the ice scoured deep hollows. The one to the north is occupied by Princes Street Gardens and the railway, the one to the south by the Grassmarket and the Cowgate. The steep slopes dropping down from the ridge to these hollows gave the town some natural protection. This was enhanced by damming the hollow to the north to create the Nor' Loch, which was drained in the 18th century, while an expanding perimeter to the south was enclosed by various defensive walls between the 14th and 17th centuries.

Many other medieval Scottish burghs were established along the line of a road leading from the gates of a royal castle—Stirling and Peebles for instance—and had a linear form. In the case of Edinburgh the restricted nature of the site, with the steep slopes to north and south, made this more pronounced. From this location you can also see the low ridge above Princes Street Gardens—farmland until after the mid-18th century—on which the New Town was built.

2. Cannonball House

A cannonball is embedded high up in the masonry of the side of Cannonball House facing the Castle. One tradition is that it was fired in the 1745 rebellion during a bombardment from the Castle after the Jacobite army had captured the city. Another story is that it marks the height to which water could be raised in the city from a source at Comiston to the south. Water was first piped to the city in 1681, and the low stone building opposite Cannonball House is a later reservoir. Before that the only sources of water for drinking and other uses were wells and the murky Nor' loch. The house itself dates from about 1630.

3. Ramsay Lodge and Ramsay Gardens

Ramsay Gardens is Victorian picturesque. Built in 1893 to a design

by Sir Patrick Geddes, the pioneer town planner, it stands on the
site of a house owned by the 18th-century poet Allan Ramsay
(Trail 3). The brightly-coloured terrace, with its timbered gables,
forms a striking contrast to the darker stonework of the tenements
on the south side of Castlehill and the Lawnmarket when seen
from Princes Street. Ramsay Lodge was originally a Georgian
terrace, remodelled in Victorian times.

4. Milne's Court

Milne's Court was an early attempt to provide more spacious
housing conditions within the Old Town. It was built between
1690 and 1700 under the direction of Robert Milne, the master
mason who designed the extension to Holyrood Palace for Charles
II. The facade of this apartment block has more uniformity of style
and more elegance than earlier ones, reflecting the more demand-
ing tastes and higher incomes of some of the city's inhabitants in
the later 17th century. The block is centred around an open
courtyard which, though small, is really the city's first proper
square—a counterpart of the residential squares of late 17th-
century London adapted to fit the cramped conditions of Edinburgh. In this sense it forms a link between older tenements like
Gladstone's Land (see below) and the elegant residential areas of
the New Town.

5. The Lawnmarket

From the top of the Lawnmarket you get a good impression of the
layout of the medieval town. The street pattern is the most
enduring feature and has changed relatively little. As in many
other medieval burghs, the single main street widens in the centre
of the town to form a market place: the change in width from
Castlehill into Lawnmarket is striking. The main street retains
this width until beyond St. Giles. The Lawnmarket was the largest
open space in the late-medieval town apart from the Grassmarket.
The name was originally 'Land market', the place where people
from the 'landward' or country areas brought their produce for
sale. City craftsmen sold their goods from the front of their own
workshops but many other traders sold from stalls in the street, as
did people bringing food and other produce into the town.

Lawnmarket and Castle from St. Giles

Originally all the market trade was accommodated in the High Street itself; looking down the Lawnmarket, you can visualise the chaos which this must have caused in such a limited space. By the 17th century the city was so large that permanent food markets were necessary and these were mostly shifted to sites down closes on the south side of the High Street below St. Giles: the location of the fish and flesh markets is commemorated in the names of closes while the grain and meal market was located behind the High Kirk itself.

In the early medieval burgh the building plots, or burgages, were laid out in long narrow strips running back from the main street in a herringbone pattern. The plots were narrow so as to give as many occupiers as possible a frontage on the main street and market area. Originally only the street frontage was built up—the 'foreland'—but as pressure for more accommodation grew new buildings, the 'backlands', were constructed, infilling the rear of the plots. This process was well advanced by the end of the 15th century. These backlands took the form of lines of houses and workshops, gable end on to the street. Access to them was provided by narrow alleys between the forelands, or sometimes running under them, which were known as 'closes', or sometimes 'wynds' and 'vennels'. The names of these could be topographical such as 'Fishmarket Close', but more commonly they came to be named after various families who occupied the forelands from which the closes led off. Wynds were common access ways while closes were private and might be shut off by gates. Semple's Close, on the north side of Castlehill, is a good example of the latter.

6. Gladstone's Land

Gladstone's Land is the best surviving example of an early 17th-century tenement block in Edinburgh. Within Britain the tenement has been seen as a characteristically Scottish form of housing. Its adoption in Scotland may reflect the country's close contact with France and Holland before the 18th century, for although tenements spread widely during the Industrial Revolution, they originated at a much earlier date. Tenements were found in other late-medieval burghs such as Glasgow, while flatted housing was built even in small towns like St. Andrews where there was plenty of space (Trail No. 11), but tenements were a particular feature of Edinburgh. Here they were a response to a chronic lack of space caused by an awkward site and the very tight circuit of the burgh limits, which barely extended beyond the Flodden Wall. Disputes between the burgh council and surrounding landowners prevented the city from adding additional land to its jurisdiction or 'royalty' before the 18th century. The population within the city walls—an area of only 140 acres—doubled in the century after 1540, producing one of the densest concentrations of population anywhere in Europe. The only way to accommodate people was to build upwards, and the scale of high-rise developments in Edinburgh by the 17th century was unrivalled. Some of the tenements which were built into the steep slope dropping down to the Cowgate behind St. Giles had six or seven storeys fronting on to the High Street and as many below facing to the south. The National Library of Scotland on George IV Bridge has a similar layout today.

Gladstone's Land was rebuilt by Thomas Gledstanes, a wealthy merchant, around 1620. The stone facade may have replaced earlier timber galleries like those on John Knox's House (see below). Inside the house, on the first floor, you can see the position of the street frontage of this earlier building. Removing the timber galleries and building a stone-arcaded front instead allowed Gledstanes to make a permanent encroachment of some 5m into the street. Nibbling away at the width of streets in this fashion was common in late-medieval Scottish towns.

On the ground floor were two shops protected by an arcade. The arcade was a continuation in stone of the old method of supporting the projecting fronts of timber buildings on wooden posts. This is the only example left in the Royal Mile, though formerly they were a common feature. Some modern ones have been constructed in the Canongate to preserve the tradition. An outside forestair on the left-hand side of the building gave access to the first floor, and from there an internal turnpike staircase ran to the flats above. A similar forestair can be seen on Moubray House, near John Knox's House. Forestairs were sometimes placed less elegantly in the middle of the frontage, cutting off light to the ground floor, a feature criticised by William Dunbar in an early 16th-century poem. An alternative arrangement was for the turnpike staircase to come down to street level in an external tower. No examples of this survive in Edinburgh's High Street, but one can be seen in St. Andrews (Trail 11). During the 1630s Gladstone's Land accommodated two merchant families and three other families. The building is now owned by the National Trust for Scotland and is open to the public.

7. James' Court, Wardrop's Court

These two courts on the north side of the Lawnmarket allow you to inspect the back of the street frontages and to see the tower staircases giving access to the upper floors. The six and seven-storey buildings around these small courtyards give a good impression of the density of population in the Old Town in the past: there is still a substantial resident population in these areas.

8. The Site of the Tolbooth

The heart-shaped pattern of stones in the roadway marks the site of the city's old Tolbooth whose storming by a mob during the Porteous Riots of 1736 has been immortalised by Scott in *The Heart of Midlothian*. The Tolbooth was almost the only public building in the Old Town before the 18th century, apart from the

Wardrop's Court, off Lawnmarket

churches. Originally the place where market tolls and dues were
collected (hence the name), it also served as a meeting place for the
burgh council, as a courthouse and as a prison. Because of the
density of building around the market place and the lack of specific
provision for any such buildings when burghs were first founded
in medieval times, it was often necessary for the tolbooth to be
built in the middle of the market place. This infilling of the market
place, albeit by a public building, often led to further unauthorised
colonisation of the market area by stallholders and shopkeepers. A
jumble of shops, called the Luckenbooths, was gradually built up
against the east end of the Tolbooth, narrowing the High Street at
this point to a mere 4m-wide lane. In other towns, such as Stirling,
this infilling of the market place was allowed to remain but in

Edinburgh, possibly because space was so limited, it was cleared away when the Tolbooth was demolished in 1817.

9. St. Giles

The High Kirk of St. Giles (it was a cathedral for only five years during the reign of Charles I) is one of the finest Scottish examples of an urban parish church, or burgh kirk. The main parish church was one of a burgh's important prestige symbols, and many of those in Scotland's larger medieval towns were rebuilt, extended and embellished between the mid-15th century and the Reformation in 1560, a period of modest but steady growth in burgh populations and prosperity. Many of Edinburgh's guilds had their own altars in the church. This explains its great width, as there were originally rows of chapels on either side of the nave. The church also benefited from endowments by individual wealthy burgesses. Although there was a church on this site from the 9th century, the oldest parts of the present structure, the four central pillars, only date from about 1120. The church developed to its present form mainly in the 15th and 16th centuries; the nave was flanked by double aisles housing various chapels. A crossing tower was built where the nave met the short transepts. The crown spire dates from 1485. This kind of spire is very much a Scottish feature and is found in a number of other burghs, as late-medieval examples or 19th-century imitations. The old stonework of the walls of the church has been hidden by a 19th-century cladding of ashlar, making the building seem more modern that it actually is. The Chapel of the Order of the Thistle was added in 1911.

10. Parliament House

The old Parliament House was completed on the orders of Charles I in 1639. Since the Union of 1707 it has housed Scotland's high courts. The buildings were remodelled between 1807 and 1810 by Robert Reid because of a need for more space. In this rebuilding the irregular but picturesque 17th-century facade was replaced by the present classical one.

11. The Royal Exchange

The Royal Exchange was the first new public building in the mid-

18th-century programme to improve the city which went on to create the New Town. It replaced an older exchange built in 1683 to the east of Parliament House but destroyed by fire in 1700. The Exchange was designed by John Adam as a meeting place where Edinburgh's merchants could conduct their business. The plan featured a custom house in the centre and incorporated over 40 shops, ten dwellings, two printing houses and three coffee houses behind an imposing facade. The building now serves as the City Chambers.

12. The Mercat Cross

The mercat cross was an affirmation in stone of a burgh's trading privileges—the very reason for its existence—and its right to hold markets and fairs. This made it the symbolic focus of the market place, the spot where people met to transact business and exchange news. Proclamations were read from its base and it was also used as a place of execution. Despite the name, comparatively few Scottish examples actually bear a cross head; more frequently the shaft is surmounted by a coat of arms or a figure, in this case a unicorn. The first mercat cross in Edinburgh is mentioned in the 14th century but the present one is much more recent. Parts of the shaft date from the 16th century but most of it is 19th century.

13. The Tron Church

The Tron Church takes its name from the nearby tron or weigh-beam where produce being brought to market was weighed. It was built between 1637 and 1641 to accommodate parishioners who could no longer use St. Giles as a result of internal alterations when it was elevated to a cathedral. It was designed on a T-plan, a layout used for a number of other 17th-century Scottish churches. Unfortunately it has suffered badly from later alterations. The south aisle was removed in the 18th century as part of an improvement scheme, while the steeple was destroyed by fire and replaced by the present one in 1828.

14. John Knox's House

Houses in medieval Edinburgh were mostly of timber-frame construction with wattle and daub panels and thatched roofs.

John Knox's House

While the street plan and the layout of the building plots have survived with relatively little change, buildings had much less permanence. The old timber-frame structures were demolished at an early date and replaced by stone ones or were destroyed by fire: Edinburgh, like most pre-industrial cities, suffered a number of serious blazes. Some traces of timber houses have been discovered by excavation. Many houses of this type were replaced in stone during the period of growing population and prosperity during the later 16th and early 17th centuries. The fashion continued, however, of adding external timber galleries to such buildings and facing over the stone fronts with Norway 'deals' or boards. During the 17th century the Burgh Council made efforts to prevent the construction of new houses of this kind because of the fire risk. Stone frontages like Gladstone's Land were the result. A number of these timber-fronted houses survived into the 19th century. A fine group in the Lawnmarket survived late enough to be captured on photograph, but only one example is left today. The building called John Knox's house—it is uncertain whether the reformer actually lived here—is a fine example of these early timber-fronted stone houses. Parts of the house may go back to the late 15th century, but it assumed its present appearance in the later 16th century when it was owned by John Mossman, a goldsmith, whose initials still appear on a carved panel. There is a fine two-storey timber gallery on the south side and there are timber gables on both the south and west facades. Further up the High Street, under pressure of demand for space, this type of house gave way to higher stone tenements like Gladstone's Land.

15. The Netherbow Port

Edinburgh remained a walled city until the middle of the 18th century. Early walls enclosed only a limited area. The King's Wall of the mid-15th century ran about halfway between the High Street and the Cowgate. Growth of the city during the 16th century led to the construction of the Flodden Wall. Building started soon after the defeat at Flodden in 1513 but continued throughout the next half-century. The defences enclosed a much larger area to the south including the Cowgate and Grassmarket and an area beyond as far south as where the Old College of the University now stands. As well as acting as a defence, the walls allowed people and goods entering the town to be controlled and supervised: for instance the gates could be closed under threat of plague. The brass plates in the roadway at this point mark the position of the Netherbow Port, one of the main gateways in the wall. This ancient gateway was rebuilt with an imposing set of towers in the early 17th century. It was still in use as a defensive barrier in 1745 but was demolished in 1764, a measure of how quickly the Jacobite threat was dissipated after Culloden.

16. The Canongate

Beyond the Netherbow Port you enter the Canongate. While the city of Edinburgh extended from the Castle to Holyrood, the royal burgh proper stopped here. The Canongate was a separate burgh, authorised in 1143 by David I who granted to the Augustinian monks of Holyrood Abbey the right to establish a burgh of their own along the 'gait' or road which led from the pre-existing royal burgh to the abbey. St. Andrews and Glasgow were originally similar foundations. The Canongate remained a totally separate burgh till 1636 with its own council, officials and guilds. There was a good deal of squabbling between the two burghs over their respective trading rights and the activities of their guilds. At that time the royal burgh acquired the feudal superiority of the Canongate which thenceforth became more closely integrated in administrative terms with the upper town though it retained some elements of its separate identity until 1856 when they were finally abolished.

In functional rather than legal terms the Canongate was an undefended suburb of the royal burgh. It was much less densely built up. 18th-century maps show that behind the street frontages there was only a modest amount of infilling by buildings and a good deal of open space with gardens and orchards. The buildings along the street were also lower and the Canongate retains its more open aspect to the present day. Because there was more space, and because it was adjacent to the palace, the Canongate was a popular place for the wealthier nobles to have their town houses; a number of these have survived. A similar cluster of town houses occurs outside Stirling Castle where the Scottish court was often based in the 16th century.

17. Chessel's Court

Chessel's Court was built in 1748. Its facade, with its symmetry and balance, reflects the change to a more stylish type of architecture, and heralds the start of the improvement of the city in the mid-18th century that led to the creation of the New Town. The overall appearance of the building, on the other hand, still harks back to the 17th century. It was restored in the 1950s as part of a scheme for renovating the Canongate which had by this time become very decayed. As you walk down the Canongate you will see many restored buildings and a number of completely new ones designed in traditional styles to blend in with the older ones. How successful do you consider the renovation work has been?

18. Moray House

Moray House is the grandest of the surviving town houses of the nobility in the Canongate. It was built around 1625—after the court had moved to London but when the Scottish Parliament and Privy Council still met in Edinburgh—for Mary, Countess of Home. It was originally designed around a large courtyard but only the north and west sides of the house have survived. Note the gallery which is carried out over the street on stone corbels: this is another example of timber construction styles being perpetuated in stone.

19. The Canongate Tolbooth

Unlike the one which stood beside St. Giles, the Canongate Tolbooth has been preserved, perhaps because with less pressure on space in the Canongate it was possible to build it into the main frontage rather than in the middle of the street. It is a good example of early civic pride—the tower, which dates from the end of the 16th century is reminiscent of a tower-house, down to the gun-loops (Trail 2). The three-storey block beside it may be contemporary or a later addition.

20. Huntly House

The name of Huntly House might suggest that it was another town house for a noble family. In fact it was originally three separate dwellings built around 1570. It was bought as an investment in 1647 by the Incorporation of Hammermen (metal workers) of the Canongate, one of the wealthier trades guilds. The building is mainly a stone one with timber gables like John Knox's House, but the jettied stories projecting over the street, supported on stone corbels, echo an older tradition of timber building. Many guilds in both the Canongate and the royal burgh of Edinburgh owned property in which they could hold guild meetings and even support impoverished guild brethren, though Huntly House was mainly let out to tenants: 17 of them in 1762. Behind Huntly House is Bakehouse Close, named after a property belonging to the Canongate bakers. The archway dates from 1570.

Huntly House, Canongate

21. Canongate Church

Comparatively few churches were built in Scotland during the
17th century, in the wake of the Reformation, but this is an
outstanding example. Its curved gables are reminiscent of contemporary Dutch architecture. Scotland had close trading links with
the Low Countries at this time, and similar styles can be seen on
gables elsewhere in the Old Town. The church was built in 1688 as
a new parish church for the Canongate. Parishioners had previously used the abbey church at Holyrood, but James VII took it
over as a chapel for the Knights of the Thistle, and the Canongate
Church was built as a substitute.

22. Canongate Manse

Further down from the Canongate Church on the same side is the manse. It was originally built around 1690 as a coaching inn. Because of the steep climb to the upper part of the city, and the obstructions caused by gateways and market stalls, Edinburgh's coaching inns were mostly located in the lower part of the Canongate and the Grassmarket which were much easier of access for wheeled vehicles.

23. Acheson House

Opposite the Canongate Church, down a close, is Acheson House, another town house, built in 1633 for Sir Archebald Acheson, a counsellor to Charles I. It was one of many town houses belonging

Acheson House, Canongate

to quite prosperous landowners which were located down narrow closes because of the shortage of available sites on the main street. Even houses with frontages on the main street, like Huntly House, might have their main entrances down a close, possibly for reasons of security.

24. Panmure House

Panmure House, the town house of the Earls of Panmure, is located up Little Lochen Close further down on the opposite side of the road.

White Horse Close, Canongate

25. Queensberry House

Queensberry House, an austere-looking building with a main block flanked by wings enclosing a small courtyard, was the last of the great town houses to be built in Edinburgh before the Union of

1707 dissolved the Scottish Parliament and Privy Council. It was constructed in the early 1680s for Lord Hatton but sold soon after to the Duke of Queensberry.

26. White Horse Close

White Horse Inn, at the rear of the close, was one of the principal inns in the Canongate. It was built in 1623 and was attractively restored in the 1960s.

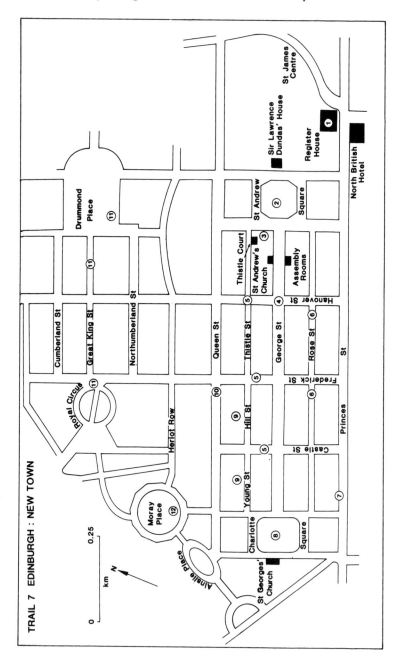

TRAIL 7 EDINBURGH : NEW TOWN

SEVEN

Edinburgh: The New Town

Ordnance Survey 1:50,000 sheet 66; 1:25,000 sheet NT 27

This trail involves a walk of about 4km.

Introduction

Ideas of Renaissance architecture and town planning spread into England during the early 17th century. On the Continent many new towns were laid out incorporating the new planning ideas, often with elaborate sets of fortifications against artillery. Renaissance town planning in Britain was more piecemeal. London expanded by the haphazard addition of large numbers of residential squares from the 1630s, but these did not form part of any integrated large-scale planning scheme. Developments in provincial towns had a similar character. Only two British towns were totally remodelled as a result of the new planning ideas: Bath and Edinburgh. The New Town of Edinburgh is the largest and, many people consider, the most magnificent piece of 18th-century town planning in Britain.

The first New Town was built between the 1770s and the early years of the 19th century. It was followed by a series of further developments during the early decades of the 19th century. Together these schemes contain miles of streets and cover an area which is many times greater than that of the Old Town. Parts of the New Town, especially Princes Street, George Street and some of the cross-streets between, have been heavily altered with their conversion from residential areas to shopping and business districts, but three quarters of the New Town is still residential and its character has been preserved from further alteration by designating it as a conservation area. The trail follows the chronological development of the New Town so that you can see how ideas of urban architecture and planning evolved from the middle of the 18th century to the middle of the 19th.

107

Origins of the New Town

The cramped, confined nature of the medieval city, and the effects which this had on its buildings, have been described in the previous trail. When the Jacobite army captured Edinburgh in 1745 the city was still sheltering behind the Flodden Wall. A desire for security may have been one factor in checking the outward growth of the capital. Probably more important were the restrictions imposed by its site, particularly northwards where the deep valley which held the Nor' Loch was a barrier to expansion. The limited extent of the 'royalty'—the area over which the city's privileges as a royal burgh operated—was also important. The boundaries of the royalty barely extended beyond the walls. The city could not expand under the control of the burgh authorities until the royalty had been extended. Some suburban growth had taken place on the south side of the city, within the area of the dependent baronial burgh of Portsburgh which was controlled by the city, but more land was needed. An ideal site was available on the far side of the Nor' Loch on the gently-sloping ridge of land which ran parallel with the Old Town—providing that the two could be connected.

Edinburgh had no public buildings of note and was chronically short of space. Some of the tenements were in a dangerous condition: one collapsed in the early 1750s and others around it had to be demolished for safety. Ideas for extending the royalty and for improving the city were in the air after the failure of the 1745 Rebellion. A major figure behind them was Provost George Drummond whose grand design for the city was published as a set of proposals in 1752. These formed the blueprint for the New Town. In 1759 drainage of the Nor' Loch was started and work commenced on building the North Bridge in 1763. In 1767 an Act of Parliament authorised the extension of the royalty to include the area known as Bearford's Parks on the far side of the Nor' Loch, the road called the Lang Dykes to the south of it (the road which was to become Princes Street) and other adjacent land which the city had purchased. All that was needed now was a design for the new town.

In 1766 a competition was held to select a plan. The winning entry was by James Craig, an unknown architect then 23 years old. His scheme was a straightforward one: a main street running east-west along the crest of the ridge linking a square at each end. On either side were two other major streets parallel to the central one, while between them ran two narrower lanes which were designed to accommodate the tradespeople who would be needed to provide services for the well-to-do inhabitants of the main streets. Mews lanes led off from these, giving access to stables and coach houses at the rear of the main properties. Other thoroughfares intersected the five parallel streets at right angles to produce a grid plan.

Craig's plan has been crticised as dull, orthodox and unadventurous. Certainly he did not incorporate some of the new planning ideas which were then in vogue, like crescents and circuses. The success of his plan lies in its superb use of the site, with the ground falling away on each side of the central street and giving fine views of the Old Town and the Firth of Forth from each intersection.

The names of the streets in Craig's New Town symbolised the union of Scotland and England under the House of Hanover. The main avenue, George Street, named after the King, linked St. Andrew and St. George Square. Parallel to George Street ran Queen Street and Princes Street. The narrower lanes between were later named Rose and Thistle Street. Two of the cross-streets were named after the House of Hanover and Frederick, George's son. Unfortunately for the symmetry of this design Edinburgh already had a George Square south of the old town, built in the late 1760s and named not after the monarch but the architect's brother. To avoid confusion St. George Square was renamed after the Queen, Charlotte.

The location of Craig's plan on the ground does not fit the site perfectly. It was not possible to locate St. Andrew Square sufficiently far to the east to allow it to have a direct connexion with the road from the North Bridge because the city did not then own all the land west of Calton Hill. The line of the old road to Queensferry also impinged on the junction btween Charlotte Square and Princes Street at the west end.

1. In Front of Register House

From in front of Register House you get a good impression of the site of the Old Town and the deep glacially-scoured hollow between it and the New Town. An important prerequisite for constructing the New Town was direct access across the valley. This was provided by the North Bridge, which was completed in

1772, and later by the Mound further to the west which was constructed from earth removed from the foundations of houses in the New Town.

Looking along Princes Street you can appreciate how the open view of the gardens and the Castle contributes to its quality. Imagine what the view would have been like if both sides of the street had been built up. This nearly happened and was only prevented by stout resistance from a body of New Town residents who challenged the would-be developers and took the case as high as the Court of Session before they won.

In front of you is the bulk of the North British Hotel, named after the railway company which had it built in 1902. The building has been regarded by some as a monstrous eyesore, but there is no denying its striking impact.

Behind you is Register House, a purpose-built archive for the public records of Scotland. These had formerly been kept in poor conditions in basements in the Old Town. Plans for a proper archive were produced in 1722 but implementation of them had to

Sir Laurence Dundas' House, St. Andrew Square

wait until the mid-1760s when government finance became available. By this time Craig's plan for the New Town had been adopted and this site was chosen to encourage further development in the area. Robert and James Adam produced the design and work began on it in 1774. Due to its high cost Register House was not completed until 1786. Its facade is a fine example of the Adam brothers' neo-classical style. It is well worth visiting the Scottish Record Office inside to see the interiors of the Legal and Historical Search Rooms, and to admire the dome, where exhibitions are often on display.

Round the corner from Register House, the St. James' shopping centre stands on the site of St. James Square, built during the last quarter of the 18th century to a plan by James Craig. The buildings were rather severe in appearance, and by the 1960s they had become so neglected and derelict that they had to be demolished, one of the few areas of the New Town where this has occurred. A plaque records the former existence of the square. The centre dwarfs Register House, dominates Leith Street and interrupts the skyline of the Old Town when seen from the north.

2. St. Andrew Square

The fine building set back on the east side of the square, now owned by the Royal Bank of Scotland, was built as a private house for Sir Laurence Dundas. On Craig's original plan it was intended that a church should occupy this site, its tower terminating the vista eastwards down George Street. Dundas had made a fortune while Commissary General to the British Army in Flanders during the 1750s. He had acquired property to the east of the site of the square before Craig drew up his plan. After the plan was approved, he succeeded in extending his lands by obtaining one of the first plots in the New Town. He acquired the rights to this key site without its exact location being generally realised. The house was completed before anyone could protest, and St. Andrew's Church had to be built on a cramped and less satisfactory position in George Street. The buildings on either side of Dundas' house were planned to be identical, giving this side of the square something of the appearance of a country house with wings and a central forecourt. The north one was built in 1769, the south one in 1781. Despite the Town Council's efforts to make the later one corre-

Georgian houses on the north side of St. Andrew Square

spond to the earlier, the builder cut a few corners with the design: can you spot them?

The column in the centre of the square supports a statue of Henry Dundas, first Viscount Melville, the influential late 18th-century politician. It was completed in 1837. Sir Laurence Dundas' town house, despite its fine appearance, is not large enough to fill the vista looking eastwards down George Street, especially today as it is overtopped by the St. James' Centre: the column provides the focus which the tower of St. Andrew's church should have done and which St. George's Church does when you look west.

From the north-east corner of the square you can see how steeply the land falls to the north, giving the residents of Queen Street a fine view across the Forth and providing a challenging site for the planners who designed the later phases of the New Town.

The north side of the square is the best-preserved one. When the first building plots in the New Town began to be taken up the Town Council imposed only a general set of building regulations. If they considered the possibility of trying to impose a greater measure of control through the design of uniform facades for the square, they did not adopt the idea. The demand for houses in the earliest years of the New Town, before it had become fashionable, was probably too limited for anyone to take the financial risk of planning large blocks of houses simultaneously. The Council merely specified that houses should not exceed three storeys on the main squares and streets, with sunk basements. The houses on this side of the square show how individual builders worked within these general guidelines. Three of the six houses are built with rubble masonry rather than ashlar (dressed stone), although this was originally plastered over. The ashlar fronts of the remaining houses may seem rather bland: this problem was solved further to the west by adding extra decorative features, and tooling the stonework in different styles on the ground floor and basement areas to break up the facades. There are differences in the height of the roofline, the positions of doors and windows, and the type of ornamentation. While this row of houses lacks the pure classical style of later developments like Charlotte Square, it has a homely appearance which is closer to the vernacular Georgian work of many smaller Scottish towns in the later 18th century.

3. Thistle Court

The block of two houses at the east end of Thistle Court was supposedly the first to be built in the New Town. The simple design, the warmth of the red sandstone rubble masonry and the open space between them give these buildings an almost rural air even though they are overshadowed by later development. This kind of court layout was not repeated in the side streets of Craig's new town, probably because it took up too much space.

4. George Street

Building of the New Town began around St. Andrew Square and moved progressively westwards along George Street, Princes Street, Queen Street, and the streets linking them. Relatively few of George Street's houses have survived unaltered without the insertion of modern shop fronts. Some have been replaced by later buildings, notably banks. The original building regulations, which stipulated that the height of frontages from basement to wall head should not exceed 14m, have been widely ignored.

A short distance up George Street from St. Andrew Square on the

Thistle Court: the first houses to be built in Craig's new town

right-hand side is the re-sited church of St. Andrew. Completed in 1787, it has a fine classical facade which deserves a less cramped site. The interior is also very attractive and is unusual in being oval in plan.

The Assembly Rooms were built by public subscription between 1784 and 1787 to provide a focus for New Town society. The portico which projects out into the street was added in 1818.

5. Hanover Street, Frederick Street, Castle Street

Most of the cross-streets of Craig's New Town have been altered by the insertion of modern shop fronts, but above the ground floor many original facades survive. The idea of designing groups of houses with balanced uniform facades had been developed by the time that Hanover and Frederick Streets were built—you can see examples, above the shop fronts, where flanking bow windows and a central feature were used to give unity to small groups of houses. The overall effect is still rather plain and simple, though. The same design, but with a much improved appearance, was used in North Castle Street. The houses on the east side of North Castle

Street, where Sir Walter Scott lived for much of the first quarter of the 19th century, are particularly fine. The quality of finish has vastly improved from the earlier houses in the cross-streets further east. Rubble masonry has given way to ashlar, and the ground-floor and basement courses have been attractively tooled or 'rusticated'.

North Castle Street

6. Rose Street

Much of the eastern end of Rose Street has been redeveloped, but some of the original houses can be seen above the shop fronts towards the western end. The quality of the stonework and the design is crude compared with adjacent houses on the main streets, and some of the buildings are flatted: can you pick out the common staircases?

7. Princes Street

Princes Street was built up rather haphazardly between the 1770s and 1805. Most of the houses were relatively plain and undistin-

guished, of two and three storeys. A group of these survives above
the shop fronts at the very western end of the street. Princes Street
was originally residential, but because of its proximity to the Old
Town it was rapidly taken over by shops, hotels and offices so that
by the 1830s many of the original residents had moved to other,
more peaceful, parts of the New Town. The street was largely
rebuilt with more substantial properties in Victorian times: Jen-
ners' department store is a fine example with its original interior
preserved, but a good deal of even this later development has been
lost and modern shop fronts inserted.

8. Charlotte Square

Charlotte Square has been called a masterpiece of urban design
and is widely acknowledged to be a major achievement in European urban architecture. Although grand in conception, it remains
human in its proportions. By the time the New Town had
extended this far west the Council, realising that their permissive
building regulations had led to a greater lack of uniformity than
had been expected, determined to create a showpiece. They commissioned Robert Adam, the foremost architect of his day, then at
the peak of his career, to design the square as a unified scheme. His
plan, produced in 1791, was for palace facades with central
classical pediments and projecting end wings. The houses were to
be further unified by ornamental features like balustrades, decorative panels and even the iron railings. The square was built up
mainly between 1792 and the early years of the 19th century. The
north side of the square is the closest to Adam's original design,
although partly due to some careful 20th-century restoration.
During and after the original building, alterations were made
which departed from Adam's plan—doors and windows were
changed and extra floors and dormer windows inserted in the roofs
against his instructions. These variations are more evident on the
east and west sides of the square. They do not detract from the fine
appearance of the square as a whole or of the individual ranges of
buildings. Notice how the pavements are raised and provided with
mounting blocks to allow easy access for carriages.

The church of St. George is on the site envisaged on Craig's
plan. Unfortunately, the Council tried to save money by dropping
Adam's design which featured a large triangular pediment sup-

Charlotte Square, north side

ported by four pairs of columns, and two small domes flanking the main one. Instead they opted for a cheaper design by Robert Reid. The dome is designed to be a replica in miniature of St. Paul's in London. The church is now West Register House, containing archives, especially maps and plans, for which there is insufficient space in the original Register House.

No. 7 Charlotte Square, in the middle of the north side, has been restored by the National Trust for Scotland. It has been carefully furnished so that it is as close as possible to its appearance when it was first occupied in 1796. A tour of the house allows you to recreate the lifestyle of the original inhabitants of the New Town, forming a fascinating contrast with Gladstone's Land in the Lawnmarket.

9. Young Street, Hill Street, Thistle Street

The lesser streets of the New Town do not have the elegance of the main thoroughfares and squares, but they do have some fine Georgian buildings. The west end of Thistle Street and its continuation into Hill Street and Young Street are the least altered of these streets. They have some solid three-storey houses many of which

Young Street: some of the less pretentious houses in Craig's new town

have been designed as matching pairs and blocks. Some are clearly flatted, but the best of them must have been affordable only by fairly well-to-do occupants. The overall effect, due to the narrowness of the street, is rather dour and austere. In the mews lanes between this street and the backs of the properties which face on to George Street and Queen Street you can find one or two examples of coach house and stable blocks with accommodation above. In one or two cases the archways of the coach houses have been preserved; in others they have been blocked up or replaced by rectangular garage doors. Additional stable blocks have been built against the backs of the Young Street properties, shutting out the light to the ground-floor rooms at the rear.

10. Queen Street

Because it was furthest from the early commercial development along Princes Street, Queen Street has retained more of its original character than the other main streets in Craig's development. It provides some excellent examples of how, within the general guidelines of the early building regulations, it was possible to achieve individuality of design of windows, doorways and decorative features like balustrades and balconies. Again, dormers have been added to some of the houses and the astragals of the original windows removed and replaced by plate glass in many cases, but the overall effect has not been lost. Notice that the widths of the frontages of the houses vary; there was no restriction on how wide a frontage could be taken up in the early phases of development, as long as the height of the facade conformed with the general requirements.

11. The Second New Town

Craig's New Town was designed as a self-contained entity with no plans for further expansion, as is shown by the lack of access to the two squares from the east and west. By the time Charlotte Square was completed, however, it was clear that demand for further development existed. The area immediately to the north and west of Craig's New Town was owned by four main proprietors. During the early 19th century each of them developed their lands as new residential areas. These developments were planned and built separately, but because they adjoin each other and the original New Town one can walk from one to the other without any real sense of discontinuity. Craig's New Town gives one a sense of sequential development when walking from east to west, as though the architects and builders were experimenting as they went. By the time the later phases of the Georgian New Town were built, they had decided exactly what they wanted and how to achieve it, so that these districts have more homogeneity about them. Each of them incorporates ideas like crescents and circuses which were not used in the first New Town.

Heriot's Hospital owned the biggest block of land north of Queen Street, and in the 1820s they began to lay out an extension to the original New Town as a speculative venture. Though many people considered that it would flop, the New Town was so firmly established as the fashionable area to live in that there was no shortage of interest. As a result, building was completed much faster than in Craig's New Town. Its plan was not dissimilar to Craig's—a central street (Great King Street) linked a square (Drummond Place) with a circus (Royal Circus), while other streets ran parallel and at right angles to form a grid. But because the whole development is situated on a sloping site it is harder to appreciate its overall unity than is the case with Craig's plan, no matter how fine some of the individual streets may appear. The main streets with their long uniform facades emphasised by extra height and decoration on the central and end blocks are very attractive, but when this idea is transferred to some of the steeply-sloping cross-streets the effect does not work very well.

The Heriot's development achieved more architectural unity than Craig's New Town not only because it was built over a shorter period but also because stricter building controls were imposed specifying the height and width of each frontage, the kind of building stone to be used, and forbidding attic storeys and steeply-pitched roofs. There was still scope for individuality in the detail of doors, windows and decoration, but only within a tightly-controlled framework. Apart from the minor streets, each block was designed as a single unit. Great King Street is laid out in four long blocks with palace facades. Buildings in some of the side streets, like Cumberland Street, are tenements rather than houses, with common entrances. This social distinction between main and side streets follows Craig's pattern.

12. The Moray Estate

A block of land lying north and west of Charlotte Square and west of Royal Circus was owned by the Earl of Moray, who decided to develop it for housing in 1822 when work on Royal Circus had just begun. The Moray estate was to be a high-class housing develop-ment, and James Gillespie Graham was commissioned to design the frontages of the houses in great detail, down to the railings, to ensure perfect uniformity. The site was an awkward wedge-shaped one, and instead of a grid layout the novel plan of a crescent, a double crescent, and an eight-sided circus linked by short connect-ing streets was adopted. Because the Earl specified the design of the

Moray Place

houses in such detail and forced the developers to adhere to his plans—he even stipulated the quarries from which the stone was to come—the Moray estate has a greater unity than any previous one. Moray Place is the most impressive private housing development in the city. Charlotte Square has a simpler classical style: Moray Place is more imposing. You may think it is a shade overdone, a little too heavy in style to be quite comfortable for private residences, but it is a magnificent achievement nonetheless, reflecting the high social standing of those for whom the houses were intended. Moray Place fails to achieve the full impact of Charlotte Square because the mature trees in the central gardens prevent you from seeing the whole design: the visual effect is rather bitty as a result. Ainslie Place, which is smaller, is better from this point of view.

New Town Society

In the Old Town there had been comparatively little social segregation: everybody was too closely packed for this. Rich and poor lived in the same close, sometimes the same tenement, sharing a common staircase. The New Town began a trend towards the creation of distinctive 'status areas' within the city which were inhabited by people from clearly-defined social strata and income levels. Although provision had been made for tradesmen and small businesses in the side streets, Craig's New Town was designed specifically as an upper-middle-class residential suburb. The flowering of Edinburgh's cultural and intellectual life in the late 18th and early 19th centuries which was such a notable feature of the Scottish Enlightenment was increasingly centred on the New Town. Apart from business connected with the law courts, people visited the Old Town less and less frequently. As more and more of the middle classes moved out, the Old Town was abandoned to the poorer levels of society and many parts of it rapidly deteriorated into slums. At the same time, the more spacious, more gracious character of the New Town's houses encouraged a more expensive lifestyle, more materialistic with more lavish entertaining, which increased the social distance between the middle classes and those below, a social distance which was reflected in the physical gulf separating the two towns.

Georgian Development in Other Scottish Towns

Although Edinburgh's Georgian New Town is unique in its size, the degree of planning and the quality of the best of its architecture, it encouraged developments in other Scottish towns. Aberdeen, Dundee and Glasgow have their own Georgian quarters (Trail 9), though many of them have been much altered by later developments. Smaller towns like Perth and Montrose also have substantial additions to their street plans dating from this period. As one moves down to smaller towns, the Georgian element tends to be represented by individual dwellings and small groups of houses rather than by large integrated schemes, but the same basic ideals of planning and architecture remain. Some estate villages like Fochabers, Grantown on Spey and Inveraray show the kind of planning found in Edinburgh's New Town on a far smaller scale, though the houses themselves are often in a more vernacular style.

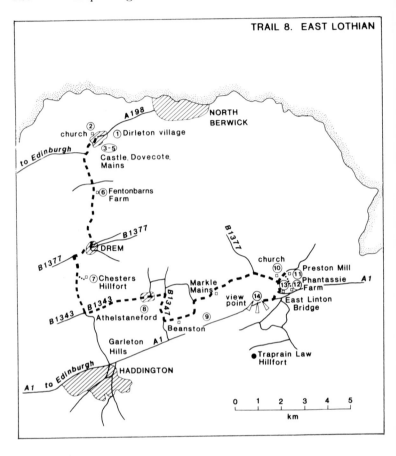

EIGHT

East Lothian: A Landscape of Agricultural Improvement

Ordance Survey 1:50,000 sheets 66–67: 1:25,000 sheets NT 57, 58

This trail involves a drive of 25km.

Introduction

The East Lothian landscape, with its large regular fields, close-cropped hedges, courtyard farmsteads and rows of farm workers' cottages, dotted at intervals with areas of woodland marking the location of estate mansions and their grounds or 'policies', is largely the creation of the later 18th and 19th centuries. Although, as we shall see, there are still many landscape features relating to earlier periods, East Lothian nevertheless epitomises the ideals of efficiency and rationality which were publicised by enthusiastic agricultural improvers—many of them East Lothian landowners—and which reached their peak in the 'high farming' era of prosperity in the mid-19th century before British agriculture was exposed to the competition of cheap grain from the American prairies. The landscape of this part of Scotland represents the culmination of efforts to create an efficient and prosperous farming system which would compare favourably with, and eventually improve upon, agriculture south of the Border. When Daniel Defoe visited the area in the early 18th century he commented on the contrast between its natural fertility and the backwardness of its farming methods. When William Cobbett travelled through East Lothian scarcely more than a century later he was profoundly impressed with the high standards of agriculture but considered that the improvers had gone rather too far in creating a regimented soulless food-factory landscape.

To appreciate what the East Lothian countryside was like before the later 18th century we have the magnificent picture provided by the Military Survey of 1747–55, a map at a scale not dissimilar to our modern 1:50,000 Ordnance Survey map (indeed, in many respects its direct ancestor). The detail of how agriculture functioned is given in collections of estate papers: rentals, leases, accounts. The arable lands lay in open fields without internal boundaries. The holdings of individual tenants and sometimes the lands of different proprietors were often scattered in strips and blocks among those of other cultivators. Some farms were held by single tenants but others were divided between two, three or more men whose shares were intermixed to give everyone a portion of both the best and worst land, a system known as 'runrig'. The arable land was divided into the infield and the outfield. The infield, the best land, usually close to the farmstead, was cultivated continuously with the aid of heavy applications of manure, producing crops of wheat, barley, oats, peas and beans. The outfield was cropped in rotation, plots being brought into cultivation for two or three years after receiving only a small amount of manure. After a few crops the fertility of the outfield fell, reducing yields below an acceptable level and the land was left to recover for a few years.

The landscape had few permanent boundaries or enclosures. It was a largely treeless patchwork in which greens, browns and yellows merged gently into each other. Even in the lowlands of the county there was still a good deal of uncultivated rough pasture: as fodder crops had not been introduced such land was essential for providing grazing for the livestock. In this open landscape the houses of the proprietors stood out because their parklands, or 'policies', were generally ornamented with plantations of trees: the fashion for this developed from the later 17th century. From the same period proprietors with an interest in improving agriculture began to experiment with new crops, better rotations and improved breeds of livestock in the parks around their houses and on their mains or home farms. By the end of the 17th century landowners were starting to enclose their home farms into large compact fields bounded by hedges and stone walls, but with limited population growth and low grain prices there was neither the capital nor the incentive to remove runrig and enclose the bulk of their estates. Some enthusiastic improvers made slow headway in this direction in the first half of the 18th century, influenced by fashion rather than profitability and a high return on their capital. By the time of the Military Survey perhaps a third of the countryside in some parts of East Lothian had been enclosed, but the main thrust of improvement came later in the 18th century when, with a growing population and rising demand, agricultural prices were higher, generating more income which could be ploughed back into estate improvement.

1. Dirleton Village (5183)

At first sight the village of Dirleton seems more English than Scottish. This is because village settlements of this size are rare over most of Scotland. Scottish rural settlement was characteristically dispersed, consisting of isolated farms and cottages with occasional small hamlet clusters rather than large villages. This may have been due in part to Scotland's physical environment: extensive areas of well-drained fertile soils, capable of supporting large communities in the past, are rare. A traditional emphasis on livestock rearing rather than arable farming, requiring less co-operation between neighbours and encouraging a more scattered settlement pattern, may also have been an influence. Where villages do occur in Scotland they are often planned estate villages from the 18th and 19th centuries rather than settlements of ancient origin (Trail 1). Dirleton, with its cottages and inns laid out around a green and dominated by an imposing baronial castle, does not seem to fit this pattern.

In south-east Scotland, from East Lothian through the Berwickshire Merse, there are, nevertheless, a number of village settlements whose origins go back to at least medieval times. These are similar in size to the small villages of Northumberland but they have no real counterpart north of the Forth. A clue to their origins may lie in their names. Most of them have names incorporating Anglian elements. The Anglian kingdom of Northumbria expanded into south-eastern Scotland early in the 7th century. Its hold over the area lasted until the early 11th century when, after the battle of Carham in 1018, the Scots pushed their frontier south to the Tweed once more. A detailed study of the elements making up these Anglian names provides clues to the extent of the influence of the Angles in this area. Place-name specialists have identified a chronological sequence of settlement names relating to their penetration of this area. The earliest known ones have endings in -ingham (Whittinghame, Tynninghame) derived from the Anglian '-ingas' (meaning 'the people of') and 'ham' (a farmstead), the first element usually being derived from a personal name. Whitting-hame is then 'the settlement of Hwita's people' or 'settlement at the place called after Hwita'. Names ending in '-ington' ('the settlement of' someone), '-worth' (an enclosure) and '-wick' (a secondary settlement) are thought to have come later. -ingham and -ington names are usually attached to places in the most fertile lowland areas, but the spread of names with -wick for example is wider, extending into the upper parts of the Tweed valley. The exact nature of the Anglian settlement is not clear, though. It has been suggested by some historians that south-east Scotland was infiltrated by substantial numbers of settlers who were used to living in comparatively large villages and who established this type of settlement in the areas which they colonised. On the other hand a relatively small elite group of Anglian leaders may have taken over the area, its settlements and population as a going concern, merely re-naming some of the places. We cannot be sure that these later villages were necessarily large when they were first established, although medieval rentals do show that some of them were substantial settlements by the 13th and 14th centuries. Nor do we know whether their early layouts corresponded with those of later times. Some of the villages in south-east Scotland have greens and a regular, planned layout, though few of these 'green villages' are as large as Dirleton. Were they laid out in this way during Anglian times, perhaps to facilitate defence, or were they the product of a later re-organisation? Many villages with greens in north-east England are now thought to have been re-organised on a more regular, planned basis after the Norman Conquest, during the 12th and 13th centuries. For these Scottish villages we do not have the same early documents to guide us. Estate rentals for Dirleton do, however, show that the village had its present layout in the 16th century, so at least its modern appearance is not the result of a late re-organisation by an improving landowner. Only excavation would help to solve this mystery. The buildings surrounding the green are comparatively recent. Most of them date from the 19th century, like the Castle Inn and the 'picturesque-style' houses with tall chimneys. These, the result of building financed by the owners of the estate, contrast with the unconsciously picturesque appearance of the cottages in Athelstaneford (see below) which were built by their individual owners.

2. Dirleton Church (513842)

The church, which stands away from the green, is obviously a late intruder into the village plan. The original parish church was located at Gullane, two miles away. It was transferred to Dirleton in 1612 because of encroachments by blowing sand. The present church is likely to have been built then or soon after. As the existing tenements surrounding the village green were already occupied, the new church had to be built on the outskirts of the village, beside the funnel-shaped loan or driftway along which animals were driven to the pasture by the seashore.

3. Dirleton Castle (516839)

Dirleton Castle is one of the most impressive baronial castles in southern Scotland. Its scale and defences are comparable with many of the more imposing medieval castles of northern England. The castle stands on a rocky outcrop commanding the village and the routeway along the coast. The right to build the first castle on this site was granted to the de Vaux family during the 12th century. The de Vaux were one of the many Anglo-Norman families who established themselves in Scotland under Anglophile Scottish Kings like David I, strengthening the monarchy and extending the feudal system as they did so (Trail 2). As on many other Scottish and English fortified sites, the first castle was probably a simple earth and timber motte and bailey which was later replaced by more substantial defences in stone. When the first stone castle was built the natural defences of the site were improved by sharpening up the rock faces of the crag and deepening the rock-cut ditch around its base. The castle was an important stronghold during the Wars of Independence, being captured by the English in 1298 and recovered by the Scots 13 years later, at which time it was partly demolished in line with Robert Bruce's policy of denying the English potential holding points in Scotland. The castle was reconstructed during the later 14th and 15th centuries. It last saw service in 1650 when it was garrisoned by a small force of royalists against Cromwell's troops. Major General Lambert obtained its surrender after a short artillery bombardment.

The castle today still presents an imposing appearance. You approach the entrance across a wooden footbridge spanning the

Dirleton Castle

fosse, on the site of the original drawbridge. The massive round
tower on your left dates from the de Vaux period of the 13th
century. The gatehouse and range of buildings to your right date
mostly from the 14th and 15th-century rebuilding under the
Halyburtons, though traces of two other 13th-century round
towers can be seen at the base of the walls. The main block on your
right incorporates the hall of the castle, with the private apartments and chapel at the far end, the kitchens towards the gatehouse, and storage areas below.

4. The Dovecote

At the corner of the wall bordering the castle is a fine example of a
dovecote. These are a common feature in East Lothian, partly
because estates in this area, although prosperous, tended to be
fairly small and thickly scattered, and dovecotes were an essential
status symbol for landed proprietors. Pigeons provided a welcome
source of fresh meat during the winter but the birds were notorious
for their depredations on surrounding grain crops. An act of the

Scottish Parliament restricted the building of dovecotes to proprietors whose lands were valued at over a certain level of annual rent. This ensured that estates with dovecotes were big enough for the birds to feed largely at the expense of the landowner's own tenants and not on the lands of neighbouring proprietors. Naturally this arrangement was not popular with the tenants whose grain was eaten by the pigeons, which they were not allowed to kill and the benefits of which went to the landlords. This example dates from the 16th century. The birds entered through a hole in the roof and nested in stone boxes inside. The projecting stone 'rat courses' were designed to prevent vermin from climbing in and destroying the eggs.

5. The Castle Mains (517839)

The mains, or home farm, of the Dirleton estate is situated immediately below the castle. A farm like this might, before the 19th century, have been run under the direct management of the proprietor to supply his household with food, or it could have been leased out to tenants. There was a mains on this site from at least the 15th century but the present farm is much more recent. A range of barns dates from 1703.

Drive west out of the village on to the A186 and turn left
towards Drem on the B345.

As you drive south you will get a good impression of the rolling, open nature of the East Lothian countryside, interspersed with large farmsteads. The one in the distance to your right shortly after you turn on to the B345 is Queenstonbank, a big 19th-century courtyard farm. Notice that the farmhouse is roofed with slate but the outbuildings with pantiles. Pantiles were first introduced as a replacement for thatch, but while they were used extensively for barns and cottages, they were not considered fashionable for more well-to-do houses until much later.

6. Fentonbarns: An 'Improved' Farmstead (514818)

New improved farmsteads, more solidly built and more efficiently laid out, were being constructed from the 1760s in this area, although most of the larger ones like Fentonbarns were rebuilt during the period of prosperous 'high farming' during the middle of the 19th century. The farmhouses, solid two and three-storey buildings, reflected the greater prosperity and higher status of the small group of men who obtained tenancies of the new large farms. The farm offices were laid out around one or more central courtyards with the emphasis on efficiency of working and minimisation of movement. Around the courtyard were grouped the cattle byres and stables, the granaries, cart sheds and barns.

Landowners in East Lothian and elsewhere in Scotland have generally received most of the credit for transforming Scottish agriculture and the rural landscape during the later 18th and 19th centuries, perhaps because they were good propagandists. The work of the tenant farmers in re-shaping the countryside and modernising agriculture was considerable and generally unsung. Fentonbarns became one of the most famous farms in Scotland during the early and mid-19th century because of the high quality of its husbandry and its great efficiency. It was tenanted by three generations of the Hope family. The grandfather began to improve the farm in a modest way in the second half of the 18th century, and his son continued the work which was completed under George Hope during the period of prosperity which preceded the influx of cheap grain from the American prairies in the later 19th century.

Fentonbarns was a large farm—about 600 acres—on some of the best soil in the county. It required a team of around 20 male farm workers and a dozen women some of whom were the wives of the ploughmen, others being Highland girls engaged on short contracts. The farm became celebrated because of the sheer drive and enterprise of its tenants. George Hope rebuilt the steading in the mid-19th century. At about the same time undersoil tile draining became possible on a large scale with the development of cheap clay pipes. Hope established a tile works on the farm which supplied not only Fentonbarns but neighbouring farms. The profits from the works paid for the installation of the drains. So celebrated was the farm and its methods that it acted as a kind of agricultural school where young men, including many from England, would come to work for a year or two before returning home to put the new ideas into practice. 'Factory farming' and 'agribusiness' may seem modern phenomena, but Fentonbarns in the middle of the 19th century was every bit a factory. The original farmhouse at Fentonbarns is in ruins, but the outbuildings, of stone rubble construction with pantiled roofs, bear the date 1874 over one of the arches—they were built right at the end of the 'high farming' period. Later outbuildings have been laid out around the original ones.

Five pairs of farm workers' cottages line the approach to Fentonbarns. The earliest phases of agricultural improvement brought little change to the living conditions of farm workers. Priority was given to rebuilding the tenants' houses, then to providing better accommodation for the livestock: better conditions for farm workers came last of all. Until well into the 19th century many of them were still living in crudely-built one-roomed huts.

Before the rationalisation of farms in the 18th and 19th centuries much of the labour was provided by living-in male and female farm servants who were normally unmarried, and by married cottars who sublet portions of the farm in return for supplying labour for an agreed number of days per week. As farms were consolidated and enlarged the cottar system declined: the cottar holdings were absorbed into the tenants' lands and the cottars became wage-earning labourers. In areas like East Lothian which concentrated on cereal growing the skilled ploughman was the

Farm workers' cottages, Drem

aristocrat of the rural labour force: he was comparatively well paid, and in addition to his wages he usually received a smallholding for growing potatoes and might also have a cow.

Only in the second half of the 19th century were farmworkers' cottages substantially improved, new ones being built with mortared stone, tile roofs and chimneys, and with two rooms instead of one. They were often built in rows adjacent to the farms which their occupants served.

This pattern of 19th-century courtyard farms and attached rows of cottages can be seen all over East Lothian. There is another good example at Drem, opposite the station, where the cottages form a particularly attractive group next to the farm steading.

7. The Chesters: Hillfort (507782)

For access to the hillfort follow the signpost from the road.

Hillforts first appear in Scotland in the 6th and 7th centuries B.C., providing evidence of a society which was becoming more unsettled with successive waves of immigrants from the continent. Most Iron Age hillforts are placed on relatively remote and high-lying hilltops which form natural defensive sites. Apart from the good state of its preservation, the Chesters has the advantage of being on relatively low ground, easily accessible by road. Its location is indeed a curious one as the fort is overlooked by a ridge to the south. If the multiple stone and earth ramparts and ditches were built as a defence against sling shots, then most of their value would have been negated by the unfavourable topography of the site. Possibly the ramparts were a status symbol as much as a serious defence. This does mean that from this rising ground you have a bird's eye view of a hillfort which is usually only obtained from aerial photographs. The fort is small compared with Traprain Law (see below), with internal dimensions of 115 × 45m, but it is enclosed by a complex series of ramparts, five lines to the north and three to the south. The entrances on the north-west and eastern sides are clearly visible. Traces of circular foundations are also evident within the ramparts: these were probably hut foundations. Some of them were probably contemporary with the fort, but others are undoubtedly later as they overlie the faint innermost rampart.

Continue towards the hills until you reach a crossroads. Turn left towards Athelstaneford.

8. Athelstaneford (5377)

As you enter the village you can see a fine dovecote on your left. It dates from 1583 and is built in a lectern style which contrasts with the round one at Dirleton. The village is attractive with its single long street bordered by a grass verge and lined with pantiled cottages. It is another example of a planned estate village (Trails 1 & 2). Sir David Kinloch of Gilmerton House, which lies a short way to the east of the village, encouraged its development in the later 18th century. He paid for the construction of the church, manse and school, leasing out plots of land on which tenants built their own cottages. This accounts for the variety of the cottages: Athelstaneford does not have the regimented appearance of some Scottish estate villages whose proprietors controlled the design of the houses as well as the public buildings. The original settlers were smallholders with plots of land for oats and potatoes and some grazing. Many of them were employed in weaving woollen cloth.

Carry straight on at the end of the main street until you reach a T-junction. Turn right and after 1km turn left on to a side road towards Beanston farm.

9. Beanston (549762) and Markle (563774): Threshing Machines

The agricultural improvements of the late 18th and early 19th centuries were not accompanied by the introduction of many mechanical innovations: this was more a feature of the later 19th century. However, one important invention, the threshing machine, formed a part of these early changes. Its introduction had important implications for rural society and the way in which labour was used. Threshing machines also led to changes in the layout of farm buildings. Before the threshing machine was developed, the normal way of separating the grain from the straw was by using a hand flail, a laborious process which occupied a good deal of time during the winter months on large arable farms.

A number of prototype threshing machines were built during the mid-18th century, but they either damaged the grain or were insufficiently robust. Credit for perfecting rather than inventing the threshing machine goes to Andrew Meikle, an East Lothian millwright, who patented his improved design in 1788. In Meikle's machine the sheaves were fed through rollers into a revolving drum which shook the grain out of the ears by velocity rather than force.

Meikle's device spread rapidly in eastern Scotland during the later 18th century because, with competition from the growing industrial centres, agricultural wages even for casual workers were relatively high and a threshing machine soon paid for itself. Meikle's original design was horse-powered. Between two and six horses walked round a circular horse-gang adjacent to the barn driving the machinery. The horse-gang was normally housed in a circular or polygonal building with open sides and a conical roof. Although some of them have been demolished in recent years they can still be seen on many Scottish farms.

Because horse-driven machines prevented the animals from doing other work when they were in the horse gang, alternative sources of power were developed. A number of threshing machines in East Lothian were driven by water power and some by wind-mills. By the early 19th century roads in the county had been considerably improved and it became feasible to bring coal quite cheaply from the mines around Tranent in the west of the county to most of the larger farms. This allowed many of these farms to install steam engines to drive their threshing machines. Farms which went over to steam power could be identified at a distance by their tall brick chimney stacks. By the 1840s there were 386 threshing machines in East Lothian; 269 of them were horse-driven, 80 steam-powered, 30 were water mills and 7 were wind-mills.

Many of the chimneys attached to steam-driven threshing machines have been demolished in recent years for safety reasons, but Beanston farm is one of those where the chimney remains. You can also see a fine barn with a range of cart sheds to the right of the chimney.

At Markle, a little to the east and further from coal supplies, the farmers kept the horse gang and did not go over to steam. If you look through into the courtyard of the farm you can see the

Cart sheds, Beanston farm

polygonal house within which the horses walked round. The group of labourers' cottages at Markle, detached from the main farmstead a little way down the road, forms an attractive group.

10. Prestonkirk Parish Church (592779)

The church of St. Baldred dates mainly from the 1770s, from the first phase of change in the countryside and a time of growing prosperity for the landowners and the larger farmers. It occupies the site of a medieval church, and part of this earlier structure, dating from the 13th century, forms the chancel. The tower was built in the 17th century. In the churchyard, to the south-west of the church, is the tombstone of Andrew Meikle.

11. Preston Mill (595778)

Before the agricultural improvements of the later 18th and 19th centuries grain mills were thickly dotted throughout Scotland, particularly in areas like East Lothian which were predominantly arable. These mills were small, crudely built and generally water-powered, though some were driven by wind power. Mills were a monopoly of the landowners whose feudal powers allowed them to 'thirl' or bind the tenants within a defined area or 'sucken' to grind their grain at a particular mill. Tenants who tried to break their thirlage by taking their grain to another mill were liable to be brought before the baron court, presided over by the landowner or his baillie, and fined. Proprietors leased out their mills to tenant millers who charged other farmers within the sucken a payment known as 'multures' for grinding their grain. Multures were a fixed proportion of the ground grain, often around a twentieth. Tenants were also required to help the miller with repairs to the fabric of the mill, its dam and lade, and to bring home new millstones. Although millers were supposed to provide a reasonable service and might themselves be summoned before the baron court for failing to do so, thirlage was generally resented by the tenant farmers and the miller was, as elsewhere, frequently caricatured as an unscrupulous rogue.

During the later 18th century multures were increasingly converted to money payments and thirlage began to die out. This allowed milling to be done on a larger scale with more investment in improved technology and bigger two and three-storey mills, as millers no longer had to cater merely for the limited number of farmers within a sucken, and had to provide a competitive service. Milling often became centred in the larger market towns. Very few

Preston Mill

country mills pre-dating the later 18th century have survived, and Preston Mill is perhaps the most attractive of them. The mill itself is likely to date from the 17th or 18th century but the kiln may be older. The mill continued working until 1957. It is now owned by the National Trust for Scotland and you can see the machinery in operation (an entrance fee is payable). The conical-shaped kiln was for drying corn: an essential adjunct to a mill given Scotland's wet climate. An exhibition in one of the mill buildings gives details of some other East Lothian mills which you may like to visit.

A short distance to the south is another dovecote; you can obtain the key for this one from Preston Mill, allowing you to see the 500 or so nesting boxes inside.

Follow the footpath past the dovecote to the farm a short distance ahead.

12. Phantassie Farm (597772)

Phantassie is another good example of an East Lothian courtyard farm built during the prosperous mid-19th century. The buildings date from the 1840s and a rather severe classical style has been adopted for the facade. It was here that Andrew Meikle built the first prototype of his improved threshing machine in 1787, though it was attached to an earlier set of farm buildings.

13. East Linton Bridge (593771)

The lower part of the bridge, its arches and cutwaters, is a good example of 16th-century Scottish bridge-building. At this time roads were worn rather than made. Bridges tended to be built adjacent to large burghs, at the lowest crossing points of major rivers, but they were also constructed along major routeways. This bridge was on the main road from Edinburgh to Berwick at the lowest point at which the River Tyne could be spanned easily. The upper part of the bridge was reconstructed in 1763 and later.

From the village of East Linton join the A1 heading towards Edinburgh. A short distance west of the village there is a lay-by with a good view over the countryside to the south including the prominent hill called Traprain Law.

14. Traprain Law (5874)

South-eastern Scotland has a dense concentration of defensive structures which are generally described as 'hillforts' although they vary greatly in size from small ones which defended a single homestead with a simple rampart and ditch, through larger ones like the Chesters which may have corresponded to defended 'villages', up to very big ones which some archaeologists would describe as 'towns'. Given the fertility of East Lothian, it is not surprising to find that it was a focus for settlement and political power in prehistoric times. The largest, and probably the most important, hillfort in the area was situated on Traprain Law, the steep volcanic hill forming a fine defensive site which commands a wide view over the East Lothian plain. The site was occupied for a thousand years or so from the later Bronze Age, through the Iron Age and the Roman occupation, into early-Christian times. As you might expect, the remains of this long occupation are complex but they are not particularly impressive when seen on the ground, apart from those relating to the last period of occupation. The site has not been excavated by modern methods and a good deal may have been lost as a result of the quarrying away of the east end of the hill.

Archaeologists have identified five, possibly six, sets of defences. The earliest enclosed a small area, about 10 acres, near the summit of the hill, and probably dates to the end of the Bronze Age. Later extensions increased the defended area so that by the time the Romans penetrated the district an area of 40 acres was enclosed, making Traprain the largest hillfort in south-east Scotland along with the one on Eildon Hill (Trail 5). While it is believed that some forts at higher altitudes may have been occupied mainly during the summer to protect herdsmen and their flocks at the summer shielings, there is no reason to suppose that Traprain was not lived in throughout the year as a major tribal centre, the capital of the tribe known to the Romans as the Votadini. The Votadini seem to have reached an agreement with the Romans, for while the fort on Eildon Hill was deserted when they first annexed Scotland south of the Forth and Clyde, Traprain continued to function. When the Romans pulled back during the mid-2nd century the fort seems to have been abandoned for a time. It was reoccupied, however, and the tribe may have remained Roman allies: repairs to the ramparts were probably due to attacks from the north by the Picts rather than by the Romans. The last set of defences is the most prominent, and consists of a massive wall 3.5m thick, of turf with stone facings, enclosing a slightly reduced area of about 30 acres. This wall is probably post-Roman in date. You may be able to pick out traces of hut foundations if you walk over the hill: the later huts were rectangular not round, relating to the period after the Roman withdrawal. There is a tradition that an early monastery was established here by St. Monenna although its site has never been discovered. If this is true, then Traprain may have continued to function as a tribal capital into the 6th century A.D., perhaps being abandoned as a result of the Anglian invasions.

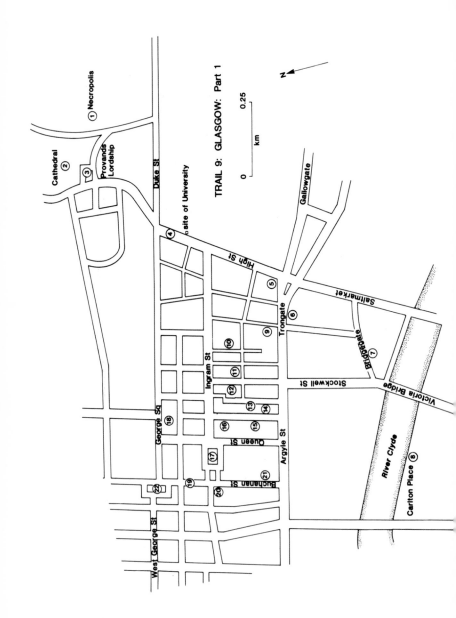

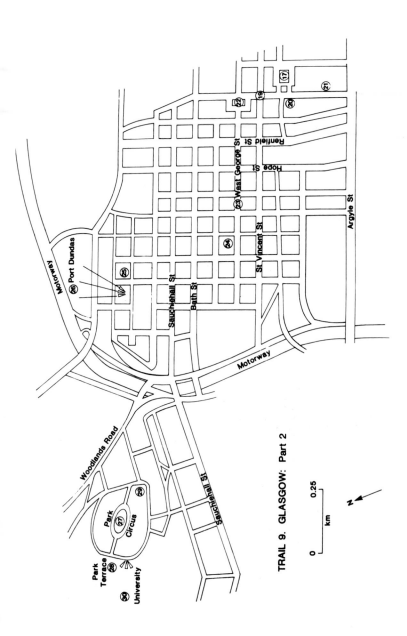

TRAIL 9. GLASGOW: Part 2

NINE

Glasgow: The Heart of an Industrial City

Ordnance Survey 1:50,000 sheet 64: 1:25,000 sheets NS 56, 66.

This trail involves two walks of 4km each which can be done consecutively or separately.

Introduction

This trail traces the development of Glasgow from its medieval origins to its position as the 'second city' of the British Empire in the later 19th century. The trail looks mostly at the city's commercial and residential development rather than at industry since, with the decline of the docks and large-scale inner city redevelopment, relatively little of Glasgow's industrial past is visible close to the city centre.

1. View from the Necropolis: Glasgow's Pre-Medieval Origins

Like St. Andrews (Trail 11), Glasgow originated as a religious centre in early-Christian times. St. Kentigern (or St. Mungo), the patron saint of the city, who lived during the late 6th and early 7th centuries, founded a small monastery here on a site which had earlier been consecrated by St. Ninian in the 4th century. Kentigern was buried here and the monastery became a place of pilgrimage, the centre of an early diocese embracing the whole of the Kingdom of Strathclyde. Successive cathedrals are thought to have stood on the site of Kentigern's tomb. Several suggestions have been put forward regarding the origin of the name 'Glasgow', and one possibility is that it is derived from two Celtic elements: 'glas', a church, and the other the first syllable of the Celtic version of Kentigern's name.

From the Necropolis on the hill above the cathedral (reached by a bridge beside the cathedral entrance) you can, on a clear day, gain a good impression of the site and situation of the city despite the alterations which have been caused by modern building. Glasgow

144

stands in the middle of a lowland basin, the 'Howe of Glasgow', surrounded at a distance of a few miles by a ring of hills and moorland. Within this basin the Glasgow area is a natural focus for routeways up and down the Clyde, through the hills from Ayrshire and the Tweed, and eastwards from the Firth of Forth. The site of the cathedral was adjacent to a routeway from Dumbarton, the capital of the Kingdom of Strathclyde, up the Clyde valley to Lanark, capital of the early sheriffdom of Lanark. The site was also adjacent to the lowest point at which the Clyde could be easily forded, where it was tidal but before it started to broaden out into the estuary. But it is important to note that the cathedral is a kilometre or so away from the river. It is likely that there was another settlement, possibly of fishermen, closer to the river from early times, a settlement from which developed the second focus of the medieval town. From the cathedral a series of terraces slopes down to the river; you can still detect the break of slope between the two main ones as you go down the High Street. To the east of the cathedral a small stream, the Molendinar Burn (from the Latin for 'mill': this was where the town's earliest water mills were sited) cuts a deep gorge through the terraces. The stream runs in a culvert today but the steepness of the valley is still apparent. This gorge made access difficult from the east and helped to direct much of Glasgow's early growth westwards.

2. The Cathedral

Although small by European standards, Glasgow cathedral was Scotland's second largest pre-Reformation cathedral after St. Andrews, a reflection in stone and mortar of the fact that this was Scotland's second diocese in rank and wealth. Although the cathedral is the product of several periods of building, its exterior seems remarkably uniform. This is partly because of its slightly unusual plan in which all aisles and chapels are contained within a single rectangle and do not protrude. The cathedral is best seen from the south-east across the Molendinar valley. From this angle you can appreciate the difficulties of the site: the steep fall of the ground at the eastern end required the construction of a massive crypt or lower church. Although the building of a crypt was partly dictated by the difficult site, it was also designed to house the tomb of Kentigern. The see of Glasgow was re-established by David I

Glasgow Cathedral

between 1114 and 1118 and a new church consecrated in 1136. This building was burnt in 1190 but its replacement was consecrated in 1197. Much of the lower walls of the nave dates from this period but the main part of the present structure dates from the 13th century. The cathedral survived the Reformation thanks to the inhabitants of the burgh who intervened to prevent it from being destroyed, and it was converted into three Protestant churches—in the nave, choir and crypt. Like so many other churches it suffered at the hands of 19th-century 'restorers' who removed the two irregular but picturesque western towers.

The existence of the monastery, the pilgrimage centre and later the cathedral would have generated custom for traders, and it is

likely that a settlement had already been established by the time
that William the Lion granted to Bishop Jocelin the right to have a
burgh with a market and later some fairs. The location of the early
burgh and the direction of its development have been disputed.
One school of thought favours early growth around the cathedral
and a gradual extension south towards the river. The other
suggests that the burgh was formally established on a new site
away from the cathedral and closer to the river around where
Glasgow Cross now stands. What is certain is that by the time we
have enough documentary evidence, in the 14th and 15th centuries, Glasgow consisted of two adjacent but distinct nuclei, the
upper town clustered around the cathedral with a mainly religious
function and the lower merchants' town near the ford and bridge.

3. Provand's Lordship

Around the cathedral were built the stone houses of the pre-
bendaries who officiated there: there were 32 of them by the
mid-15th century. The only one which remains is Provand's
Lordship, the manse of the prebendary of Barlanark. The house
was originally built around 1471 but it has been much altered since

Provand's Lordship

then: many of the windows are clearly 18th-century by their size and regularity. Provand's Lordship may have been larger than some of the other manses because it probably housed some of the inmates from the adjoining St. Nicholas' Hospital. The house is built with undressed stone, and the rear of it, with three crow-stepped gables, is probably closest to its original appearance, although even here the present form of the building appears to date from the later 17th century. Until the 16th century at least there appears to have been a contrast between the stone-built houses of the upper town, reflecting the power and prestige of the church, and the timber-frame ones of the merchants' town. By the 17th century the lower town had been rebuilt in stone with houses not dissimilar to this one.

As at St. Andrews the bishop, and from 1491 the archbishop, had his palace or castle beside the cathedral. At Glasgow this took the form of a motley collection of buildings immediately to the west of the cathedral centred on a four-storey tower and surrounded from the early 16th century by a curtain wall with towers and a large gatehouse. After the Reformation it fell into ruin. Most of the stone was robbed for other buildings and the remains were finally removed in the later 18th century.

4. The High Street

Because Glasgow had two distinct centres, its plan was more complex than that of many medieval Scottish towns. A north-south road, the present High Street, ran from the cathedral pecincts towards the ford. Two routes crossed it at right angles, the upper one along the line of Rottenrow and Drygate, the old route from Dumbarton to Lanark, and the lower one along Trongate and Gallowgate following the river. The ecclesiastical settlement grew up around the upper crossroads, the merchants' burgh around the lower one. Between the two was an area of open ground which was only gradually filled in to link the two settlements. The early trading settlement near the river had a T-shaped plan extending along the modern Trongate and Gallowgate and to the south towards the river. The High Street ran fairly directly to the original ford but the first wooden bridge, recorded in the late 13th century, and its early 15th-century replacement in stone, was slightly downstream of this, roughly where the modern Victoria

Bridge stands. From the southern end of the merchants' town a new street, Bridgegate, was built running diagonally to the bridge.

Parts of the area to the east of the High Street between the two settlements were acquired by the Dominican friars in the 13th century. In 1450–1 Bishop Turnbull obtained permission to found a university whose first buildings were on the Black Friars' lands. These were replaced during the mid-17th century by a more imposing set of college buildings, fronting on the High Street, with several acres of gardens behind. Unfortunately, they were demolished in 1870 to provide a site for a railway station. Only the name of a side street, College Street, remains to point to the site of Scotland's second oldest university. Illustrations of the buildings indicate that they were particularly fine examples of 17th-century Scottish architecture. The facade which faced the High Street has, however, been preserved in a curious and altered form by being wrapped round four sides of the Pierce Lodge on Gilmorehill where the new university buildings were constructed. The layout of the Neo-Gothic Victorian university (see below), centred around two quadrangles with an asymmetrically placed tower in between, copies the plan of the 17th-century college. Many of the older buildings in and around the High Street were removed in the 1870s and 1880s by railway companies seeking land, or by the City Improvement Trust as slums.

5. The Tolbooth

The junction of the High Street with Trongate and Gallowgate is still known as Glasgow Cross. For centuries it was the centre of the trading settlement whose growth gradually eclipsed the cluster around the cathedral, particularly after the Reformation. The growing prosperity and civic pride of the burgh were reflected in the construction of a new five-storey tolbooth in 1626. The tolbooth served as a meeting place for the burgh council, a courthouse and a prison: only the steeple remains today.

6. The Tron

Two other spires are virtually all that is left of the pre-18th century burgh. In Trongate is the steeple of the Tron church dating from the late 16th century with 17th-century additions. The tron, or weighbeam, was actually housed in the base of the tower after a fire in the late 18th century destroyed the church. When the church was rebuilt slightly to the south, the detached steeple was pierced with arches at the base and left as a monument.

7. Bridgegate

In Bridgegate is the steeple of the Merchants' Hall, dating from 1659. The merchant and trades incorporations of most of Scotland's larger burghs provided help for impoverished members and their families, but in Glasgow this system became more formalised with the construction of merchants' and trades halls which were used for meetings, social gatherings, and to house the needy. The original trades hall has not survived but its replacement is described below (no. 13).

8. View Across the River

From the bottom of Bridgegate you can look across the river to what was an early suburb, the barony of Gorbals, whose lands were acquired by the town in 1649. In the late 18th and early 19th centuries a number of adjacent sites south of the river were laid out as speculative residential developments: Kingston, Tradeston, Hutchesontown and Lauriestown. Unfortunately, these middle-class areas were rapidly invaded by industry and were abandoned by their original occupants to poorer and poorer inhabitants. In this process the spacious terraced houses were subdivided into a multitude of flats, and eventually some of the worst housing conditions in the city resulted. One of Lauriestown's finest facades has survived in Carlton Place, two long palace-fronted blocks facing the river which were built from 1802 onwards.

9. Candleriggs: The 18th-Century Merchants' Town

During the 16th and 17th centuries Glasgow's slow but steady growth of population was accommodated mainly by infilling the existing building plots in the burgh and by using up the surviving open space between the merchants' town and the cathedral area. In 1652 a serious fire destroyed almost a third of the town and the council ordered certain industries whose activities posed a fire hazard to move to the fringes of the burgh as a safety measure. Glasgow's candlemakers located themselves beyond the burgage plots to the west of the High Street on some of the previously cultivated rigs of the town's arable land. The site became known as Candleriggs and survives in a street name.

Scotland had started to develop trade with England's North American and Caribbean colonies before the Union of 1707. Sugar refining and rum distilling were early industries which brought in large profits: some of the early sugar houses were also located in Candleriggs. After the Union Scotland could engage in trans-Atlantic trade openly. Much of the prosperity and growth of the city in the first two-thirds of the 18th century was due to the tobacco trade. The considerable fortunes amassed by some Glasgow merchants, the 'Tobacco Lords', in this trade led them to move out of their cramped accommodation in the old town and build large mansions in the area west of the High Street and north of Trongate. A number of streets in this area—Buchanan Street, Glassford Street, Miller Street—are named after prominent tobacco merchants who originally owned mansions in this area and through whose property the streets were laid out between the 1760s and 1780s. Under pressure of the demand for space the mansions of the Tobacco Lords were demolished to make way for more densely-packed commercial property. Despite the regular street plan of this part of Glasgow the area grew in a very haphazard manner as the commercial centre of the city pushed steadily westwards with offices and later warehouses filling in behind.

10. Brunswick Street

Candleriggs best preserves the character of the 18th-century commercial town with rows of simple, rather severe warehouses with shops below dating from the last decade of the 18th century. Brunswick Street also has offices and warehouses from this period.

11. Wilson Street

At 60, Wilson Street a block of warehouses may have been designed by Robert and James Adam around 1790. There was originally an arcade on the ground floor of this building: the attic storey is a later addition.

12. The Trades House

Glassford Street has the new Trades House, designed by Robert Adam in 1794. The cramped site and the insertion of modern shop fronts have rather spoiled the effect of this fine building.

13. Virginia Street

Virginia Street has some more ornate buildings from the early years of the 19th century. 31–35 Virginia Street was the tobacco exchange, built in 1819 after the peak of the tobacco boom, and a good example of the many commodity exchanges which formerly existed in this area. The exchange is now an arcade: you can still see the window at one end where the auctioneer is said to have sat.

14. Miller Street: A Merchant's House

At 42, Miller Street is a survivor—a fairly modest one—of the merchants' houses which dominated this area before the spread of commercial property. It was built in 1775 but the attics are later.

15. Arthur's Warehouse

This remained an area of offices and warehouses even after the commercial centre of the city moved further west. Miller Street has some fine ornate warehouse blocks from the 19th century. No 81, Arthur's Warehouse, dates from 1854 and is Georgian in style with restrained decoration.

16. Miller Street: Warehouses

Number 37, Miller Street, built only a few years later than Arthur's Warehouse, is in a highly ornate Italian style: originally it had ground-floor arcades.

17. The Royal Exchange

Glasgow more than Edinburgh developed layouts of public buildings in small squares, framing the vista down long streets. The Royal Exchange, now Stirling's Library, is a good example of this.

George Square; the original terraced houses have had an additional floor and attic storey added to them

The classical portico dates from 1827–32, but inside this you can see the facade of what was perhaps the grandest of the original merchants' houses in this area, built for William Cunningham in 1778 and later converted to form the front of the Exchange.

18. George Square

In 1772 the town council bought the lands of Ramshead and Meadowflats lying west of the High Street and north of the Candleriggs-Virginia Street area. A more regularly planned housing area was laid out on this land focusing on George Square which, although not the city's first residential square, was certainly its most impressive. George Square is so much the commercial heart of the city today that it is difficult to imagine it as a quiet residential area surrounded by terraced houses with a large garden in the centre. Yet, if you look at the facade of the Diplomat Hotel on the north side of the square, and ignore the top storey which is a later addition, you will get some idea of the character and scale of the original terraces which were built between 1808 and 1818. The houses must have been rather small for the huge size of the square, and the later, high buildings, including the boldly-designed City Chambers, built between 1883 and 1888, are more in proportion. The square did not survive for long as a residential area: it was too close to the commercial area west of Candleriggs and it was taken over for office accommodation.

19. Buchanan Street

Buchanan Street marks the westward limit of the late 18th-century city and its largely unplanned expansion. Beyond it are the larger, more carefully designed gridiron layouts of the late Georgian and Victorian residential areas. Buchanan Street has remained the hub of the city centre, linking its two main shopping areas, the one on Trongate-Argyle Street, originally the working-class area, a westward extension of the old medieval market, the other along Sauchiehall Street catering for the middle-class carriage trade. Buchanan Street has a fine collection of public and private buildings, especially on its west side, many of them dating from the second half of the 19th century.

20. The Stock Exchange, Buchanan Street

The flamboyant Italian design of the former Stock Exchange (1875) is especially notable.

21. Argyle Arcade

Argyle Arcade (1827) is an early example of construction in cast iron.

22. St. George's Church

St. George's church (1807) frames the view down West George Street and was originally more imposing as it was not overlooked by the tall buildings on either side.

The first walk ends here. The second one is the same length but involves more climbing.

West George Street; a Georgian terraced house survives between later, more ornate Victorian buildings

23. West George Street

The 18th-century town is on fairly flat land, sloping gently from George Square towards the river. West of Buchanan Street the topography changes dramatically, with a profound effect on the townscape. The city extends over a series of hills of moulded glacial drift called drumlins. These hills are characteristically oval in plan, like eggs in cross section, with a steep face towards the north-west (the direction from which the ice came) and gentler slopes to the south-east. They can be up to 30m high. Over these rounded hills and the hollows between has been laid a grid pattern of streets producing an effect which in places rivals that of San Francisco, giving a distinctive character to streets which might otherwise have been boring. The area from Buchanan Street towards Blythswood Square was developed during the early years of the 19th century. There was less conscious planning of the housing than in the new town of Edinburgh (Trail 7), but a high standard of design was nevertheless maintained. Many of the original Georgian villas and terraces have been demolished to

F

make way for commercial property but West George Street has some survivors: no. 196, built around 1830, is one of the best, but towards Blythswood Square are a number of terraces dating from the 1820s and early 1830s.

24. Blythswood Square

Blythswood Square, though almost entirely offices now, has hardly been altered. The square may lack the distinction of some of those in the Edinburgh new town—it is roughly contemporary with the second new town and the development of the Moray Estate—but it is nevertheless impressive, with some subtle design features. Notice how the spacing of the windows in the central blocks is not quite even. They are grouped into threes in order to distinguish each house from the others, but the difference in spacing is so slight that the effect is absorbed unconsciously.

25. Hill Street: Tenements

Across Sauchiehall Street is Garnethill, another drumlin, but a very different townscape, for this area was largely built up with tenements. Glasgow tenements, which proliferated in the later 19th century, have acquired a bad reputation for poor housing conditions. However, by the middle of the 19th century they were becoming acceptable as middle-class accommodation, though often in three-storey blocks rather than the four-storey working-class tenements. Some of the middle-class tenements can be hard to distinguish from the late Georgian terraces which served as their model. Tenement architecture presented its own problems. Georgian terraces of individual houses could achieve a balance by grading the sizes of the windows, with the largest on the first floor and the smallest on the second. This could not be done for tenements where each storey was a separate flat. The answer to preventing such buildings from having a top-heavy appearance was to keep the windows the same size on all floors but to make them seem graded by means of the ornamentation around them. Decoration was concentrated on the first floor and reduced progressively upwards. Grouping of the windows also helped to reduce the monotony of tenement streets, as did breaking up the facades by using bay windows. In Hill Street the tenements date from c1845. One of the tenement flats on the south side of Hill Street near its western end has been preserved by the National Trust for Scotland as it was earlier in the 20th century and is open to the public.

26. View of Port Dundas

From Garnethill you have a view northwards across an area which has been extensively redeveloped in recent years. Formerly it was an industrial and tenement area but it has been transformed with the construction of the urban motorway along the line of the Monkland Canal. An unfortunate result has been the creation of a good deal of derelict and undeveloped land. Above the motorway you can see the warehouses at Port Dundas. In the 17th and early 18th centuries Glasgow suffered on account of its poor communications with Edinburgh and eastern Scotland in general. The road across the Forth-Clyde isthmus was vital but often poorly maintained, while the sea passage around the north of Scotland was long and dangerous. Under the circumstances it was hardly surprising that proposals for a canal between the Forth and Clyde estuaries should find favour with the city's businessmen. The Forth and Clyde canal was constructed as far as Port Dundas by the mid-1780s and it gave rise to a broad belt of industry in the area where the motorway now runs. The canal was joined to the Monklands Canal in 1790, a short but important canal linking the city to the North Lanarkshire coalfields and assuring Glasgow's industries a fuel supply. Today the Forth and Clyde canal carries no traffic and much of the Monklands Canal has been filled in to make way for the motorway, but the buildings round this once-thriving canal port survive to remind us of the importance of water transport in the past. Most of the buildings are bonded warehouses today but originally they included a distillery, grain mills and a sugar refinery. The old custom house stands at the eastern end.

27. Park Circus

Woodlands Hill, the next drumlin to the west of Garnethill, is different in character again, forming a particularly striking piece of urban design. Much of the hill was built up in the 1850s as a unified development under the direction of the architect Charles

Wilson, who contoured his roads around the hill rather than using a grid. The centrepiece of the development is Park Circus. The circus is really a flattened oval which gives a particularly long and fine facade on the north-eastern side. The overall style of the houses is in many ways Georgian but the detail—the patterned stonework and ornamental string courses—is Victorian.

28. Park Terrace

The outer curve of the hill to the west, Park Terrace, is markedly different in style and there is no doubt about the Victorian design of the houses here. Each one is distinctly marked off from its neighbours, each having a two-storey bay window. The roofs are higher and steeper in pitch than in Park Circus, almost French in style, and every third house in the terrace is given greater prominence.

29. Trinity College

The other end of the hill is crowned by the Free Church College (now Trinity College) whose three towers are a landmark from many angles. The College, dating from 1856, was also designed by Wilson.

30. View of Kelvingrove Park and the University

From Park Terrace you have a fine view over Kelvingrove Park and the University, one of the few Gothic Revival buildings in Glasgow. Started in 1866, the design is a mixture of styles—Scottish and possibly Flemish—with a tower which many feel to be too tall for the height of the facade.

The trail ends here, and you can get a bus back to the city centre by walking down from Woodlands Hill to Woodlands Road or Sauchiehall Street. The trail has only considered the development of the city of Glasgow until about the middle of the 19th century. Huge areas of post-1850 development extend beyond the areas covered in these two walks, but most of them are beyond reasonable walking distance of the city centre, and the more modern sections of the city are increasingly similar to those of other British cities. If you are driving around Glasgow, look out for the areas of tenement housing: many of them have been renovated recently: the far end of Woodlands Road towards the University is a good example.

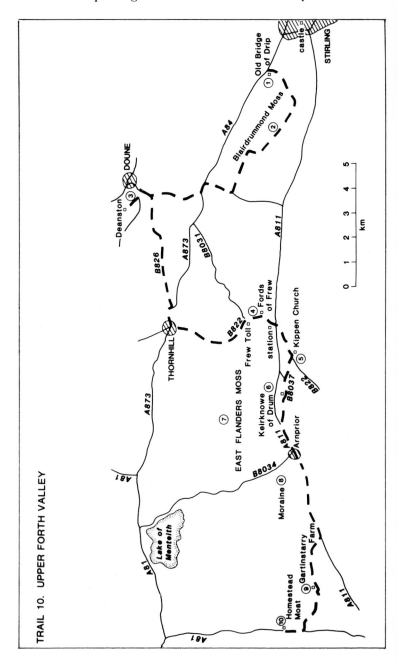

TRAIL 10. UPPER FORTH VALLEY

TEN

The Upper Forth Valley: A Landscape of Reclamation

Ordnance Survey 1:50,000 sheet 57; 1:25,000 sheets NN 60/70,
NS 49/59, 69/79

This trail involves a drive of 45km with an optional
introductory viewpoint at Stirling Castle.

Introduction: The View from Stirling Castle

If you stand on the battlements of Stirling Castle and face westwards you look across the wide, level plain forming the upper
valley of the River Forth. On one side it is bounded by the steep
northward-facing escarpment of the Campsie Fells, while to the
north lies the low broken hill country separating this basin from
the valley of the River Teith, with the southernmost Highland
peaks as a backdrop. The River Forth meanders sluggishly across
this broad lowland, and you may find it difficult to imagine it as it
once was, soon after the end of the last glaciation, a sea estuary with
extensive mud flats exposed on either side of the channel at low
tide. The modern estuary of the Forth, near the Kincardine Bridge,
gives a good impression of what the area above Stirling must once
have looked like.

This trail, more than most of the others in this book, is concerned with the evolution of the topography of the area described.
In the past man was often directly influenced by the character of
the physical environment in which he lived, particularly when his
technology was relatively primitive. The peculiar character of the
development of this former estuary produced a physical geography
which discouraged settlement and hindered communications for
thousands of years. On the other hand, man's ability to alter his
environment eventually reached such a level that major transfor-
mations of the landscape in this area became possible. The
reclamation of the peat mosses of the Upper Forth valley in the late
18th and early 19th centuries is a particularly striking example of
the kind of landscape changes which were taking place throughout the Lowlands at this period.

The landscape development of this area is related to changes in sea level which occurred at the end of the last Ice Age. When the ice sheets finally retreated from Scotland some 10,000 years ago, the land surface which had been depressed by the weight of the ice began to recover. However, the relatively rapid return to the sea of huge quantities of water which had formerly been locked up in the ice sheets covering huge areas of Europe and North America produced an immediate phase of high sea level relative to the land which drowned this former river valley. Then as the land surface, free of the weight of ice, slowly began to recover and rise, the level of the sea relative to the land began to fall. As sea level in the estuary dropped, a series of successively lower beaches was cut and the estuary became narrower until it was only a thin ribbon, probably about as wide as the belt of country over which the present River Forth meanders. As the various beaches became abandoned by the sea, peat started to form on top of them.

Then, around 8500 years ago, the balance between the rising land and sea changed yet again: the rate of uplift of the land slowed down but water was still being added to the oceans from decaying ice sheets in northern Canada. This reversed the fall of sea level and caused the estuary to be flooded once more to its full width. The former beaches and their peat cover were buried by mud flats of fine marine clay, called in this area 'carse clay'. At the maximum of this last transgression of the sea, the shoreline lay near the village of Gartmore 26km above Stirling, at an altitude of around 15m above present sea level. At this time, with the basin of Loch Lomond also flooded by the sea, Scotland was almost cut in two and there was a gap of only about 8km separating the two inlets. In this huge estuary whales sometimes became stranded and their bones have been uncovered, some bearing the tool marks of prehistoric man. About 5500 years ago the relative sea level began to subside again with the final melting of the ice sheets and the continued, though by now slow, rise of the land surface. The mud flats which had filled the valley were abandoned by the tide. A forest cover developed on them but as the climate became wetter, later in prehistoric times, the trees were killed off and a thick layer of peat, sometimes reaching depths of 6 or 7m, began to accumulate. The upper Forth valley became one of the largest expanses of lowland peat moss in Scotland, an area which was unattractive to settlement because of the wet conditions, and was also difficult to cross.

Settlement and communications were mainly confined to the slopes above the valley down to the later 18th century when large-scale reclamation work began.

From Stirling take the A84(T) westwards.
Leave the A84 just beyond the new bridge, at 769956, turning left on to a side road which cuts back sharply towards the old bridge.

1. Old Bridge of Drip (770956)

The name 'Drip' derives from the nearby former peat bog Drip Moss and is a perfect description of the character of this area before reclamation started.

The bridge is a good example of 18th-century engineering. The arches are graduated in size, forming an attractive, symmetrical structure built of red and grey sandstone rubble brought in from the edge of the carselands. The bridge was built around 1770 on the initiative of local farmers who contributed to the cost of its construction. It was built to allow the farmers on the north side of the carse lands to have easier access to coal which was mined near

Old Bridge of Drip

Stirling, and lime for agricultural improvement, which was obtainable from around Sauchie, to the south. The bridge replaced a dangerous ford, and its construction greatly encouraged agricultural improvement and facilitated marketing. Ramsay of Ochtertyre, a local landowner, remarked in his memoirs that the building of the bridge allowed ordinary farmers to burn more coal than gentlemen had been able to afford 40 years earlier.

The nearby farm at Hill of Drip is a modern one but the site is typical of many on the northern edge of the former peat mosses: on an elevated site, in this case a mound of glacial debris, some five metres above the level of the former mosslands.

Continue along the minor road.

2. Blairdrummond Moss: A Landscape of Reclamation (7695-7797)

In the mid-18th century the valley of the upper Forth was a backward and remote area. Settlement was mainly confined to the slopes above the peat mosses although it was appreciated that the carse clays, once exposed from beneath the peat cover, were extremely fertile. There had been a good deal of small-scale piecemeal reclamation around the edge of the mosses where the peat was shallowest: the peat was cut away for fuel and some of it was cultivated as what the local farmers called 'burntland'. This involved ditching the peat moss to let the surface dry out, paring the upper layer of the peat off, piling it into heaps, burning it and then scattering the ashes. A crop of oats was then sown in the ashes and returns were often very high because of the concentration of nutrients in the burnt peat. This process could be repeated year after year until the cover of peat had been burnt away, exposing the clay below which could then be cultivated in a normal fashion. This type of reclamation was, however, very haphazard and slow.

In 1767 Lord Kames began to undertake large-scale, planned reclamation on his estate at Blairdrummond. His intention was to remove the peat cover over extensive areas so that the fertile carse clays could be properly farmed. He started off by giving a tenant a long lease of eight acres of peat moss. He charged no rent at all for the first seven years and only gradually increased it thereafter as the farmer cleared more land and brought it into cultivation. Kames slowly extended this scheme so that by 1775 he had 25 smallholders at work on the mosslands, the later ones being required to tackle the areas with a deeper peat cover but being compensated by having the land rent-free for the first 19 years of their lease. When Lord Kames died in 1782, 52 small farmers were at work. His son continued the reclamation scheme and, by 1790, 115 crofts had been leased, many of the new ones going to Highlanders who had been brought in from more remote parts of Perthshire. The farmers on the edge of the carselands gave the newcomers the scathing title of 'moss lairds', but the value of the reclaimed land was high, while the crofters also made money from selling the peat. By 1817 about 1200 acres of mossland had been cleared and nearly 1000 people were living on the carse area of the estate. The surrounding farmers soon changed their tune and became eager to buy out the smallholders to extend their own farms. Many of the small farmers sold out at a considerable profit and some went off to Canada to undertake further pioneering. The process of amalgamating the small crofts into larger units continued throughout the 19th century so that the landscape is now one of large farms rather than small units.

As you follow the minor road onwards past the old Bridge of Drip you are driving along Westwood Lane, one of the roads which were built through the carselands to open it up for settlement. The individual crofts were laid out in herringbone fashion on either side of these moss roads, with the houses beside the road forming a pattern similar to that of a Hebridean crofting township (Trail 16). At 759948 you can see a good example of one of the later 19th-century farmsteads which replaced the first simple moss cottages. The track which runs past it to the north-west is Nailer's Lane, one of the earliest areas of reclamation on the shallower peat. The track ends at a ruined farm in the middle of nowhere, but in 1813 there were as many as 24 separate crofts along this lane, each with its own cottage. The smallholdings have since been amalgamated to form larger holdings and the cottages have been demolished. Westwood Lane formed the boundary of the Blairdrummond estate; on your left the land belonged to the Meiklewood estate and was reclaimed as part of a separate scheme. The densely settled landscape of small crofts which marked the first phase of reclamation has gone almost entirely. Something of the original pattern of croft boundaries can be seen along Rossburn

Lane between 737965 and 725970 in the regular layout of drainage ditches and field boundaries. Each strip was once a separate small farm. With holding amalgamation came enclosure, the planting of hawthorn hedges and the laying of tile drains though the land still waterlogs easily. One of the modern farms at 737965 still bears the old contemptuous name of 'Mosslaird'.

The first houses built by the crofters were simple turf huts: the soft peat surface would not bear the weight of anything more solid. Later they rebuilt their homes more substantially using bricks made from the carse clay which they had exposed. These later brick houses, like the turf ones which they replaced, have vanished but if you look carefully you may be able to see some traces of brickwork in the outbuildings of the more recent farmsteads, or as ruins in the middle of the fields. As the smaller units became amalgamated into bigger farms throughout the 19th century, the large modern steadings which you can see in the landscape today were built. The carselands were originally cultivated very intensively with rotations which included crops of wheat, barley, oats, beans and rye grass for hay. The importance of arable farming in the 19th century is reflected in the square buildings attached to the barns which protected the horse gins that drove the threshing machines (see Trail 8). Built of sandstone rubble like the main farm buildings and roofed with pantiles or corrugated iron, these are now redundant but still survive on many of the steadings, notably along Kirk Lane (722979). Today only a small portion of the former mossland survives as Ochtertyre Moss at the wooded area north of Rossburn Lane.

When you reach the B8075 in the centre of Blairdrummond Moss turn right to regain the A84(T).

The method by which the peat cover was removed involved the cutting of deep channels down to the clay. These drained southwards to the River Forth. The peat on either side of the channels was cut away in great blocks which were tipped into the ditches to float down to the river and then down the estuary. This continued until 1873 when the practice was prohibited due to complaints from inshore fishermen that the peat rafts were fouling their nets. In order to obtain a sufficient head of water in the channels to float away the peat Lord Kames erected a 9m-diameter water wheel at the Mill of Torr (742989). This lifted water in buckets from the River Teith into a pipe and then into a canal which fed into the system of ditches. The waterwheel remained in operation from 1787 to 1839, and the main channel from it can be seen crossing the A84 road at 731980 before running along the edge of the woodland area south of the road.

3. Deanston (715015)

Continue west on the A84.

It is worth diverting a short distance from the former mosslands to the outskirts of Doune. The medieval castle there is well known, but equally interesting is the little industrial community of Deanston on the south bank of the River Teith, reached by a minor road which leaves the B8032 immediately after its junction with the A84.

The term 'Industrial Revolution' often conjures up images of large factories powered by clanking steam engines located in the heart of dirty, overcrowded, rapidly-growing towns. For the earliest phases of industrialisation in Scotland, however, nothing could be further from the truth. Factories were relatively small and depended on water, not steam power. As a result the earliest factories had to be located where there was a good head of water and this often led to their being established in remote rural areas far from existing towns. Only later did the spread of steam power begin to confine industries such as cotton manufacturing to coalfield locations or sites adjacent to canals where coal could be brought in cheaply.

Fast-flowing Highland streams at the point where they entered the Lowlands were particularly attractive locations for early cotton-spinning mills. Early mill sites included Stanley, on the Tay above Perth, the River Ericht near Blairgowrie, and this example at Deanston. The River Teith was particularly suitable for early water-power based factories because its flow was regulated by Loch Katrine, preventing the level of the stream from dropping too low in summer. The site of the mill at Deanston was carefully chosen by the first owners to provide a good head of water. It began operating in 1785 under the direction of John Buchanan and his son Archibald, linen yarn merchants from Glasgow who were diversifying into cotton. They were in close contact with English pioneers of machine spinning, notably Sir Richard Arkwright: John Buchanan acted as Arkwright's agent in Scotland while Archibald had served an apprenticeship at Arkwright's famous cotton mill at Cromford in Derbyshire. Later the Buchanans joined forces with James Finlay, another merchant, to form the firm of James Finlay and Co., one of the most important companies in the Scottish cotton industry. At first the mill relied on labour from nearby Doune, but in order to attract and retain a suitable labour force the mill owners were forced to provide housing adjacent to the factory. The result was the present community which has survived with relatively little alteration. At one time the village had a population of over 1000.

The earliest mill surviving at Deanston is the six-storey red sandstone block dating from 1827 which is now used as a distillery. Nearby are the weaving sheds and the house for the waterwheels. The centre of the village consists of rows of solid sandstone cottages with two storeys and an attic—but if you walk round to the back, you will see that some of them are flatted. Upstream from the mill you can see the lade. The earliest weir on the Teith which channelled water into the lade was at 712019, but in the 1820s a new

Mill cottages, Deanston

weir was built further upstream at 703027 to provide a greater head of water. In the early 1830s four new water wheels of 12m diameter were installed at the mill, and these continued to operate until 1949 when they were replaced by water-driven turbines. This shows that despite their relatively remote location some of the larger water-power mills like Deanston were able to remain competitive throughout the 19th century and it was only in the post-war period with the general rundown of the textile industries in Scotland that production at Deanston ceased and the mill was converted to a distillery.

Return to the A84. Follow it back towards Stirling for half a kilometre, then turn right on to the B826 and continue to Thornhill. From Thornhill follow the B822 going south.

4. The Fords of Frew: Communications in the Carselands (670960)

It is easy to imagine how much of a barrier the peat mosses of the upper Forth valley provided to communications before reclamation got under way. The old routes ran round the edges of the carselands on the higher, better-drained ground, and relatively few roads crossed the valley from one side to another. The B822 road from Thornhill to Kippen was originally built in the early 19th century to link both sides of the valley. Like many of the new roads which were built in Scotland in the later 18th and early 19th centuries, it was a turnpike, a road built by a private trust on which tolls were charged to recoup the costs of construction and provide a return to the investors. The tolls were collected at toll barriers which usually consisted of a gate across the roadway, with an adjacent cottage or tollhouse for the keeper. While the gates themselves have long since vanished, the place name 'toll' often survives, and sometimes the tollhouses as well. There is a good example at Frew Toll (667967). Like most tollhouses it is a single-storey cottage with its windows placed to give the keeper a good view of traffic on the road.

Stirling Bridge was the lowest crossing point of the River Forth, the focus of most north-south traffic and a key location in many military campaigns, as is shown by the number of battles which have been fought in its vicinity. Further upstream the most widely used crossing point was the Fords of Frew. This was the route used by Montrose's army in 1645 and by the Jacobites in 1745 when Stirling Bridge had been partly demolished by the government forces. In later times this was one of the main crossing places for drovers bringing cattle south from the Highlands. The site of the ford was at 670960, a short way downstream from the later Bridge of Frew. The location is marked by the name of the nearby farm, Fordhead. You may be able to make out a hollowed track leading away from the south bank of the river just to the west of the farm. Near it there is a small block of sandstone marked with the Roman numeral VI (670960). This is thought to mark the distance in miles along the old road to the southern boundary of the parish. If you look to the south you can see a great embayment in the scarp face of the Campsies. This is the Spout of Ballochleam; the road climbed over it and then across the hills towards Glasgow.

At 664957 you can see the remains of the former Kippen railway station. In 1856 the North British Railway Company opened a line from Stirling to Balloch skirting the southern edge of the valley, with a branch line to Aberfoyle. The traffic on the line never lived up to expectations and passenger services were abandoned as early as 1934 with the coming of motor bus services to the area. The railway era lasted barely 80 years in this district, and now most of the bus services have gone too.

Follow the B822 south to Kippen.

5. Kippen (6594)

The three villages of Gargunnock, Kippen and Buchlyvie which are strung along the slopes above the carselands may not be spectacular but they nevertheless contain many interesting examples of plain, solid, no-nonsense rural houses from the later 18th and early 19th centuries. In Kippen, at 653949, you can see the remains of the old parish church: only the west gable and portions of the side walls survive. The building dates from at least the late 17th century and may be earlier. The gable end is crowned with an attractive bell cote supported by four miniature classical columns and surmounted by a weathervane. One of the oldest houses in the village, known as Taylor's Building, is situated in Old Glasgow Lane, just off the main village street. It has a symmetrical three-

Bell tower, Kippen old parish church

storey facade but is on an oblong rather than a square plan. It is a good example of the style of larger village housing in Scotland from the early or mid-18th century.

Take the B8037 westward out of Kippen.

6. Motte: Keir Knowe of Drum (636953)

This site is situated a short way north of the road in thick woodland.

Mottes, the remains of medieval earth and timber castles, were considered in detail in Trail 2. Most early castles of this type incorporated an artificial mound, sometimes shaped around a pre-existing hillock. Keir Knowe of Drum is a good example of how a natural site could be adapted for the same purpose with relatively little modification. The site overlooks the ancient postglacial shoreline of the carse and sits on top of the former cliff some 15m above the plain. A tributary valley cutting down through the cliff has formed a promontory which is partly cut off by a smaller side gully. Excavations have shown that this site has been levelled and modified to provide the site for a wooden tower similar to those which have been found on top of artificial mottes. The perimeter of the levelled area was defended by a bank and palisade and, on the west side by a drystone wall.

From above the trees you have a good view over the mosslands to the north.

7. East Flanders Moss (6298)

The peat mosses in the western, higher part of the Forth valley have not been as extensively reclaimed as those further east. This was due partly to the more remote location of the area which was further from market centres and sources of agricultural lime. Also, the peat was generally deeper here and the mosses wider, making it harder to float the peat away. The result is that the modern landscapes of the eastern and western parts of the Forth valley are very different. In the eastern part of the valley virtually all the peat has been removed, leaving only small islands like Ochtertyre Moss, surrounded by cultivation. The reclaimed carselands are crossed by a dense network of minor roads which often have a regular, rectilinear layout, with roads down the centre of the carse linking all the farms together. To the west reclamation has been more piecemeal in character. Instead of through roads linking the various farms together, dead-end roads run to the individual farmsteads which are located close to the edge of the moss, giving the settlement pattern a pioneer, frontier appearance. Huge areas of peat moss covering several square miles remain. East Flanders moss, between the Thornhill-Kippen and Port of Menteith-Arn-prior roads, has preserved most of the original, character of the pre-18th century mosslands. The centre of the moss is trackless, marshy and difficult of access but a good impression of its bleak, empty character can be gained from the view along the higher parts of the B8037 to the west of Kippen.

Rejoin the A811 and continue west.

8. Arnprior: A Complex Glacial Moraine (6194)

The B8034 from Arnprior to Port of Menteith runs through an area of hillocks and ridges separated by marshy hollows contrasting markedly with the flatness of the valley further east. The ridges form one of the best examples in Scotland of a terminal moraine, the debris which accumulated at the margin of a glacier. The ice sheets of the last glaciation melted downwards and back into the mountains so that around 13,000 years ago there may have been no ice left in Scotland. However, between about 10,800 and 10,300 years ago there was a return of cold conditions. Ice began to form in the mountain corries once more, coalescing to form major ice streams in the valleys. A large mass of ice built up in the Western Highlands until only the summits of the higher mountains showed above it. The ice flowed into the basin now occupied by Loch Lomond and down the forth valley as far as Arnprior. Its maximum limits are represented by this belt of deposits which divided the eastern and western parts of Flanders Moss and holds back the Lake of Menteith. Much of the moraine is composed of sands, gravels, and in places marine clay lifted from the bed of the former estuary and transported by the ice. The debris has been heaped in a series of ridges some of which are up to 30 m high. Most of these ridges are features known as 'kames', deposits of sand and gravel which were washed into crevasses in the ice by meltwater streams and were dumped as mounds when the ice melted. Many of the hollows in between are 'kettle holes' marking the location of blocks of stagnant or 'dead' ice which eventually melted. The streams of meltwater pouring from the snout of the glacier deposited huge fans of sands and gravels to the east of the moraine. The moraine and the higher parts of this fan remained above the level of the encroaching postglacial sea and the subsequent growth of peat so that this was an attractive area for early settlement and for communications. The B8034 road across the valley follows the moraine, and Cardross House and its surrounding policies are located on the sloping outwash fan. From Arnprior the moraine curves westwards towards Buchlyvie.

Continue west along the A811 and after 4km turn right on to the B835.

9. Gartinstarry (553938)

On the north side of the B835 about a mile west of Buchlyvie, Gartinstarry is a fine example of a later 18th-century farmstead. It is thought to date from 1789 and the facade has been little altered.

At the junction with the A81 turn right and drive north for 1km.

10. The Peel of Gartfarran (536954)

Medieval settlement in this area was mainly concentrated on the well-drained land above the carses. This is shown by a number of mottes marking the site of former motte-and-bailey castles, of which Keir Knowe of Drum was one. But there was some attempt to colonise the fringes of the peat mosses which at least had the advantage of providing sites which could be readily defended by water. This phase of settlement is shown by the survival of two well-preserved homestead moat sites. One, on the western margin of East Flanders Moss (618989), is rather remote but the other one, which is marked as the 'Peel of Gartfarran' on Ordnance Survey maps, is only 100m from the Glasgow-Aberfoyle road. It is one of the best-preserved earthworks of its kind in Scotland. Its shape is trapezoidal, the diagonals measuring about 50m internally. The central area is surrounded by a prominent ditch from 8 to 12m wide at the top with a bank of material thrown up on either side. The inner bank is up to 5m wide and in places is up to 1m high, but it is faint in several places. You can see the original entrance in the middle of the west side with a causeway crossing the ditch. There are other gaps in the banks but these are later in date. The moat and banks were the defences of timber hall or manor house belonging to a small landowner. Finds of pottery within the banks date from the late 13th or 14th centuries, which fits the known chronology of such sites (see Trail 2). The bank would originally have been surmounted by a palisade and the moat would have been filled with water. The site has not been excavated and the remains of the timber buildings in the centre may well have been destroyed by later cultivation; you can see traces of ridge and furrow ploughing inside the banks (see Trail 5).

The area east of the moated site is one of the largest surviving extents of peat moss. Reclamation here has been even smaller in scale than on East Flanders Moss, but the appearance of the peat moss has been greatly altered by the cutting of surface drains and by large-scale afforestation.

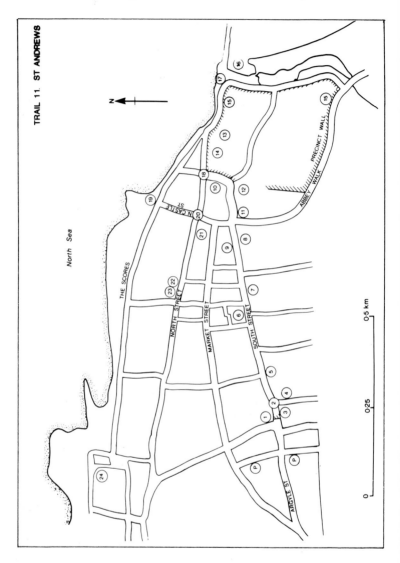

ELEVEN

St. Andrews: A Medieval Burgh

Ordnance Survey 1:50,000 sheet 59; 1:25,000 sheet NO 51.

This trail involves a walk of about 3km.

Introduction

In many larger Scottish towns it is difficult to reconstruct the character of the medieval burgh from the fragments which have been left by the developments of the Industrial Revolution and modern periods. St. Andrews has, however, preserved more of its medieval street pattern and buildings than any other larger burgh and it provides an opportunity to see how a medieval town was originally laid out and how it developed.

Parking is available on either side of Argyle Street, the street leading to the West Port.

1. The West Port

Medieval towns are often thought of as having been defended by impressive curtain walls and gateways, but this was often not the case. In Scotland, while some early burghs seem to have been protected by simple wooden palisades and earth banks, very few towns rebuilt their defences in stone later in the medieval period. Edinburgh (Trail 6) and Stirling were exceptional in this respect and most burghs were undefended against attack. In terms of their trading privileges it was, however, important for burghs to delimit the area of their freedom and monopolies, and to regulate as far as possible traffic coming into the town to stop people from evading tolls on produce which was brought to market. For this purpose gateways, or ports, were often constructed in otherwise undefended burghs, and the West Port of St. Andrews is the best surviving example in Scotland. It was built in 1589 on the site of an earlier gateway and was supposedly modelled on the now-demolished Netherbow Port of Edinburgh (Trail 6). Despite its towers

West Port

and gun loops it was a toll barrier rather than a serious defence. The other main streets of St. Andrews had similar ports which have not survived; this one was extensively restored in 1843. The gateways also allowed the burgh authorities to control entry to the town during outbreaks of plague.

2. South Street

Once inside the West Port you look down South Street right across the medieval town to the precincts of the cathedral. The plan of St. Andrews consists of three main streets which converge on the cathedral: South Street and North Street with Market Street running between them. The streets which run north to south at right angles are much narrower; some are mere alleys. This contrast was emphasised before the 19th century by the old street names. The main east-west streets were called 'gate' from the Anglo-Scandinavian word for 'street', while the connecting access ways were known as 'wynds'. The only north-south 'gate' was Fishergate (now North Castle Street) which led from the castle, emphasising the importance of the route to the bishop's residence.

This kind of street plan with several main streets running approximately parallel, linked by narrower access ways, is found in some other east-coast Scottish burghs such as Perth and Crail. It has many similarities with the layout of planned medieval towns elsewhere in Europe and is more complex and developed than the single main street, widening in the middle into a market place, which is characteristic of many other medieval Scottish burghs, including Edinburgh.

3. South Street: Houses

The white-painted house between the West Port and Louden's Close preserves an external forestair, showing that it was originally built as a flatted dwelling. Visitors to Scotland during the 17th and 18th centuries often remarked that the Scots tended to live in apartment housing of this type in the countryside as well as the towns. It increased the number of families that could be housed in a limited area, but while this was an important consideration in larger towns, in a small burgh like St. Andrews where there was plenty of open space the building of houses in this way was not necessarily a response to a lack of room for building.

3. Louden's Close

The two houses on either side of the entrance to Louden's Close are typical of many older houses in St. Andrews. They are built of local rubble masonry with dressed stone surrounds to the windows and doors, and are roofed with pantiles which in Scotland, as well as England, reflect a distinctively east-coast tradition. The mellow red tints of pantiled roofs brighten many of the Fife burghs. The high, steeply-pitched roofs have been pierced at the rear with dormer windows.

Medieval towns had their property boundaries laid out in long, narrow plots called burgages. In medieval times to be a burgess, or freeman, of a burgh it was necessary to acquire a burgage tenement and build a house on it. Naturally every burgess, whether craftsman or merchant, wished to have a plot with a frontage on the market place or one of the main streets. In order to give as many people as possible a share of the street frontage burgages were normally made very narrow, running back from the main street in a long strip. Originally the burgage plots were only built up along the street, the space at the rear being occupied by gardens, orchards and even agricultural smallholdings. As time went on and the population of the town grew, new blocks of burgages might be laid out on the fringe of the town, but the rear of existing plots might also be infilled with houses and workshops running at right angles to the street. Louden's Close provides a good example of this with infilling on either side and part of the old cobbled surface preserved. Because the burgages on this side of South Street were so long it was possible to build extensively behind the street frontage and still leave room for gardens and open space. As a result, infilling had begun as early as the 16th century and is clearly shown on John Geddy's bird's-eye view of c1580.

Access to the street had to be provided by alleyways or 'closes' running through the buildings fronting the street. You can see another row of buildings infilling a burgage further to the east, and you also get a good impression of the long, narrow character of the plots by the lines of the intervening property boundaries which have a standard width of around 9m.

5. The Blackfriars' Chapel

During the later medieval period the mendicant orders or friars established friaries in most of the larger Scottish burghs. Because they were dedicated to poverty they had little money and were not able to compete for the more expensive town-centre locations. They usually settled at the edge of the built-up area. The friaries were dissolved at the Reformation during the 1560s and their lands came into the hands of the burgh or of surrounding landowners. Very few remains of burgh friaries survive, and this chapel is one of the best examples in Scotland. The Dominican friary at St. Andrews was founded in 1464, but the Dominicans probably did not acquire this site until 1518. The location of the friary marks the furthest extent of St. Andrews to the westward at this time. The burgages which include Louden's Close represent a later addition to the town which leapfrogged the friary property.

The surviving remains are of a chapel which was added to the north side of the friary church in 1525. A house of the Franciscan (Grey) friars was founded in St. Andrews in the 1460s between North Street and Market Street. Its location is commemorated by the modern Greyfriars Gardens but very few traces of it remain.

6. The Burgh Kirk: Parish Church of the Holy Trinity

During the late 15th and early 16th centuries Scottish burghs, and in particular their merchants, were prosperous in a modest way. This prosperity was reflected in many burghs by the building and embellishment of impressive burgh kirks in which the various guilds often had their own altars. The church of the Holy Trinity dates from this period, though it was substantially restored during the 19th and 20th centuries. Only the tower remains of the 15th-century church. Its solid, almost castle-like air hints at the prosperity of St. Andrews as a religious and a trading centre in the decades before the Reformation—a position of prosperity which it was to lose thereafter.

Religion played a major role in the lives of the inhabitants of medieval towns, and in St. Andrews it is easy to see how the various institutions of the church dominated the property and buildings of the burgh. The entire layout of the town was influenced by the location of the cathedral, but within the burgh in addition to the burgh kirk there were the friaries, the colleges of the university which had been founded by the church, and also much urban property belonging to various organisations. For example 67–69 South Street formed part of the burgh tenements owned by the Knights of St. John.

7. St. Mary's College

This college of the university was founded in 1537 by Archbishop Beaton on the site of the earliest university buildings. Since 1579 it has concentrated on the teaching of theology. On the north side is the Principal's house, and the west side is occupied by classrooms with a fine bell tower.

8. South Court

South Court is another example of how infilling along the rear of burgage plots could occur. The houses, which date from the mid-17th century, were skilfully restored in 1972 by the Saltire Society.

Principal's house, St. Mary's College

9. Buildings on the North Side of South Street

In contrast to the modest two-storey houses towards the West Port on the edge of the old town, those at the cathedral end of South Street are grander with three or four stories. St. Andrews contains many houses dating from the late 16th and 17th centuries. This period marks a major phase of rebuilding with a transition from the use of timber-frame construction to stone. However, many of these buildings were re-fronted in the 18th century to give more stylish and uniform facades so that the overall appearance of the older part of the town is Georgian rather than earlier. You can see examples here of houses which have been completely re-faced in dressed stone. Others have preserved their older rubble masonry with dressed stone mainly around the windows and doors. If you look closely at some of these, and other examples elsewhere in the burgh, you can see that the large Georgian windows are later insertions and that there are traces of earlier smaller windows and other decorative features.

10. Dean's Court

Dean's Court was the residence of the archdeacons of St. Andrews. The buildings date from the 16th century and have been restored as a hall of residence for the University.

11. St. Leonard's College

The relics of St. Andrew attracted many pilgrims, and in medieval times a hospital was built to accommodate them on this site. Later it was converted into a nunnery and in 1512 to a college of the university.

12. The Pends

The Pends (the name means a vaulted or covered passage) originally formed the main gateway to the cathedral precincts, and the arches are an important survival of a precinct wall dating from the 14th century, most of which was replaced by the later 16th-century wall. The 16th-century house behind the Pends was occupied by Mary, Queen of Scots on her visits to the town.

13. Church of St. Rule or St. Regulus

The impressive tower and a small part of the nave are all that remains of the early 12th-century church of St. Rule. The building has been dated to about 1130–50, and it is thought that it may have been designed to receive the remains of an early saint, possibly in the fine stone sarcophagus dated to about 900 which is preserved in the museum near the base of the tower. The style of St. Rule's is very individual and it was not necessarily typical of Norman cathedrals in Scotland. The tall square tower has a definite Northumbrian air and it is believed that the masons who built it came from Yorkshire and also worked on the church at Wharram le Street there. There are similar towers in Scotland at Dunblane cathedral, Muthill and Dunning. The church belonged to the Augustinian monastic order but its tall, narrow proportions must have made it an unsatisfactory monastic cathedral.

14. St. Andrews Cathedral

It might seem surprising at first that St. Andrew was chosen as Scotland's patron saint rather than, say, St. Columba or St. Ninian, for St. Andrew never set foot in Scotland. The story goes, however, that during the early 8th century a stranger arrived in Scotland with some bones which he claimed were those of St. Andrew. He convinced Angus, king of the Picts, who had a shrine built on the spot where the relics had been brought ashore. A Pictish royal monastery was then established around the shrine, and when in 908 the only bishopric in Scotland was transferred here the importance of St. Andrews as a religious centre was confirmed.

The cathedral was built as a replacement to St. Rule's on an altogether grander scale. It served both as the cathedral church for the diocese of St. Andrews and as the church of the Augustinian monks in the attached priory. Founded in 1161 and consecrated in 1318, it was a cathedral of the first rank. The nave, with 14 bays, made it the largest church in Scotland and one of the biggest in Britain. Its size emphasises the importance of St. Andrews as the seat of Scotland's archbishopric. Despite its ruined condition the remains of the cathedral are impressive. You can obtain a good bird's-eye view of its layout from the top of the tower of St. Rule's. The east gable dates from the 12th century. The original west front was situated further west than the present one. It was destroyed in a storm and the replacement dates from the late 13th century. On the south side of the cathedral the layout of the cloisters and the surrounding buildings of the priory are also clear.

15. The Precinct Walls

The walls which delimit the cathedral precinct are the finest surviving example in Scotland. They were constructed in 1520 on the foundations of an earlier 14th-century wall which enclosed an area of about 30 acres. Along the south stretch of the wall in Abbey Walk you can see a distinct contrast in the masonry halfway up the wall. The lower part of the wall is probably the originally 14th-century one, the upper part its later replacement. The circuit of the wall has 13 of the original 16 towers and is defended by gun loops. The section facing the harbour is perhaps the most impressive.

The original boundary or jurisdiction of the cathedral and the earlier monastery lay to the west of this precinct wall, running from Abbey Street towards the castle. This area included within its bounds the hospital of St. Leonards and a good deal of residential property.

16. The Harbour

The importance of St. Andrews as a religious and educational centre encouraged a prosperous trading community, and in the 16th-century bird's-eye view of the town mentioned above the harbour, which dates from medieval times, is filled with shipping. Although foreign trade fell off in the later 17th and 18th centuries, the coasting trade remained important and the harbour was improved at various times in the late 18th century, mid-19th century and at the turn of the present century. A little fishing is still carried on.

17. St. Mary's Church

As has been mentioned, the earliest Christian settlement on the peninsula dates from the 8th century. Nothing remains of this early monastery, but the church of St. Mary, whose 12th-century foundations are in a picturesque location overlooking the harbour, is probably a later building on the same site. St. Mary's was a lineal descendent of the early monastery because it belonged to the Culdees, the Celtic monks who were eventually replaced by the Church of Rome and the Augustinian monks. The Culdee cell survived into the 14th century alongside the priory, from which they were excluded.

18. Site of Former Market Place

The small triangular area at the east end of North Street has been identified as the probable site of the earliest market place in St. Andrews and also as the location of the small settlement which preceded the planned medieval burgh. The site lay entirely within the area of the religious community of Kinrimund and probably grew up as a fishing village and service centre for the monastery with its parish church located at the eastern end of the settlement

Cottage with external forestair, North Street

before the cathedral was built and with the market place in the centre. After the foundation of the burgh the site was clearly too restricted and the market was later moved to Market Street. This area still retained a vestige of its market function in the Fish Cross. This part of the town housed a small but distinctive fishing community in later times. Around the old market area you can see other fine examples of 17th-century housing, again with outside forestairs. Those on the south side have preserved some of their original windows but those on the north side have had larger ones inserted during the 18th and 19th centuries.

19. The Castle

The castle occupies a strong defensive position on the cliffs to the north of the town. On the side facing the burgh there is a deep ditch, crossed by a drawbridge. Originally there was an outer gatehouse too. Most of the surviving remains date from the 16th century but the first castle on this site was built around 1200 as a residence for the bishop. It changed hands several times during the Wars of Independence but was rebuilt and continued to act as the residence of the archbishop of St. Andrews. The castle was badly damaged in the siege of 1546–7 when a group of Protestants including John Knox seized it and held out for a year against royal forces aided by the French. After the siege the damage was repaired by Archbishop Hamilton who had the present front range of the castle built. A particularly interesting feature of the castle is the survival of a rock-cut mine and counter mine dating from the siege of 1546–7.

20. Market Street

Market Street is the only one of St. Andrews' three main streets which does not extend to the cathedral precincts. This, and the layout of the burgage plots, suggest that Market Street is a later insertion between North and South Streets, designed to provide more space for the town's markets and fairs than the original site next to the precinct wall. There was probably originally a back lane along its line providing access to the rear of the plots which fronted on to North and South streets. This has been enlarged to form an oval market place. The bird's-eye view by Geddy shows the market cross, pillory and weigh beam standing in the middle of the market place and the tolbooth or town house at its western end.

21. House in Market Street

The house on the south side of Market Street just west of its junction with South Castle Street is a good example of how burgh architecture coped with the problems posed by the restricted site and narrow frontages provided by the burgage plots. The building is gable end on to the street, built like so much of St. Andrews with rubble masonry and dressed stone facings. The gable is crow-stepped, a style characteristic of small Scottish burghs.

22. St. Salvator's Chapel

The University of St. Andrews, the oldest in Scotland, was founded in 1411 using buildings on the site of the later St. Mary's college. Its earliest college, St. Salvator's was founded in 1450 by Bishop Kennedy who also established the grey friars. The frontage on the street including the chapel and tower is all that remains of the original college buildings.

Market Street: house with narrow frontage

23. House Adjacent to St. Salvator's

The house immediately west of the chapel has preserved its original tower staircase sticking out into the street. This was a common style of housing in the larger Scottish burghs during the 17th century.

24. The Old Course

The Old Course is the oldest golf course in the world: records of its
use go back to the 15th century. The Royal and Ancient Golf Club
was founded in 1754 and remains the ruling auhority on the game.

The Development of the Medieval Burgh

The trail has taken you from the edge of the medieval burgh to its
pre-medieval origins and back again, so you have now seen
evidence relating to all its phases of growth. The layout of St.
Andrews has been partly conditioned by its site on a rocky promontory with cliffs to the north and the Kinness Burn to the south. The
pre-burgh nucleus of the settlement was known as Kinrimund, a
Pictish monastic community at the end of the promontory with
royal connexions: the name means 'head of the King's ridge'. This
monastery, dating from the mid-8th century, pre-dated the foundation of the burgh by four centuries. The lines of medieval North
Street and South Street converge on the church of St. Mary which
overlies the early monastery, and it is probable that both these
streets had their origins as Dark Age trackways. It has already been
suggested that an early settlement grew up along the line of North
Street, mainly within the cathedral precincts, focusing on an area
which became the market place of the early burgh. Between 1144
and 1153 Bishop Robert established a new planned settlement or
burgh. It pre-dated the new cathedral by a few years, but both
cathedral and burgh may have been part of the same grand design.
The plan of the new burgh was simple—the settlement was laid
out along two streets, the modern North and South Streets,
converging on the cathedral precincts. Burgage plots were laid out
on either side of these streets with a standard width of 12 paces. A
narrow back lane gave access to the rear of the plots between the
two main streets.

The next phase of development involved the laying out of a new
market place along the line of the lane between the two original
main streets. A charter authorising the transfer of the market from
its original location dates from between 1189 and 1198. Between the
13th and 15th centuries the burgh was extended westwards along
the line of the three main streets by laying out further blocks of
burgages with a standard width of 9m. The positions of the

Blackfriars and Greyfriars friaries mark the limits of this phase of growth.

A further extension of the burgh, principally along South Street, took place in the 15th or 16th century up to the position of the West Port. The bird's-eye view of the town, drawn in about 1580 by John Geddy, shows that these were still effectively the limits of the town in the late 16th century apart from a small suburb just outside the West Port.

Although St. Andrews still has a strong medieval character, it is a thriving town today. The University has a strong influence on the town and attracts students from a wide area to continue in a modern context the tradition of learning that dates from 1411. The town's trading and to a lesser extent its fishing activities continue too. Trade is boosted by the large numbers of tourists who visit the town, providing support for a wide range of shops but particularly the woollen mills, craft shops and hotels. Golfing too draws a large number of people to St. Andrews. It is the preservation of so much of St. Andrews' past activities and of the town itself which has encouraged its continuing prosperity in the 1980s.

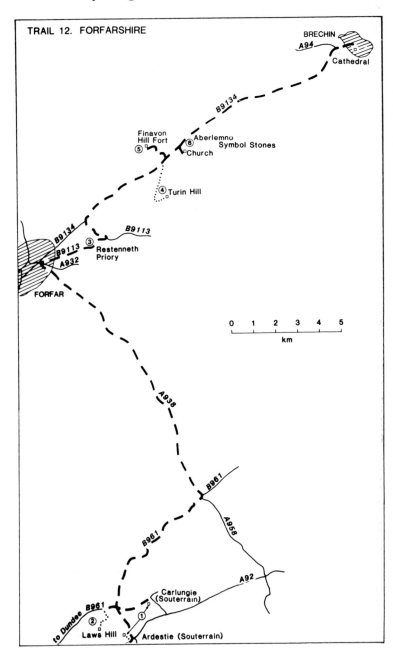

TRAIL 12. FORFARSHIRE

TWELVE

Forfarshire: In Search of the Picts

Ordnance Survey 1:50,000 sheet 54; 1:25,000 sheets NO 43, 44/45, 45/55, 53/63

This trail involves a drive of 52km with some short optional walks.

Introduction

This trail consists of a drive across the old county of Forfarshire from the outskirts of Dundee to Brechin. It can be followed in reverse if you are travelling south from Aberdeen. Its theme relates to the Picts, in many ways the most obscure and enigmatic of the early peoples who merged to form medieval Scotland. This section outlines what little is known about them so that you can appreciate some of the problems involved in trying to identify their handiwork in the landscape.

The name 'Picti', or 'painted people', first appears in the work of a Roman author, Eumenius, in 297 A.D., referring to the inhabitants of eastern Scotland north of the Forth. We do not know what they actually called themselves. During the first Roman penetration of Scotland the Roman commander Agricola had defeated a tribe known as the Caledonii, occupying north-east Scotland. To the south of them were various tribes who appear to have merged to form a confederation known as the Maeatae. At a much later date there are still signs of a continuing distinctiveness between northern and southern Pictland on either side of the Mounth, the barrier of hills which separates the lowlands of Forfarshire from those of the North-East. These two tribal groups, who occupied the area which became the heart of Pictland, were derived from the Bronze Age population of the area with an admixture of Iron Age immigrants. They seem to have spoken two languages: in the south one which had been fairly recently introduced, a form of Celtic which was allied to Welsh, Cornish and Breton, and in the north an ancient pre-Celtic language. The Picts, then, were a mixture of peoples rather than a homogeneous group. Strictly speaking, Pictland included the whole of Scotland north of the Forth and the Kingdom of Strathclyde, apart from those areas of the west coast which were settled by the Scots from Ireland from about 500 A.D. onwards. Areas like the Northern and Western Isles seem to have had some different cultural traditions from the core of Pictland and may have been linked with it only peripherally.

Written references to the Picts are few, oblique and nearly all from non-Pictish sources. The first mention of the Picts in 297 is mere chance, so that there is a problem in deciding when the 'Pictish' period really begins. By the 6th or 7th centuries this loose tribal grouping had been united into a single kingdom. This independent kingdom came to an end in 843 when the Scottish King Kenneth mac Alpin united the throne of the Picts with that of the Scots of Dalriada. Yet even this event was not as final as historians once believed. The Picts had been in contact with the Scots of Dalriada for centuries before this union, often at war but frequently with peaceful links as well. They had indeed been converted to Christianity from the west by monks from Iona (Trail 13). Many Irish influences can be detected in the Pictish monasteries, their sculpture and alphabet. On the other hand Pictish elements survived (probably more often than is realised) into medieval times although the Pictish language fell out of use.

If the Picts are difficult to pinpoint historically, the same is true of their legacy in the landscape. 'Pict' is really an historical rather than an archaeological concept, and given that their cultural background was so diverse, it is unreasonable to expect that their surviving traces will be homogeneous and easy to identify.

1. Ardestie and Carlungie: Souterrains (502344 & 511349)

Souterrains have long presented a puzzle to archaeologists because nobody was sure of their purpose or even of when they were built. They are underground chambers, lined with stone slabs and generally curving. They can be up to 60m long. It is now thought that they were originally covered with timber and thatch roofs. Souterrains occur in the heartland of the Picts in eastern Scotland between the Tay and the Moray Firth but they are also found more widely in northern and western Scotland, where they are often marked on Ordnance Survey maps as 'earth houses' (Trail 17). They also occur in Ireland.

At one time archaeologists thought that they were houses, conjuring up images of the Picts as a race of burrow-dwellers. Excavations within the last 30 years have shown, however, that souterrains were associated with groups of circular huts at the surface. In some instances the entrances to the souterrains can be shown to have been situated inside a hut which was larger than the remainder in the group. Souterrains were re-interpreted as underground storehouses, probably for grain (although their use as cattle byres has also been suggested). This change of opinion as the result of new excavated evidence shows the dangers of drawing interpretations of landscape features purely from what has survived to the present day. In these examples the living part of the settlement above ground has been obliterated by later cultivation and the storage areas have survived only because they were below the surface and had been built more substantially with stone rather than timber to prevent the underground walls from collapsing due to the pressure of the soil.

As far as dating was concerned it used to be thought that souterrains dated from the period of the Pictish Kingdom from the 6th to the 9th centuries, but again new archaeological evidence has shown that they were earlier, having been built during the first two centuries A.D. Curiously, some of the excavated examples had been deliberately filled in with soil and their roofs dismantled, apparently by the inhabitants of the associated settlements who continued to use the sites. This occurred around 200 A.D. and has provided yet another puzzle. The way in which the souterrains were linked with specific huts in the settlements, and the fact that they almost always occur singly rather than in small groups, suggests that they were kept under the control of an individual rather than being a communal facility. Perhaps they were used for storing tribute? One suggestion is that the Roman army, on its periodic forays north of the Antonine Wall, may have instituted a system of requisitioning grain from the local inhabitants to feed its troops, and that the souterrains were storehouses for this levy. The souterrains were then cheerfully filled in by the inhabitants when the Romans finally withdrew. More convincingly, it has been proposed that as society in this area gradually became more complex, developing into the earliest phases of the historical Pictish Kingdom, the surpluses which had previously been creamed off by village headmen were now being taken by a higher social group and concentrated more centrally, perhaps at sites like Forteviot and Scone which were to become Pictish royal centres.

So souterrains are not really 'Pictish' at all but relate to the immediate ancestors of the historical Picts. Nevertheless we have already mentioned that many of the settlement sites continued in use after the souterrains were filled in, and there is evidence, admittedly rather sparse at present, that on some sites occupation continued down to the 7th or 9th centuries.

Although there are many souterrains in southern Pictland, the two excavated examples at Ardestie and Carlungie have been preserved and are under official protection. North of the farm of Mains of Ardestie, at 502344, one of them is located in the middle of a field and can be reached by a footpath. Without its roof the souterrain appears as an open, stone-lined trench but you get a good impression of its shape and layout. A drainage channel ran down the centre of the floor of the souterrain, and its main entrance was immediately adjacent to the largest of a group of four huts which were spaced closely together beside it.

A little over 2km away at Carlungie there is another example, also in the middle of a field and accessible by a footpath (511349). The main part of the souterrain is more sharply curved than the one at Ardestie, forming a U-shape. It seems to have had an entrance at each end, while a narrow passage leads off from the centre of the U-bend. Excavations showed a cluster of eight huts on the surface, and the site may have been occupied for some 200 years after the souterrain was filled in

2. Laws Hill: Fort and Broch (491349)

This site can be reached by a walk of 2.5km there and back. If you do not wish to do this walk continue the trail at No. 3.

Just over 1km to the north-east of the souterrain at Ardestie is Laws Hill. *Park your car at Drumsturdy (491349) and follow a minor road to the south. Turn right and go past Laws Farm to the summit of the hill.* On the summit is a fort whose ramparts were originally supported by a framework of timbers. The wall is up to 9m thick and is faced with stone blocks with a rubble core. The fort is oval in shape, about 120m long and 60m wide. At either end there are additional defences. At some time the timbers supporting the wall were set on fire and the intense heat has fused the stones together into a solid glassy mass. This process is known as 'vitrification'. It was once believed that such forts had been set alight deliberately to produce a solid wall but it is now considered to have been the result of attack or of accidental fires. Until fairly recently it was believed that all forts with ramparts of timber-laced construction, including all vitrified forts, dated from the Iron Age. Excavations of a fort at Burghead in Moray have produced radiocarbon dates for the timber-laced structure well within the Pictish period so that each of the hillforts within Pictland now needs to be considered separately as far as its date is concerned. In the interior of this fort, however, you can see the foundations of a broch which seems to have been built at a later date than the fort, as it partly overlies the vitrified wall. Enough is known about brochs (Trail 16) to place them as contemporary with or slightly earlier than the nearby souterrains. This particular fort, then, must be Iron Age rather than Pictish.

Return to your car. Follow the B961 eastwards and then north to its junction with the A938. Turn left on to the A938 towards Forfar.

If many of the souterrain sites continued to be occupied in later centuries, then the location of surviving souterrains may provide some guide to the later distribution of settlement during the Pictish period. Place names also tell us something about Pictish settlement. Throughout Pictland from Fife to the Black Isle you can find places whose names contain the element 'pit'. This is thought to derive from a Pictish word meaning 'a share' (of land) and to denote settlements which were functioning in later Pictish times: the 9th and 10th centuries. Detailed examination of their distribution shows that they occur in lowland situations with a marked preference for good, well-drained soils which would have been particularly suitable for arable farming. They are rarely found near the coast, which suggests that other types of settlement names may have been used in such locations. The second element in these 'pit' names is usually Q-Celtic, the language introduced by the Scots who took over the Pictish Kingdom in the 9th century. This would suggest that the 'pit' names are relatively late in date, having been created at a time when Scottish immigrants were moving into the area. The fact that 'pit' means a share must also indicate that there were larger units of landholding and settlement, and possibly smaller ones too. After the merging of the Scots and Picts some characteristically Scottish place-name elements were introduced, including 'bal' (a farmstead) which may have replaced 'pit' for some settlements.

The fact that a 'pit' name, Pitairlie, is attached to a farm less than 1km from Carlungie suggests that there may have been continuity of settlement from the souterrain users onwards in this area. As you follow the B961 uphill from Pitairlie you can look eastwards along the slope which marks the edge of the lower eastern end of the Sidlaw hills. Along the lower part of this slope, on well-drained ground, you can find more 'pit' names on the map, Pitlivie and Pitcundrum, as well as some 'bal' names. After you join the A958 you have reached a rolling plateau up to 200m high. There are no early settlement names with 'pit' or 'bal' elements here. If you look at the names of the farms that you pass you will see that most of them are simple topographic descriptive names like Backhills, Mosston and Smallburn, using words which were characteristic of medieval Scots rather than of earlier times. This is an indication that this higher-lying area was settled at a much later date than the surrounding country with its scatter of 'pit' and 'bal' names. Documentary evidence confirms that this area, now Carmyllie parish, was only settled during medieval times.

From the centre of Forfar follow the B9113 eastwards for 2km to the next site.

3. Restenneth Priory (482517)

The ruins of the priory are situated just off the B9113 road east of Forfar. Restenneth was a priory of Augustinian canons and was probably founded during the reign of David I in the 12th century. The ruins of the choir of the priory church probably date from this time. To the south of the church is a walled enclosure marking the site of the former monastic cloisters and associated buildings. It is the tower of the church which is worth a closer look, though. The top, a fine broach spire, a type which is uncommon in Scotland, is quite late in date, possibly 15th century. The upper part of the tower itself may date from the 12th century but the lower part is earlier. The give-away is the south door at the base of the tower. This narrow, round-headed entrance is pure Anglo-Saxon. It is thought that the base of the tower formed part of an early Pictish church built for King Nechtan mac Dereli in 710 by masons brought from Northumberland. The date is significant as it marks the period when the Christian church in Pictland adopted the usages of the Northumbrian church, following the Synod of Whitby (Trail 13), bringing the churches of the two areas into closer contact.

Continue east along the B9113 for 1km. Turn left on a minor road leading north to the B9134. Turn right on to this, towards Brechin.

4. Turin Hill: Fort (513535)

This site involves a walk of 4km there and back. If you do not wish to do the walk continue the Trail at No. 5

The best way to reach this hilltop fort is from the north by a track which leads off from the B9134 at 524549, past Back of Turin farm, and which continues as a footpath towards the summit of the ridge, a walk of about 1.5km from the main road. On a clear day the view from the top, towards Strathmore to the north and over Rescobie Loch to the south, is reward enough, but the hilltop is also occupied by an interesting sequence of forts. To the south the ground is so steep that defences are hardly needed, but to the north you can see a double line of ramparts enclosing an oval area about 300 × 120m—similar in shape, but larger than, the fort on Laws Hill. Inside this, but overlying the defences on the south-west side, is a much smaller oval stone-walled fort with a single rampart which was probably timber-laced. Within this second fort, and again overlying its rampart in turn, is an even smaller ring-fort or dun, about 30m in diameter, with a stone wall about 9m thick. The first fort may date from the early Iron Age, and the second may be contemporary with the one on Laws Hill. The ring fort is clearly later; two other similar-sized forts, less well preserved, can be seen about 150m to the east and west of this one. Small forts like these occur widely in the heartland of the Pictish territory but are also found on the margins of Pictland and on the west coast. Some of them may have been built before the Pictish period and have remained in use, but one or two examples have certainly produced evidence of Pictish occupation, though others, on the western margins of Pictland, may have been built by the Scots pushing eastwards.

5. Finavon: Hill Fort (507557)

The hill of Finavon, on the other side of the valley to the north of Turin Hill, has another hillfort which is well worth visiting because it is so easily accessible. *Half a kilometre along the B9134 from the track to Turin Hill, a minor road leads off to the left (516553). Follow this road over the crest of the hill. The fort is on an outlying hillock to the north.* Finavon is another example of a vitrified fort. Like the ones on Turin Hill and Laws Hill it is oval in shape, a plan which is a distinctively Tayside one and which might point to a common origin. The fort consisted of a single timber-laced rampart which was originally 6m thick, with additional defences at the eastern end. The remains of a well can be seen in an enclosure inside the ramparts. Excavations in the 1930s suggested that the main rampart may originally have stood nearly 5m high on the downslope side of the hill. A line of timber buildings had been constructed against the inner side of the wall. It is possible that the vitrification which can be seen in places was caused by an accidental fire among these buildings rather than by attackers. More recently, radiocarbon dating has shown that the fort was occupied between about 400 and 600 B.C. so that it is certainly pre-Pictish.

Return to the B9134 and continue towards Brechin for 0.5km.

6. Aberlemno: Pictish Symbol Stones (523555 & 523559)

The most frequent and at the same time the most puzzling feature associated with the Picts is the sculptured stones which can be found throughout eastern Scotland from Fife to Orkney with marked concentrations in Forfarshire, parts of Aberdeenshire and Easter Ross. They can occur singly or in groups, on their own in the middle of fields or in churchyards. Archaeologists have divided Pictish symbol stones into three groups according to the types of motifs portrayed. Class I stones are upright boulders on which have been incised various abstract and animal symbols. Class II stones are more carefully prepared and dressed slabs on which a cross has been carved, generally in relief, on one side while the reverse side has symbols similar to the Class I stones and sometimes also human figures. Class III stones are similar to the last type but with only the cross and none of the other symbols.

The crosses indicate that the Class II and III stones date from after the conversion of the Picts to Christianity, in the 8th century. Class I stones are considered to be pre-Christian, from the 5th to the 8th centuries. The problem with these stones is that their function, and the meanings of the symbols which they carry, are obscure. Various interpretations have been put forward; one suggestion is that they were memorial stones. Few of them seem to be directly associated with a burial but many of them may have been moved from their original locations. Another theory is that they were property markers, delimiting the boundaries of the lands belonging to various tribal groups, which are represented by combinations of symbols. The Class II stones, with crosses, might have indicated the limits of ecclesiastical lands or of a tribal group that had been converted to Christianity. When the various combinations of symbols are mapped there does not seem to be any discernible pattern, but it is likely that the stones which now survive are only a fraction of those which once existed; new ones are still being discovered. Yet another possibility is that the stones were set up to commemorate dynastic marriages and alliances. Class I stones are much more common in the North-East and there are fewer in southern Pictland, while there are more Class II stones here than in the North-East. This may reflect a shift in cultural and political domination from north to south with the unification of the two areas.

A good deal depends on what the various symbols were designed to show. A study of the ones used on the Class I and II stones has highlighted some interesting characteristics. The same symbols are used throughout Pictland; these include animals such as horse, boar, bull, stag, wolf, fish, snake and eagle which would have been familiar to the sculptors, and also two mythical creatures which archaeologists have labelled the 'Pictish beast' or 'swimming elephant' and the 'Pictish S-dragon'. The use of animals as tribal badges or totems is recorded from many primitive societies, and

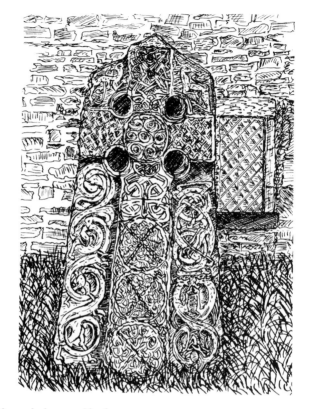

Pictish symbol stone, Aberlemno

this may have been their function here. The other designs include identifiable objects such as combs and mirrors and also what seem to be complete abstracts to which archaeologists have attached names like Z-rod, V-rod, notched rectangle, tuning fork etc. The way in which the symbols appear fully developed and completely standardised throughout Pictland suggests that they may have had a long previous history in some other medium. This could have been wood, but skin is also a possibility, remembering that the Picts' supposed custom of tattooing themselves is thought to have led to their Roman nickname 'the painted people'. Professor Charles Thomas has argued recently that the designs originated as tattoos which designated a person's tribe and status. He considers that the Picts began to copy the custom of erecting memorial stones

from Christian North Britain and Ireland, or from Roman examples, and that these personal symbols were transferred to the stones,
just as many 18th-century Scottish tombstones have the tools of a
person's trade carved on them. The symbols which depict objects
like combs and mirrors seem to be derived from earlier Iron Age
artefacts rather than objects in current use: another example,

Pictish symbol stone, Aberlemno churchyard

perhaps, of the very conservative nature of Pictish society. All the theories which have been put forward to explain the symbol stones rely heavily on analogy and surmise, so that we will probably never know for certain what their purpose was; in many ways this makes them even more fascinating.

At Aberlemno you can see some particularly fine examples of Pictish symbol stones carved in red sandstone. One of them stands in the churchyard, just off the B9134 to the right at 523555. This example is clearly a Class II stone because the front has a cross surrounded by an interlacing ornament of serpents. The reverse side of the stone has some of the classic Pictish abstract symbols at the top—the Z-rod, notched rectangle and triple disc—while below is a dramatic hunting scene with galloping horsemen and figures on foot with spears and bows.

Two other stones are located beside the B9134 in a small walled enclosure at 523559. One is an example of a Class I stone, the other a Class II stone nearly 3m high. The front has a cross with an angel carrying a book on either side, in a pose which is either mourning or adoring, depending on your preference. The design of the cross has many parallels with the high crosses on Iona (Trail 13) and reflects clear Irish influences. On the reverse side at the top of the stone are more abstract symbols: the crescent and V-rod, with a double disc and Z-rod below. Under this there is another hunting or battle scene.

If you are staying in the area you may wish to visit two small museums with collections of Pictish symbol stones at Meigle, between Blairgowrie and Alyth, and at St. Vigeans on the northern outskirts of Arbroath.

Continue along the B9134 to Brechin.

7. Brechin: The Cathedral and Round Tower (596601)

Today a small market town, Brechin may not have the air of a cathedral city, but near the town centre you will nevertheless find a cathedral. This was originally a Pictish monastic site and became the centre of a diocese around 1150 when the old Pictish bishopric of Abernethy was split up. Most of the older work of the cathedral

Round tower, Brechin Cathedral

dates from the 13th century, but the building was radically altered during a 'restoration' in 1806–7. At this time the north and south transepts were demolished and the aisles were widened. The outer walls of the aisles were raised so that the whole building could be covered with a single roof of continuous pitch, hiding the clerestorey windows above the nave. The cathedral had continued in use as the parish church after the Reformation but the choir had been allowed to fall into ruins. In 1900–2 the choir was rebuilt and roofed, and new transepts erected on the original foundations.

The most distinctive feature of the cathedral is the slim pencil-like round tower which rises like a minaret from the south-west corner. This is one of only two round towers in Scotland; the other is at Abernethy. Round towers originated in Ireland, partly, it is thought, as bell towers and lookout posts against the Vikings. Their entrances were set above the ground for protection and were reached by wooden ladders which could be pulled up. Sometimes the base of the tower was solid for several feet up to make it fire-resistant. The towers may also have been used as refuges, and in this sense they were like tall thin brochs (Trail 16) or tower houses (Trail 1). The tower at Brechin is thought to date from around 1000 A.D. and was attached to a former Pictish monastery. The doorway is over 2m off the ground. The sides of the door slope towards the top, a characteristic feature of Irish towers. Above the entrance is a crucifixion and on either side two figures, possibly bishops. The tower is some 30m high, tapering slightly towards the top. There were two internal timber floors resting on projecting courses of stones and lit by small windows. At the top are four larger openings facing the cardinal points of the compass to let the sound of the bells ring out across the countryside.

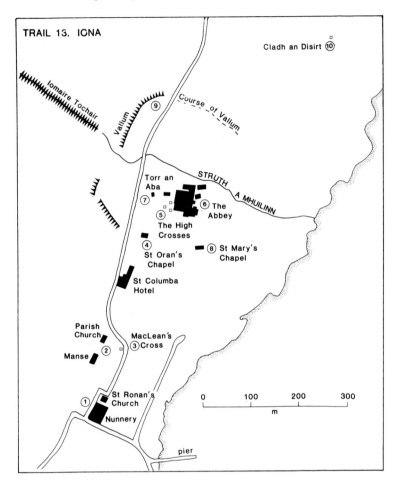

THIRTEEN

Iona: An Early-Christian Monastic Site

Ordance Survey 1:50,000 sheet 48; 1:25,000 sheet NM 22

The trail involves a walk of about 2.5km around the Abbey of
Iona and its associated features. Iona can be reached by
passenger ferry from Fionnphort at the south-west tip of Mull,
or by day excursion cruises from Oban. Cars are not allowed
on the island.

Introduction

This trail is designed to show the very long-term continuity of
occupation which can be found on many Scottish sites, whether
lay or ecclesiastical. In the case of Iona this continuity spans some
1,400 years of Christian worship, interrupted at times but always
renewed because of the sanctity of the site. On the other hand this
long-continued use of a site provides difficulties when it comes to
understanding the landscape remains, as those from earlier periods
tend to have been obliterated. Archaeologists and historians are
often faced with a dilemma when studying sites such as early-
Christian monasteries. On the one hand there are examples which
have been abandoned and never re-occupied. These may be far
more obvious in the landscape; but are they really representative?
On the other hand, the more 'typical' sites are the most likely to
have remained in use and there may be less to see and interpret.

Certain places radiate an atmosphere of peace and tranquillity,
and one senses that Iona would still possess this quality even
without its holy associations. Looking across the Sound of Iona,
turquoise where the granite sand and shingle lie close to the
surface, towards the hills of Mull one can appreciate why the
island attracted a group of monks who had left their homes in a
self-imposed penitential exile. What is perhaps harder to appreciate is why a site which seems so remote today should have become
the most important and influential early-Christian monastery in
north Britain. To understand how this happened we need to look
briefly at the origins and spread of Christianity within the British
Isles.

Christianity, having become established in Roman Britain, seems to have survived the withdrawal of the legions in areas like Wales, the South-West, and Cumbria, which were not immediately affected by the Anglo-Saxon settlement. The church retained its administrative structure of bishops and dioceses; a particularly vigorous diocese centred on Carlisle is thought to have expanded its missionary activity into Scotland in the 5th and 6th centuries, establishing further dioceses in Galloway, the Tweed basin (probably centred on Old Melrose: Trail 5), the Firth of Forth and the Glasgow area (Trail 9). The Picts, north of the Forth, remained pagan. The Irish annals record that Patrick, the son of a Roman official, was kidnapped from Cumbria by raiders and brought to Ireland when he was about 16. After several years he escaped to the Continent, became ordained as a priest and returned to Cumbria. In 432 he went back to Ireland as a missionary. There were probably already some Irish Christians before Patrick returned, and the conversion of the island was accomplished remarkably peacefully. It is curious that Ireland, the one part of Western Europe which the Romans did not attempt to subdue, was nevertheless taken over by Roman beliefs and ideas in the shape of Christianity. Ireland became a repository of classical learning when the barbarian invasions disrupted the old ways of life and organisation throughout the Roman Empire.

St. Patrick brought to Ireland a church which was organised on the basis of dioceses and bishops, like the surviving church in western Britain. This structure was superimposed on the tribal framework of 5th-century Ireland, the tribal territories becoming ecclesiastical units. By the end of the 5th century, however, a new force began to affect religion in the west: monasticism. The idea of living a devotional life under ascetic conditions in remote areas, whether as a hermit or as part of a group, originated in countries around the eastern Mediterranean in the 4th century as a reaction to the growing slackness and materialism of the town-based church. The fashion spread rapidly to the West, reaching south-west England first, then South Wales and Ireland. The idea of 'families' of monks living together fitted well into a society where kinship was of paramount importance. It was from Ireland that parties of monks spread out with the dual objectives of spreading the word of God by missionary activity and doing penance by living a life of hardship in remote places.

The desire for isolation and mortification can be seen in the remote rock-bound monasteries off the west coast of Ireland. The search for remote and uninhabited locations took groups of monks in their leather curraghs to Faroe, Iceland, and just possibly Greenland and beyond. Around northern and western Scotland archaeologists have found promontories, some of which are extremely difficult of access today, and isolated stacks whose summits require rock-climbing techniques to reach, with the remains of single huts or small groups of cells. These are probably the remains of hermitages, or in some cases small monasteries, from early-Christian times. The sites were clearly chosen for their inaccessibility, and on some of them seabirds must have been the main component of the monks' diet.

On the other hand large monasteries were founded in places where they could be more closely in touch with the local population. Such centres had an important evangelising role. At a time when sea travel was much easier than journeying overland Iona was in a central location for the entire Western Isles, and was easily reached from Ireland. Contact with Ireland was important throughout the development of the early-Christian monastery on Iona and, as we will see, these contacts continued into medieval times.

The monstery on Iona was founded in 563 by Columba, a prince of one of the ruling families of Ireland and one of the heirs to the High Kingship at Tara. He went into a self-imposed exile after a dynastic quarrel at home, but the monastery was probably established to serve an existing Christian population among the Scots of Dalriada who had migrated from Ireland. Columba himself achieved a formidable reputation in his own lifetime. As the community on Iona expanded, other daughter houses were established on Jura, Tiree and beside Loch Awe, while other independent monasteries were also founded among the Western Isles, on Lismore, Eigg and Bute. A disciple of Columba's, Cormac, brought Christianity to the Northern Isles around 575, and monks from Iona are also credited with converting the Picts. When Oswald, King of Northumbria, ascended the throne after a period of exile which included a stay on Iona, he sent for a bishop from the island, Aidan, who founded the monastery at Lindisfarne. His successors there were also monks from Iona. From Lindisfarne in turn other monastic communities were established in Northern England and Southern Scotland. It was in Northumbria that the

Celtic church, which had been cut off from the mainstream of ecclesiastical life on the Continent for a century or more, came into contact with the mission which had been established by St. Augustine, pushing northwards. Major disputes over important points of church procedure were settled at Whitby in 664 in favour of the Roman church. Although the influence of the Celtic church in northern England declined after this, close contacts continued between Ireland, Iona and Northumbria. These can be traced in the artistic styles of monuments like the high crosses of Iona. The golden age of Celtic monasticism was over by the 7th century as the monasteries began to acquire lands and to squabble over them. The Viking raids, which started at Iona in 795, finally caused the eclipse of the Celtic church. As a result of these raids the main part of the Iona community returned to Kells in Ireland, but some kind of religious presence continued on the island. A new phase in the religious history of Iona began around 1200 with the foundation of a Benedictine abbey and a nunnery. So sacred was the location of the early monastery considered to be that the later abbey was founded within its precincts, perhaps over the shrine of Columba. The same continuity of tradition can be seen at Lismore where the cathedral of the Diocese of Lismore and Argyll was built within the boundaries of the monastic enclosure. The abbey on Iona fell into decay after the Reformation but travellers and antiquarians began to rediscover the island during the 18th century. At first many of them thought that the surviving buildings dated from Columba's time, but in fact much of what you will see on the island relates to the medieval abbey. Nevertheless, there are still clues in the landscape to the character of the early monastery.

1. The Nunnery and St. Ronan's Church

Medieval nunneries were generally less well endowed than the major abbeys. As a result their churches were smaller and simpler, their living quarters more modest. Because of this few of them survived the Reformation; most have left little trace in the landscape. It is strange that one has to come to Iona to get a good impression of what medieval nunneries throughout lowland Britain must have been like. Although Iona's nunnery is in ruins, enough remains for you to reconstruct the tightly-grouped complex of buildings. The nunnery is thought to have been founded at about the same time as the abbey (around 1200) and by the same man, Reginald, son of Somerled, ancestor of the Lords of the Isles. The first prioress was supposedly Reginald's sister. The original nucleus of nuns probably came from Ireland where houses of Augustinian canonesses like this one were numerous. The layout of the nunnery fits the general European pattern, but many aspects of its style seem to be Irish, and masons from Ireland may have helped to build it. While the abbey became endowed with widely scattered lands, the nunnery was only granted a block of estates in Mull, along with the southern, rocky part of Iona itself.

Like the abbey, and in common with medieval abbeys elsewhere (Trail 5), the nunnery comprises a church with an attached cloister surrounded by living quarters. Most of the remains date from the 13th century but the refectory on the south side of the cloister and the vanished west range represent a 15th-century rebuilding, when the cloister was enlarged. The range of buildings on the east side was the dormitory block. You can detect differences in the stone used in the 13th and 15th-century buildings. The rebuilt 15th-century cloister was surrounded by an elaborately-designed arcade,

The nunnery, Iona

remains of which can be seen in the nunnery museum in St. Ronan's Church. The nunnery church is a simple rectangle with an aisle on the north side. You can see where the arcade of the nave was blocked up during 15th-century alterations.

The adjacent building, St. Ronan's church, was the medieval parish church of the island, indicating that there was a substantial lay population here as well as the monks. It dates from the late 12th or 13th century. Like other medieval churches in the West Highlands it is small, plain and unadorned. It has been re-roofed and is now a museum housing many carved stones and grave slabs from the area round the nunnery and the burial ground to the north.

2. The Parish Church and Manse

The 19th-century parish church which replaced St. Ronan's possesses something of its simplicity in a more sophisticated style. It was built in 1828 to a design by the engineer Thomas Telford, following a Parliamentary act of 1824 authorising funds for the building of 42 new churches and their manses in the Highlands. Telford is better known as a builder of bridges, roads and canals, but the Commission for Highland Roads and Bridges, for which he was chief engineer, was the only group engaged in large-scale construction projects in the area at this time and it was entrusted with the work. You can find virtually identical churches from Islay to Sutherland. They were built because the increase in population in the Highlands in the late 18th and early 19th centuries rendered many existing churches too small, while some large parishes needed extra churches to serve their growing communities. On Iona there was the additional reason that the medieval church had been in ruins for a long time. The manses were designed as single-storey buildings with projecting wings, but this one has had an extra storey added at a later date.

3. MacLean's Cross

In front of the parish church is the first of the famous high crosses of Iona. It does not date from the time of Columba, though: MacLean's Cross is medieval, probably late 15th century. It does, however, represent a local tradition of stone carving which continued on the island from early-Christian into medieval times and which can also be appreciated from the sculptured grave slabs in the abbey museum. The cross seems to be in its original position at the meeting place of three medieval causeways which linked the nunnery and abbey to the two principal landing places. The side arms of the cross have suffered some damage, although they were probably originally fairly short, but the intertwining, plaited design of the shaft is well preserved. On the west side, facing the church, is a crucifixion scene. The name of this cross, unlike some of the older ones, is probably authentic; it is thought that it was carved for a member of the Clan MacLean, although exactly who is uncertain.

MacLean's Cross, Iona

4. St. Oran's Chapel and Reilig Odhrain

The chapel, with its entrance framed by a rounded arch decorated with a chevron and beak-head motif, is older than the nunnery or the abbey, probably dating from the later 12th century. It is thought to have been built as a private chapel and mortuary for Somerled, or his son Reginald, supposedly the founder of the abbey. It remained the burial place for the Lords of the Isles in later medieval times, stressing the importance of their patronage and protection to the monastic community. The layout of the building, with the doorway in the west gable rather than the south wall, and the style of the arch, closely parallel contemporary Irish work another indication of the continuing links between Iona and Ireland.

The burial ground of Reiling Odhrain is named after St. Odhrain, a cousin of Columba. It was a cemetery in early-Christian times although it continued to be used well into the Middle Ages. The best of the early-Christian and medieval grave markers and slabs have been removed to the abbey museum but some remain here. It has been suggested that this was a lay burial ground (though only for people of higher social status) and that the monastic burial ground may have been closer to the abbey. This may explain why the burial ground is on the edge of the monastic precincts rather than within them, though an alternative explanation is that the site of the monastery itself has been moved over time.

Beyond the Reilig Odhrain you can see a cobbled causeway leading to the abbey. This was uncovered following excavations in 1962; the spaces between the large red granite cobbles were probably filled up with gravel when the road was in use.

Excavations during the 1970s in the area between the Reilig Odhrain and the abbey have provided many insights into the early Columban community. It is clear that the island was inhabited at various stages throughout prehistory and that the area of raised beach on which the abbey stands had been settled and cultivated long before the arrival of the monks. Traces of timber buildings were discovered relating to the earlier phases of the monastery, and the material filling in a ditch, which perhaps marked the earliest boundary of the monastery, contained wooden and leather articles, including shoes and a purse, which had been preserved because the ground was waterlogged. There was probably a workshop and tannery nearby.

5. The High Crosses

In front of the west door of the Abbey stand two crosses and the stump of a third which are among the best examples of early-Christian free-standing or 'high' crosses in Britain. The clustering of three such important monuments here probably indicates that the main focus of the early monastery, Columba's shrine, was located close by. St. John's Cross, standing closest to the abbey, is a replica. The original one, in several fragments, is being conserved and repaired. The remaining two crosses, St. Matthew's, of which only the lower shaft remains, and St. Martin's, are originals. Other crosses were also erected elsewhere on the island; fragments of two of them from the Reilig Odhrain are preserved in the nunnery museum, and the base of another one sits on the summit of the low rocky ridge, Torr an Aba, opposite the west door of the Abbey.

Free-standing crosses may have developed from pagan standing stones; such stones, inscribed with the ogham alphabet, are known from pre-Christian Ireland. They gradually acquired the cross motif which grew in importance until the slab became a cross. The grave of the founder of a monastery may often have been marked in this way, and it was a natural extension of this idea to raise such crosses at the centre of a monastery as a more general symbol. Free-standing crosses were used for different purposes in early-Christian and medieval times. They might act as preaching crosses, gathering points for a community where monks held services. At times when it was not normal to mark the graves of ordinary people, large churchyard crosses served to commemorate all. Crosses were also used as boundary markers for church lands and were often mentioned in medieval charters in this context. Roadside crosses might mark places where coffins were rested while being carried to the parish church. They could also serve as guides for travellers. Within the precincts of monasteries they might act as focal points, commemorate important locations, such as saints' graves, or encourage the monks to meditate. Like later ecclesiastical art, their designs can tell us much about their markers and where they got their ideas from. Because of their size and weight they have rarely moved far from their original site so that they are more clearly identified with particular localities than, for instance, manuscripts or metalwork, which are more portable. The famous Book of Kells, for instance, has had its origins located from Northumbria to Ireland, although there is some agreement that it was probably written and illuminated on Iona; but there is no doubt that these crosses were carved on the island.

High crosses seem to have developed first in Ireland. Their prototypes were probably wooden because many of the structural and design features of early stones ones—mortice-and-tenon joints and even 'nail heads' incorporated into the design—seem to be a hangover from wooden examples. The ring heads of these crosses probably derive from supports for the arms of wooden crosses used in processions. On the other hand, some elements in the design of such crosses came from metallurgy. The original wooden crosses may have had outer coverings of decorated sheet metal, whose designs were copied in stone. Early crosses were decorated in a variety of abstract motifs but later ones, like those of St. Matthew and St. John, were sculpture crosses with biblical scenes carved on them. St. John's Cross, with only one biblical scene, is transitional. St. Martin's Cross is carved from a single block but the original St. John's cross was made up of eight separate pieces. In this example the ring was not original but was added later, possibly after the original cross had collapsed.

6. The Abbey

Although the abbey has been extensively restored during the present century, the layout of the medieval buildings has been retained and every effort has been made to preserve and enhance the surviving medieval stonework. To the left of the west entrance to the church you can see a small chapel which has been named 'Columba's shrine'. This was once a separate building, and although only the lower parts of the walls are original, it seems to have been a chapel or oratory dating from as early as the 9th or 10th centuries. Tradition claims that it is built on the site of Columba's tomb, which is quite possible although there is no proof.

The Benedictine abbey was supposedly founded by Reginald, son of Somerled, around 1200. In its early days it was moderately prosperous, being endowed with lands which were scattered through the Western Isles and the mainland from Kintyre to North

West front of the Abbey, Iona

Uist. Nevertheless, it was very much an outpost of medieval monasticism, and the abbey depended heavily on the support of the Lords of the Isles who were buried in St. Oran's chapel. As with the nunnery, many of the decorative features indicate contact with Ireland and probably the use of Irish masons. The plain style of the early church is best seen in the north transept of the building. The early church had a simple cruciform plan with a long, narrow nave, but during the 13th century the church was extended eastwards above an undercroft with north and south aisles. At the end of the 13th century grandiose plans were laid for a huge southern transept with an eastern aisle. The building of this was abandoned

H

at an early stage of construction but some of the foundations can be seen outside the church on its south-east side. Following this there was little alteration to the church until the 15th century when its entire south wall was demolished and a new one built, giving a wider nave and chancel and a new south aisle. As at Melrose (Trail 5), there is a marked contrast between the severe Romanesque style of the earlier church and the elaborate decoration of the later rebuilding. Evidence for these changes can be seen clearly in the masonry inside the church. Iona was remote from the mainstream of medieval monastic life, and the architecture and decoration of the church strongly reflects local traditions within the Western Isles as well as contacts with Ireland.

After the Reformation the church became derelict but in the 1630s efforts were made to restore its east end as a cathedral for the diocese of the Isles. At this time the south choir aisle and nave were abandoned and separated from the rest of the church by walls blocking up the arcades. The upper parts of the nave walls were probably demolished to provide stone for the new blocking walls, and further deterioration of the structure occurred during the 18th century. The ruins were repaired to prevent further decay during the later 19th century under the direction of the 8th Duke of Argyll. Restoration of the church began in 1902, and the other monastic buildings were rebuilt mainly after the Second World War. The original monastic buildings were added to the first church and date from various periods. As at Melrose (Trail 5), the cloister has been placed to the north of the church rather than on the south side as was normal, because of access to a water supply in this direction for flushing the drains and latrines. The west range is almost entirely modern, being much larger than the medieval block which stood on this side of the cloister. The eastern range, facing it, is 13th-century with 15th-century alterations and was originally the dormitory with the chapter house below. On the north side is the refectory and beyond the cloister the abbot's house and latrines. Detached to the north is a building which was probably the infirmary. To the east there is also a small detached chapel, St. Michael's, dating from the late 12th or 13th century. It may have been constructed to serve as a place of worship while the abbey was being built. It has been converted to a museum in which the best sculptured stones and grave markers from the Reilig Odhrain have been preserved.

7. Torr an Aba

The well in front of the abbey was once thought to date back to Columba's time, but excavation has indicated that it was sunk in the 16th century. Immediately in front of the west range of the cloister are the foundations of another building now laid out as a garden. Again, this was once believed to have been part of the pre-medieval monastery, but it has been shown to have been the bakehouse and brewery of the abbey. Facing the west side of the abbey is a low rocky ridge, Torr an Aba. On its summit the remains of a small circular stone hut can be seen. It would be attractive to interpret this as the remains of Columba's own cell. Adomnan's 'Life of Columba' suggests that he had one in a 'high place' within the monastery for private meditation, but the archaeological evidence is not conclusive; the hut could have been built at a variety of periods.

8. St. Mary's Chapel

South-east of the abbey are the ruined walls of another building about which little is known. It may have been a chapel and seems later in date than the earliest phases of the medieval abbey. A branch of the stone causeway leads to it, suggesting that it was quite important. It may have been used by pilgrims visiting the island.

9. The Vallum

Early-Christian monasteries in Ireland were always surrounded by a boundary, often an earthen bank with an outer ditch, and in some cases a stone wall. Sometimes this 'vallum' or perimeter was derived from the wall of a pre-existing fort but its function was not defensive; rather it was a spiritual and legal boundary defining the monastic area, within which the abbot's word was absolute and beyond which the monks might not be allowed without permission. The buildings of these early monasteries were originally of timber, and even where they were later replaced by stone the small chapels and cells have survived only occasionally. The vallum, surviving as an earthwork or incorporated into later boundaries, is often the best indication on the ground of the site of a former early-

Christian monastery. The location of one on Lismore has been traced by the survival of a circular boundary even though it is mostly composed of relatively recent drystone walls. The one at Iona is more rectangular in shape and encloses an area of about 20 acres, comparable to many Irish examples. A short way along the road which runs north from the abbey you can see on your left the earthworks which form the best-preserved section, with a massive bank, outer ditch, and small bank beyond. However, if you examine it in detail you will see that it is not just a simple earthwork; within the angle at the top are humps and bumps which seem to be old gravel workings and also the remains of a small rectangular cottage and its associated enclosures, from comparatively recent times. The vallum seems to have run eastwards from here below the road and towards the sea. Its traces are hardly visible on the ground but show up from the air. The eastern limits of the enclosure are harder to determine; they have been ploughed out by long-continued cultivation. Immediately west of the road which passes the abbey, on the west side of a rocky hill, there are further traces of the vallum with an earth rampart and a ditch cut in solid rock. To the south its limits are uncertain because it has been obliterated and because between the abbey and the burial ground excavations have shown a multiplicity of boundaries. In this area the original vallum may have been replaced by a later ditch on a different line. The location of the high crosses and 'St Columba's shrine' support the idea that the focus of the early monastery was the same as that of the medieval abbey, but recent excavations have suggested an alternative, that the original cluster of monastic buildings lay beneath and just to the north of the burial ground and that the community later expanded northwards towards where the abbey now stands. Certainly, it is hard to believe that the massive earthwork to the north-west of the abbey was the work of Columba and his handful of monks. It is more likely to date from a later phase of the early-Christian monastery when the community had grown substantially. If so, then the original area of the monastery may well have been smaller than that enclosed by the vallum which can be traced today. Further excavations might help to solve the problem but the long occupation of the site has produced a very complex stratigraphy while much of the earliest remains has undoubtedly been obliterated by later building and cultivation.

From the well-preserved northern corner of the vallum you can see a ridge running north-westwards. This is an artificial causeway which crosses an area which, before drainage in the mid-18th century, was a loch. The causeway stood at its southern end and may have acted as a dam; the small stream which flows out from this marshy area and runs just north of the abbey powered the medieval corn mill. The causeway may also have provided a dry route for the monks to reach the cultivated lands beyond, but whether it is medieval in date or earlier is uncertain.

10. Clach an Disirt

On the coast half a kilometre north-east of the abbey is Clach an Disirt. You can see the foundations of a small rectangular building with an enclosure which, on the south-west side, has a stone wall with two large upright granite blocks marking the entrance. Elsewhere a low turf bank indicates the limits of the enclosure. The building may be a medieval chapel, and the enclosure a burial ground, but the name indicates that originally the site was a hermitage, perhaps a place of retreat for the early-Christian monks, beyond the limits of the monastery.

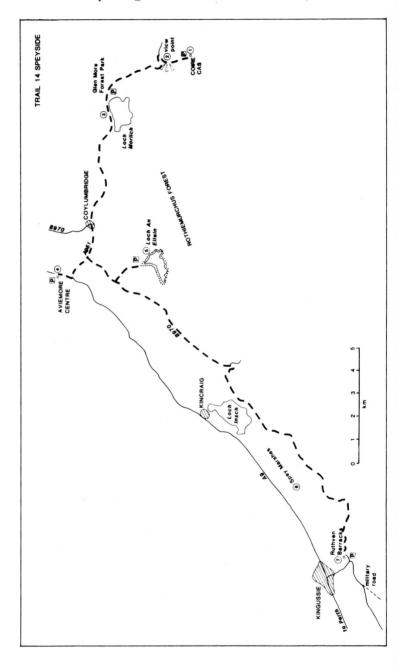

FOURTEEN

Speyside: Ancient Woodlands, Tourism and Conservation in the Landscape

Ordnance Survey 1:50,000 sheets 35 & 36. Most of this trail is covered by the 1:25,000 Outdoor Leisure Map, 'High Tops of the Cairngorms'.

This trail involves a drive of about 40km with some short optional walks.

Introduction

The Aviemore district, with its skiing facilities and wide range of summer attractions, is the most visited tourist area in the Scottish Highlands. It contains two very distinctive types of large-scale habitat which are of national importance: the arctic/alpine environment of the Cairngorm plateaux and the native pine forests on the lower slopes above the Spey. Each of these has an assemblage of plant and animal species which are unique in Britain. There are also some significant habitats at a smaller scale, like the Spey marshes between Kingussie and Kincraig or the celebrated osprey eyrie at Loch Garten. Both the summit plateaux and the pine forests are under pressure today because of the influx of visitors. The influence of man on the Cairngorm tops has been comparatively recent, but he has been exploiting the woodlands and modifying their character over a longer period. In looking at the historic landscape it is easy to forget that the vegetation cover can be partly or wholly the product of human activity, just as much as more obviously man-made elements like farmland and buildings. One theme of this trail is to show how the physical environment of the area has developed since the final retreat of the glaciers at the end of the last Ice Age, and the extent to which man has intervened to alter the landscape since then.

In these trails the term 'historic' is often used with a dimension of centuries rather than decades, but we must remember that history is constantly being created and that to understand how man has shaped the landscape we need to consider not only the distant—and possibly more romantic—past but also more recent times. The 1960s were an important period in the evolution of the landscape of the Aviemore area with the development of large-scale tourist and skiing facilities. Already, after the oil price rises of the 1970s and the world economic recession of the 1980s, even the 1960s are beginning to take on a rosy romantic glow. Another theme of this trail is the impact of tourist developments on the landscape in modern times, and we raise some questions regarding the conflict between the conservation of landscape as a natural resource and the exploitation of its tourist and recreational potential.

1. The Car Park at Coire Cas (989061)

The car park, at an altitude of 640m, lies in a transition zone between the true mountain environment of the Cairngorms above and the valley with its pine forests, heather moor and marshes. If you are visiting it on a clear day in summer, look up to the head of the corrie for snow patches. These are not permanent although they often persist well into the late summer if the weather is cool and cloudy. They rarely last right through to the following winter, but other more sheltered beds elsewhere in the Cairngorms sometimes survive for several years, only melting in particularly warm summers. The permanent snowline is not very far above the summit plateaux, and it would take only a modest drop in average annual temperatures for large permanent snow beds to appear. Indeed, in the 17th and 18th centuries, the culmination of a cold phase in Europe which has become known as the Little Ice Age, it is probable that large permanent snow beds did exist in the Cairngorms and elsewhere in the Scottish mountains, though it is unlikely that there was enough accumulation to start forming mini-glaciers. The snow beds in Coire Cas, perhaps more than any other feature, warn visitors that the Cairngorm plateau above is a harsh environment more comparable with the arctic tundra than any other parts of the British uplands. *If you take the chairlift to the Ptarmigan restaurant and then walk up to the summit make sure that you wear suitable clothing and take the appropriate equipment with you. If you are unsure about what you need, read the safety notices at the bottom of the chairlift.*

The effects of this cold climate in the past and at the present time can be seen in the frost-shattered boulders which mantle the left-hand side of the valley above the foot of the chairlift. You may also be able to make out faint terraces on the right-hand side of the valley above the White Lady Shieling. These are due to the process of solifluction, the slippage of water-saturated surface debris over a frozen subsoil, a process which continues today in winter and spring.

The vegetation around the car park and up the valley sides is also transitional. There is a good deal of heather (*Calluna vulgaris*) and bilberry (*Vaccinium myrtillus*) which only gives way to true arctic/alpine flora at a higher level. You can even find one or two stunted conifers struggling to survive. They have been found at up to 840m in some places. This is an indication that trees can grow in this area at higher altitudes than you normally find them. The treeline around the Cairngorms is kept artificially low for reasons which will be discussed below. On the opposite side of the valley from the car park you can see that the surface skin of peat covering the gently-sloping ridge above the stream has been eroded into gullies or 'peat hags'. If you walk over in this direction you should be able to find the remains of trees at the base of the peat, indicating that this whole area was wooded before the peat cover began to form. During the warmest part of the post-glacial period the general treeline may have been as high as 790m in this area.

Although Coire Cas had previously been used for skiing on a small scale, the real development of the sport only occurred after 1961 when the road and chairlift were opened. Looking up from the car park you can see how the introduction of the ski facilities has affected the vegetation cover. If you walk up the valley or take the chairlift you will see that the pistes have been cleared of boulders and re-seeded with grasses, as have those areas which have been badly trampled or churned up by vehicles. The re-seeding has not always been completely successful, a reminder of the fragile nature of the mountain vegetation cover and the thin soils below. If you take the chairlift and walk up to the summit of Cairngorm you will see that efforts are being made to confine walkers to the well-worn footpaths because of widespread damage to the vegetation of the plateau. The chairlift has increased the number of visitors to the summit a hundredfold. Conservationists are concerned that the operation of the chairlift, especially in summer, is having serious long-term effects on the vegetation cover over wide areas of the Cairngorm-Braeriach summit area. Once the thin soil cover is disturbed it is very slow to form again. The breeding areas of rare birds like the golden eagle are also being inadvertently disturbed by the influx of visitors. Food left by the tourists attracts lowland birds like crows which then stay to rob the eggs of mountain birds. Because of these problems and others, like foot-path erosion, plans to extend the skiing facilities beyond Coire Cas and the neighbouring valley of Coire na Ciste have been strongly opposed by environmentalist groups.

2. The road down from Coire Cas (987073)

Drive down from the car park and stop in one of the roadside parking areas where you have a good view over Loch Morlich and the Glen More Forest Park. At the end of the last glaciation the whole of the basin below you was filled with a lobe of ice which had pushed in from the Spey valley rather than coming from the northern corries of the Cairngorms, whose glaciers were much smaller. This ice gradually became stagnant as it melted. The meltwater escaped along the edge of the ice and eventually, underneath it. The deep valley of the Allt Mor below you was carved by glacial meltwater in this way, as was the deep gorge which cuts through the ridge of Airgiod-meall on your left (965065). The meltwater could not escape westwards because the Spey valley was still blocked by the main stream of ice. Instead, it flowed eastwards into Strath Nethy through gaps in the hills to your right and, later, as the ice surface melted down further, through the pass of Ryvoan in front of you. These streams laid down extensive deposits of sand and gravel on top of the moraine deposited by the glacier. The result, when the ice melted, was a landscape of gravelly terraces, knolls and ridges separated by poorly-drained hollows. This landscape was colonised by vegetation as the ice disappeared, and as the climate became warmer the pine forests developed. You can see remnants of these below you today.

You are looking over Glenmore Forest Park, one of the largest areas of Forestry Commission land in Speyside, with about 3850 acres planted. The forest originally belonged to the Dukes of Gordon, but large-scale exploitation of the timber started later here than in other Speyside woodlands, probably because Glenmore was more remote, making extraction of the timber more difficult. In 1783 the timber in the forest was sold by the Duke of Gordon to two Hull merchants. Timber was at a premium for shipbuilding during the Napoleonic Wars, and between 1783 and 1805 large areas of the forest were felled. The timber was collected in Loch Morlich before being floated down the River Luineag to the Spey. A good deal of work had to be undertaken in removing rocks and deepening the river bed for this to be practicable. The timber was then rafted down the Spey to Garmouth on the coast which developed a thriving shipbuilding industry. Timber was also sent further afield to Hull and the Thames. The timber industry declined during the later 19th century and the forest was converted into a sheep range. The sheep nibbled the young seedlings and killed them off so that there was little natural regeneration of the forest. Most of the mature pine trees which you can see in Glenmore—those which have not been planted—are over 150 years old. The First World War brought a great increase in the demand for timber and a narrow-gauge railway was constructed from Loch Morlich through the Sluggan Pass to the Spey to bring out the timber. In 1923 the land was sold to the Forestry Commission who began a major programme of replanting. It was found that the native Scots Pines were no longer regenerating themselves very well, and other non-native species of conifer including Sitka Spruce, Lodgepole Pine, Norway Spruce, Larch and Douglas Fir were planted. Felling of this planted timber has only commenced in the 1980s and large-scale extraction will not begin until the next century, emphasising the long-term nature of forestry as a commercial activity.

The edge of the forest below you is marked by a sharp boundary along a deer fence. After the Forestry Commission took over, the forest was fenced to control the deer which damaged young seedlings. In places you can see that there is a scatter of trees beyond the boundary fence where saplings have managed to establish themselves despite the grazing pressure. The treeline has been kept artificially low partly because of the effects of grazing over a long period. During the 18th century cattle were the most important livestock in the area; animals were reared for their meat and were driven south to be sold to English buyers at the cattle trysts of Crieff and Falkirk, many of the animals ending up in London. The Lairig Ghru, the deep pass which cuts through the Cairngorms to the west of you, was an important route for droving cattle to the south. In summer the animals were grazed on shieling pastures in the high corries of the Cairngorms, and additional animals were also brought in from the lowlands to utilise the mountain grazings. This put pressure on the upper levels of the forest. During the 19th century most of the Speyside forests were turned over to large-scale sheep farming: sheep were even more effective in preventing the natural regeneration of the woodlands. In the later 19th century, when sheep farming was no longer economic, the woodlands were converted into deer forests to maximise their sporting potential. Deer had always grazed in the woods but before the 18th century their numbers had been kept in check by wolves; in the 19th century deliberate feeding of the deer increased the size of the herds, putting greater pressure on the forests. These varied kinds of grazing pressure have had the effect of lowering the treeline; where grazing has been intense over long periods the forest has contracted as the old trees have died off and new ones have failed to replace them. The treeline could be pushed much higher than its current level today—it is commonly around 500m—but the trees at these higher levels would be small and stunted and it would not be a commercial proposition to plant them. If you look to your right you will see an area of experimental planting on the slopes of Carn Lochan na Beinne (010080) divided into small square plots to test the capabilities of different species at extreme altitude. Some of these trees grow at up to 680m.

3. Loch Morlich (9609)

The area around Loch Morlich provides a good example of how forestry and outdoor recreation can be successfully combined. The Forestry Commission have turned the area into a forest park to encourage rather than restrict visitors. Sailing, windsurfing and fishing are available on the loch which also has some fine beaches: the local granite decomposes to form a fine sand. Within the forest there is a youth hostel, a caravan/campsite, and an outdoor training centre. Various walks and trails have been laid out in the woods and these provide a good introduction to the complex nature of a forest whose history of exploitation has been very varied. From the last vantage point it is easy to distinguish the main areas of native Scots Pine from the introduced conifers which are lighter in colour. A walk through the forest will show you that it is made up of a mosaic of smaller habitats. The details of the vegetation of the native pine forests will be considered below, but for the moment, notice the contrast between areas of natural Scots Pine where the trees are large and wide-spreading with twisted, reddish branches, and areas which have been planted where the trees are closer set, straighter and with fewer branches below the level of the main canopy.

4. Aviemore (8912)

Aviemore started off as an inn on General Wade's military road (see below). After the railway from Perth to Inverness was opened in 1863 it developed as a small tourist centre. The northern part of the village has a number of substantial stone villas dating from this period. In the early 1960s, with the development of the ski facilities at Coire Cas, plans were made to turn Aviemore into a large resort which could cater for both summer and winter visitors. The Aviemore centre, opened in 1966, was the result. It is a complex of hotels, timeshare apartments, self-catering chalets, restaurants, shops, entertainment and sporting facilities which is unique in Britain, but many people feel that the centre is an eyesore in such a rural setting. The hotel blocks can be seen clearly from the car park at Coire Cas and from the summit of Cairngorm on a clear day. The best panoramic view of the centre can be obtained from Craigellachie, the hill above Aviemore on the opposite side of the A9, which is a nature reserve with an attractive nature trail through birch woodlands.

5. Loch an Eilean and Rothiemurchus Forest (8907)

From Inverdruie, between Aviemore and Coylumbridge, take the B970 south for about 2km and follow the sign for the loch along a minor road to your left until you reach a large car park. Do not take the minor road from Inverdruie to the loch via Blackpark as it is poorly surfaced and has two gates across it.

The walk around the loch (about 4km) provides one of the best introductions to an area of native pine forest which has been little affected by artificial planting. The castle on the island in the loch

Castle, Loch an Eilean

dates from the 15th century and was held successively by the Mackintoshes, the Gordons and the Grants. It was supposedly the last nesting place in Scotland of the osprey before its extinction and subsequent re-establishment.

The Speyside forests are one of the largest remnants of a type of woodland which was much more widely distributed in Britain several thousand years ago. At the end of the last glaciation the first trees to establish themselves over what was a tundra landscape were birch with some aspen and rowan. As conditions became warmer pine began to move in and replace birch throughout the south of England. Pine and birch were both active colonisers of new ground because their light seeds were readily spread by the wind, and both types of tree were hardy, being able to withstand low temperatures and thrive on thin, poor soils. At a later date, with much warmer conditions and the gradual development of deeper, richer soils, birch and pine woods were replaced over most of England by mixed deciduous woods in which oak, elm and lime were among the most important species. In Scotland oakwoods became established in the valleys with alder in wetter areas. Above this pine forests covered the lower slopes, sometimes mixed with birch, while birch often formed a belt on its own at the uphill margins. Man has mostly removed the valley oakwoods and replaced them

Mature pine forest, Rothiemurchus

with plantations, while grazing and a deterioration of the climate, with the onset of wetter conditions and the growth of peat during the first millennium B.C., caused a retreat of the uphill margins of the woodlands.

Large-scale exploitation of the pinewoods for commercial purposes was delayed because of the inaccessibility of the area. By the 17th century the Lowlands had become virtually treeless; the medieval forest cover had been stripped off without any organised replanting, and towns on the east coast depended on imported timber from Norway for their needs. Some efforts were made to use the pinewoods of the Western Highlands, which were accessible by sea, for shipbuilding and charcoal iron smelting, but the Speyside woods were not opened up until the early 18th century. In 1728 the York Buildings Company, a rather shady group who dabbled in all sorts of industrial enterprises in the Highlands after the 1715 rebellion, bought 60,000 trees in the forest of Abernethy, further down the valley, from Sir James Grant and started commercial logging. They cleared away various obstructions on the Spey which allowed the timber to be floated down to the coast. As well as various sawmills they built an iron smelter near Nethy Bridge, using local charcoal and iron ore brought by the military road over the Lecht Pass from Tomintoul. They went out of business a few years later in a spectacular crash, but they had demonstrated the potential of the area for forestry. Rothiemurchus was developed for timber rather later in the 18th century, but at the peak of production, during the Napoleonic Wars, timber was bringing in an annual income of between £10,000 and £20,000 to the estate. In 1813 sawmilling was centralised at Inverdruie. To float the logs down to the Spey, lochs like Loch an Eilean and Loch Morlich were dammed to raise the water level. Sluice gates could then be opened to release a controlled flood which would carry the logs downstream if the normal water level was inadequate. Gangs of raftsmen came up the Spey from Ballindalloch to float the rafts of timber down when water conditions were right. This early forestry was wasteful and unsystematic so that the forest was seriously damaged. Only from the 1820s was timber extraction done on a more systematic basis. There was prolific regeneration of young trees after the early 19th-century felling, and many of the trees in the forest today date from this time. Sheep and deer reduced the numbers of young saplings later in the century, although with greater protection in recent years more young trees have been springing up.

As you walk round the loch you will get a good idea of the characteristic vegetation patterns of these native pine forests. They consist mostly of pure stands of pine although there are some birch trees among them in places with occasional rowans and alders in wetter areas. The trees do best on the drier knolls and hummocks. In places the pine woods are very thick and the canopy lets little light through to the forest floor so that there is little ground vegetation. More characteristically, the forest is open and the ground flora is a mixture of dwarf shrubs, principally heather and

Rothiemurchus: the fringes of the native pine forest on the lower slopes of the Cairngorms

bilberry with some grasses, and sometimes juniper. The moister hollows between the hummocks may contain bog communities with sphagnum moss and cotton sedge. On the west side of Loch an Eilean the area has been improved for pasture and the ground is covered with grasses and some bracken rather than heath. As you walk round the eastern side of the loch you can see the higher and more remote parts of the forest straggling up the slopes of Creag Dhubh. You are walking through woodland which, although it has been modified by man, is a direct descendant of the first full forest cover to be established throughout Britain at the end of the Ice Age. Most of Rothiemurchus Forest lies within the Cairngorm National Nature Reserve, an area of 258 sq.km. created largely by agreements between individual landowners and the Nature Conservancy Council regarding how the forests should be managed. In the areas of native pinewood no foreign species are being introduced, and deer are controlled to encourage the growth of new seedlings.

Return to the B970 and turn left along it.

6. The Spey Marshes (8103-7700)

From the higher points of the B970 between Feshie Bridge and Ruthven you have good views over the flood plain of the Spey. You can see that efforts have been made to drain the marshy bottom land by the cutting of a series of drainage channels and throwing up embankments to try and protect the area from flooding. In the early 19th century agriculture in this area was put on a more commercial footing. Much of the land was turned into large sheep farms, and many townships of small farmers were cleared to make way for sheep. Some of these abandoned townships are still visible in the landscape today; they are marked on the 1:25,000 map but are generally remote and difficult of access. At the same time efforts were made to improve the arable side of farming and to extend the cultivated area on the valley floor. The Spey had always been liable to severe flooding, and from the map you can see how settlement avoids the flood plain and clings to the higher ground above. The drainage schemes which were carried out in the first half of the 19th century were successful for a while in providing additional crop land from what had formerly been only hay meadows. However, the expense of maintaining the drainage system and embankments proved to be too great in relation to the return, and the land was left to revert to flooded pasture. The area between Kincraig and Kingussie has become an important marshland habitat with reed swamps and some willow scrub fringed in places by birchwoods with a shrub layer of juniper. 1200 acres of these marshes form an R.S.P.B. bird reserve. Access to hides for bird-watching can be obtained at the R.S.P.B. reception centre on the B970 a short way east of Ruthven Barracks.

7. Ruthven Barracks (764997)

Ruthven Barracks stands on an artificial mound which was originally topped by a castle belonging to the Comyn family, and later in the 14th century to the infamous Wolf of Badenoch, an illegitimate son of Robert II, whose achievements included the burning of the town and cathedral of Elgin in 1390 following an argument with the bishop. The castle on this site in the 17th century was burnt down during the Jacobite rebellion of 1689. In 1721 the Hanoverian government erected the barracks as one of a

Ruthven Barracks, Kingussie

series of outposts in the Highlands. The barracks at Ruthven were
designed to house a company of infantry and, after the completion
of the military road down Speyside, the stable block on the north
side was added to allow dragoons to patrol the road. The barracks
were designed as a 'listening post' rather than as a defensible
fortress, but you can see that the perimeter wall is pierced with
loopholes for musketry. At the start of the 1745 rebellion most of
the garrison was withdrawn by General Cope to augment his
forces when he passed en route for Inverness after failing to
intercept the Jacobite army. A sergeant and a dozen soldiers
successfully defended it against 300 Jacobites who, having no
artillery, were unable to make an effective attack on it. In 1746 the
barracks were captured by the main Jacobite army and were burnt.

The barracks stood close to the line of General Wade's military
road which crossed the Spey nearby. The river has removed all
traces of its course over the flood plain. The network of military
roads laid out by government troops after the 1715 uprising, and
extended after the 1745 rebellion, formed the first purpose-built
network of roads in the Highlands. The roads were built from 1725
onwards, in a hurry and not always very well, and were aligned to
aid troop movements rather than to serve the areas through which
they passed. Nevertheless, they began the process of opening up the
Highlands and can be seen as one of the first examples of the
penetration of outside influences into the area, contemporary with

Ruthven Barracks: well and barrack block

the start of commercial exploitation of the Spey woodlands. The military road down the Spey valley has been largely obliterated or overlain by more modern roads so that while the line of the road can generally be followed, the actual features on the ground are of a later date. For those who would like to walk a section of the road which has been little altered, a track runs from the B987 at 751991 towards Luibleathann. Since the building of the new section of the A9 it is impossible to reach this spot direct from Ruthven, and you will have to go round by Newtonmore.

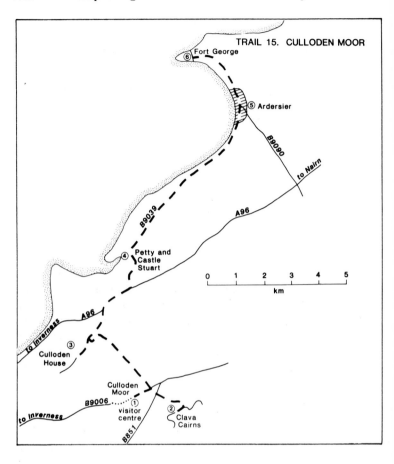

FIFTEEN

Culloden Moor: The Landscape of a Battlefield

Ordnance Survey 1:50,000 sheet 27; 1:25,000 sheets NH 64/74, 65/75

This trail involves a drive of 20km with an optional walk.

Introduction

Historical events like battles, or even an entire campaign like the Jacobite Rebellion of 1745, are short-term episodes which usually have little direct impact on the landscape. Battlefields, even modern ones, can be disappointing to visit because there is often very little to see and because the landscape has often changed so much since the battle was fought that it is difficult to visualise the site as it was at the time of the conflict. On the other hand even a short-term military episode may have indirect longer-term repercussions on the landscape such as the construction of new roads and defences. The Jacobite rebellions of 1715 and 1745 led to the building of a network of military roads throughout the Highlands linking a series of forts and garrisons (Trail 14). The alignments of the roads built by General Wade and his successors have sometimes been abandoned, but in many places they form the basis of the modern road system. Some of the forts, like the one at Inverlochy, have vanished; others, like Fort George (see below), remain as impressive monuments in the landscape.

The battlefield of Culloden, along with Bannockburn, is probably one of the most emotive historical sites in Scotland, yet it was not marked out until late in the 19th century, while its landscape has changed greatly since 1746 as a result of agricultural improvement and afforestation. On the other hand, such is the power of the folk myth of Scottish history, which much popular writing and tourist literature eagerly helps to sustain, that the 1745 Rebellion has become surrounded in a romantic haze. The battlefield is worth a visit as an insight into how the Scots see their own history and how they project it to visitors through the features marking the

241

site of the battle and the exhibition in the National Trust for Scotland centre nearby. Bannockburn too has a visitor centre to keep the legends alive, but here the battlefield has been engulfed in suburban development and has been changed out of all recognition since 1314. At least at Culloden it is possible to gain some impression of what the Jacobite army, tired, hungry and ill-led, faced on that cold April day in the last major battle on British soil. This trail looks at some of the features of the landscapes around Culloden which are associated with the 1745 rebellion and at how interpretations of history have shaped the site today. Mindful that the battle was an extremely transient event in an area which had been settled for thousands of years, we will also be considering features from other periods.

1. Culloden Moor (742451)

We do not propose to describe the campaign of 1745–6 nor the course of the battle of Culloden itself. This has been done on innumerable occasions with varying degrees of accuracy. The exhibition at the National Trust for Scotland centre will give you an outline of the events while the bookstall will offer you a selection of more detailed reading. Our aim is to explain why the battle was fought here, to discuss the character of the site, and to show how it has changed since 1746.

The site on which the battle was fought was selected by Prince Charles Edward Stuart and was ill-chosen in many respects. The retreating Jacobite army had been based at Inverness for two months. After the Duke of Cumberland's forces had marched from Aberdeen and had been allowed to cross the major obstacle of the Spey without opposition, it was clear either that a battle would have to be fought near Inverness or the Jacobite forces would need to disperse into the mountains and continue the campaign as a guerilla war. Lord George Murray, the most accomplished of the Jacobite commanders, wanted to bring the Hanoverian forces to battle on the east side of the River Nairn where the ground was higher, steeper and more boggy. This would have made it difficult for the Duke of Cumberland to bring up his artillery and would also have restricted the use of his cavalry while at the same time offering the Jacobites the best opportunity for making the most of the Highland clans' traditional form of attack the wild downhill charge with the broadsword after an initial volley of musketry. But Murray was on bad terms with the Prince by this stage of the campaign and he was overruled. The Prince chose Culloden Moor on which to fight the first battle in which he had commanded in person, and set up his headquarters at Culloden House below the moor to the north-west.

Culloden Moor is a flat-topped ridge running north-east to south-west between the Moray Firth and the valley of the River Nairn. The land fell away on either side of the moor but its crest was completely open, giving the Hanoverian army plenty of room to deploy in parade-ground style and offering little impediment to the movement of their cavalry and artillery. The Jacobite army was drawn up where the moorland narrowed between two sets of enclosures with stone and turf walls. The idea was that these would protect the wings of the army and prevent Cumberland's dragoons from outflanking them. This was reasonable up to a point but it overlooked the possibility that if the enclosures were once breached and broken into, the walls which ran at right angles to the Jacobite front and second line would provide excellent cover for troops who could then rake the clansmen with musket fire.

Once chosen, the site of the battlefield played a major part in the Jacobite defeat, even granted that their troops were mostly in poor condition after an arduous night march to make an abortive attack on Cumberland's camp at Nairn, and after being almost unfed for two or three days due to a failure of the supply system. The open moor gave Cumberland the opportunity to use his cannon with devastating effect, causing severe casualties before the two armies even engaged. Once the enclosure walls facing the left wing of Cumberland's troops had been breached, his cavalry were able to outflank the Jacobite right and threaten their rear. The walls also provided cover for Wolfe's battallion and the Campbell Highlanders to fire into the right wing of the Jacobite front line from the side as they attacked Cumberland's left. Once the battle was over the level ground allowed the Hanoverian dragoons to pursue the Jacobite fugitives with ease. There is little point in speculating what the Jacobite army might have achieved had they fought on ground of Lord George Murray's choosing, but there is no doubt that the choice of Culloden Moor doomed their efforts to failure from the start.

Today it is difficult to gain an impression of the lie of the battlefield or of its character in 1746. In the early 19th century the moor was enclosed into an area of regular rectangular fields, and in 1835 a new road—now the B9006—was built through the centre of the battlefield. Because the quality of the land was relatively poor much of it has been planted with conifers in the present century, although efforts are now being made to open up the area around the immediate site of the battle to restore something of its earlier appearance. The best general view of the area is from the B9006 near the King's Stables at 734449. The left wing of the Jacobite third line, consisting mainly of cavalry without mounts operating as infantry, was located just to the east of here. You can look over fields which lie to the north of the battlefield proper but which at least give you an impression of how the open country might once have looked. The 18th-century cottage of King's Stables postdates the battle and derives its name from the fact that some of Cumberland's dragoons, guarding the area after the battle, picketed their horses nearby.

The National Trust for Scotland centre stands just to the east of where Cumberland's left wing was located. The walls which provided cover for the Argyll regiment and Wolfe's troops, and the enclosures through which the Hanoverian cavalry advanced towards the Jacobite rear, are no longer visible, having been replaced

Old Leanach Cottage

by larger, more regular enclosure walls. The cottage of Old Leanach is one of the few identifiable features from the time of the battle. Although it was altered later and has been heavily restored, it gives a good impression of what the better sort of rural housing looked like in this area in the mid-18th century. It is thatched with heather, which was more durable than straw and better suited to a wetter climate. Although it looks primitive it was, in fact, a comparatively well-to-do farmhouse in its day, and many of the poorer houses in this area at the time of the battle would have been constructed largely of turf. The building was inhabited into the early years of this century but it owes its preservation solely to its connexion with the battle. Innumerable other traditional 'peasant houses', some of which were recorded in early photographs, survived down to the late 19th or early 20th century and were then demolished to make way for better accommodation, usually leaving very little trace in the landscape today. Old Leanach cottage has been preserved solely by a fluke of location and association, but this is not uncommon with such historic features in the modern landscape: Burns' cottage at Alloway in Ayrshire is another example.

The area where the fiercest fighting occurred, where the Jacobite right wing and the Hanoverian left came to hand-to-hand conflict with broadsword and bayonet, lies on either side of the road a little to the west of the visitor centre and the old cottage. It is shown by a prominent cairn and markers identifying the graves of members of various clans who were buried close to where they fell. The location of the graves of the Hanoverian dead is unknown, and this in itself shows how tradition has shaped the appearance of the battlefield today. The cairn and most of the markers were only placed there in 1881, ironically by the then laird of Culloden, a descendant of Duncan Forbes of Culloden, a staunch Hanoverian supporter. Interest in preserving the battlefield was kindled by a lingering romanticism for the Jacobite cause which by this time had become perfectly respectable as the Stuart line had been extinct for a century. The grave markers were placed according to local traditions, and it is not difficult to appreciate that the locations of the graves of the clans were remembered while the burial place of the Hanoverian soldiers was not. If you read the guidebook to the battlefield you may be struck by the vagueness of the links between certain events and places on the battlefield. This is partly due to the varying and sometimes totally conflicting accounts of the battle produced by eyewitnesses. There is not even any agreement about Prince Charles' location during the battle.

The next site can be visited by car, but if you would like to walk, leave your car in the car park at the battlefield; the round trip is about 5km. In either case, follow the B9006 east for half a kilometre to a crossroads, turn right and keep straight at a second crossroads, down into the valley of the River Nairn. Cross the stream and take the first turning on your right; the site is half a kilometre along this road on the right.

2. The Clava Cairns (758445)

The major prehistoric site at Clava consists of three large cairns at 758445. They appear to have been laid out as a single unit and show no signs of subsequent modifications. They are the best examples of a distinctive group of cairns which cluster around the north-eastern end of the Great Glen. The two outside cairns are passage graves with a stone-lined passage leading into a circular central chamber. The cairns are surrounded by kerbs with stone circles beyond. The central monument does not have a chamber and is of a type known as a ring cairn; it too is set within a stone circle, three of whose stones are joined to the cairn by causeways. The passages of the two outer cairns both have the same alignment, south-west towards a point on the horizon where the sun would have set in midwinter some 4,000 years ago. This, and the combination of stone circles with chambered tombs, shows that there was an overlap between the two types of monument; in Trail 18 we discuss how in Orkney the chambered tombs appear to have been distinctly earlier than the megalithic stone circles.

So far the Clava cairns have not been securely dated, so that it is not quite clear how they fit into the general chronology of such monuments in Britain. Radiocarbon dates for charcoal in a pit beside one on the outskirts of Inverness gave a date of c4000–3700 B.C. which may date the cairns approximately. If this is true, they come fairly late in the sequence of megalithic monuments. The tombs at Clava have many features which are identical with a group of passage graves in Ireland known as the Boyne group, and it has been suggested that the cluster of monuments around Inverness may have been built by colonists from Ireland.

Return to the crossroads at 749452 and carry on northwards towards Balloch. After passing through the village turn left. You will see the grounds of Culloden House on your right after about 1km.

3. Culloden House (721465)

In the mid-18th century Culloden House was the home of Duncan Forbes, laird of Culloden and Lord President of the Court of Session. He was the government's most formidable supporter in the north of Scotland. During the 1715 rebellion Forbes had helped his sister-in-law to defend the house during an unsuccessful seven weeks' siege by the Jacobites and had afterwards assisted in the recapture of Inverness for the government. In 1745, with the first news of Prince Charles' landing, Forbes hurried north to Culloden to do what he could to hinder the rebellion. He wrote personally to many clan chiefs attempting to persuade them not to declare for the Stuarts and to either stay at home or actively join the government side. He may have succeeded in reducing support for the Jacobites, and his importance as a thorn in their side is shown by their efforts to capture him, including mounting an unsuccessful surprise attack on the house with 200 Fraser clansmen. After they

Culloden House

were beaten off, Forbes made Inverness the focus for pro-government resistance in the north. When the Jacobites retreated to Inverness, Forbes retired into Ross-shire to carry on the fight, leaving his house undefended. Prince Charles may well have chosen Culloden House as his headquarters before the battle specifically because it was Forbes' home. It is ironic that the final battle of the rebellion should have been fought on the doorstep of the man who had done more to hinder the Jacobite cause than any other Scotsman.

In the mid-18th century Culloden House was a partly fortified mansion dating from the mid-17th century with two battlemented towers flanking the central block and surrounded by a solid stone wall. In 1772 most of the old house was demolished, to be replaced by the present classical mansion which incorporates some of the stonework of the earlier house at the base of its central block. The proportions of this house, with its balanced facade and flanking side pavilions, make it one of the most perfect small country houses of its period in Scotland. The architect is not known; the style is very similar to work done by the Adam family, and as they were involved in the construction of Fort George (see below) until 1769, it is possible that they may have had a hand in the design, but the link is not proven. The Forbes family lived here till 1897. Culloden House is now a hotel.

Retrace your route and continue past Balloch to join the A96. Turn right and continue for about one and a half kilometres. Turn left on to the B9039.

4. Petty and Castle Stuart (739499)

Moray is another part of Scotland which is rich in early medieval earth and timber castles (see Trail 1). At Petty you can find a motte right next to the parish church. It was common in medieval times for church and castle to be closely associated in this way, as the parish church often developed from the private chapel of a major landowner. The church is the traditional burial place of the chiefs of the Clan Mackintosh. Castle Stuart nearby (741498) is a tower house which was built in 1625 for the third Earl of Moray. It has been restored for use as a private house.

5. Ardersier (7854)

The old name for this village was Campbelltown, named after a branch of the West Highland family who acquired the lands of Cawdor and who developed this site as a burgh of barony in 1623. The burgh does not appear to have been a particularly flourishing one and much of Ardersier's growth came in the later 18th century with fishing and servicing the garrison at nearby Fort George. At the north end of the village the modern B9039 and B9006 roads meet. Both of them lie on the direct line of 18th-century military roads, one a branch from Fort George to Inverness, the other a main through route linking the fort with Perth and Dundee via Braemar. It was started in 1749, the year after work began on the fort. Although the 18th-century military roads which were built in Scotland often had to take circuitous routes through rugged country, where the ground permitted the engineers laid them out in long straight stretches, reminiscent of Roman roads. The line of the B9006 south-east of Ardersier is a good example.

6. Fort George (7656)

Fort George is the best example in Scotland, indeed in Britain, of an 18th-century artillery fortification. The policy of building forts in the Highlands to counter potential rebellion had been initiated by Cromwell, who established a fort at Inverlochy and another at Inverness. The earthwork fort at Inverlochy was rebuilt in stone in 1690 and renamed Fort William after William III. After the 1715 rebellion the government undertook further work. A chain of forts was created in the Great Glen by strengthening Fort William and by building a new fort at Inverness, named Fort George after the king, on the site of the present Castle Hill. The Cromwellian fort nearby had been dismantled in 1661 after the Restoration. Another fort was built at Fort Augustus, halfway down the Great Glen, between 1729 and 1742. Other smaller holding points such as Ruthven Barracks near Kingussie (Trail 14) were designed as 'listening posts' and were not expected to be defended against a serious attack. Although the forts were built in the modern fashion, they were not particularly strong and some of them, notably Fort Augustus, were overlooked by higher ground. The government miscalculated in assuming that any Highland rebels would not have artillery. After the Battle of Prestonpans Prince Charles did have an artillery train, though a shortage of experienced gunners severely reduced its usefulness. Although Fort William held out with some difficulty, Fort Augustus and Fort George both surrendered fairly quickly, the former after its gunpowder magazine had been detonated by a lucky shot, the latter after attempts to lay a mine under the ramparts had been started. The Jacobites took care to demolish much of the ramparts at Inverness.

After Culloden it was decided initially to rebuild Fort George on its original site. However, its location was cramped and inconvenient. Instead a new Fort George was planned some way to the east on a promontory curving into the Moray Firth. The site was far more secure and could be easily supplied by sea. It was first planned in 1747 and finally completed in 1769. This time there was no underestimation of any potential future threat. The army built the strongest possible fortress using the most advanced technology of the day. While some of the earlier Highland forts had been built in a hurry with a minimum of expense, the new Fort George was designed as a textbook example of military engineering.

To appreciate the layout of Fort George it is necessary to understand how the science of fortification changed after medieval times with the development of weapons using gunpower. Larger medieval castles depended mainly on high curtain walls and towers placed, if possible, on sites which were difficult to undermine or approach with siege engines and scaling ladders. The development of artillery which could hit hard from a distance revolutionised matters. Defence in depth rather than height was now required to keep cannon as far from the main walls as possible. Ramparts needed to be immensely thick rather than high to withstand the impact of prolonged bombardment. During the 16th century fortification developed as a specialised science, and through to the 19th century the same principles applied, only with increasing refinement. In protecting a fortress from direct attack the need was to cover all the area around the walls and eliminate areas of 'dead ground' which could shelter the attackers.

The new systems of defence were designed to allow defenders to concentrate overwhelming firepower on attackers who got close to the ramparts, while providing platforms from which cannon could engage the more distant batteries. A key element was the

Governor's House, Fort George

diamond-shaped or arrow-headed bastion connected to the thick
curtain wall by a narrower recessed neck. The bastions mounted
cannon to keep attackers at a distance while guns in the recessed
necks, the flankers, could fire along the curtain wall and rake the
face of the opposite bastion, whose angle was carefully calculated
to allow this. Such systems of defence became standard around
larger and more strategically important towns on the Continent,
and many excellent examples survive. In Britain, much more
secure from foreign invasion, it was rare to build expensive town
defences of this kind, apart from some temporary ones thrown up
during the Civil Wars. The best example of a town fortified in this
way is Berwick-on-Tweed, whose Tudor fortifications were designed to protect it from the Scots. This type of defensive system in
Britain was confined mainly to forts built for coastal defence, and
to control the Highlands.

As you approach Fort George you can see that the defences have
been concentrated on the landward side, looking towards the
Highlands rather than seawards. You come first to a huge V-

shaped outwork surrounded by a ditch. This was known as a ravelin and was designed to keep attackers well back from the curtain wall. You can appreciate the scale of the defences at Fort George when you realise that the area of the ravelin alone is greater than that of many larger medieval castles. It was designed with an open back so that if it was captured it was open to fire from the inner defences. In front of the ravelin is a covered way from which troops could sally out to attack besiegers. Behind the ravelin is the great ditch crossed by a single bridge leading to the main gate which pierces the massive curtain wall. If you can imagine yourself as an attacker on the bridge or scrambling around in the ditch, you can see how anyone who penetrated this far was exposed to a crossfire from the bastions on either side as well as direct fire from the wall in front of you. Inside the fort are the barrack blocks, designed to accommodate up to 2,500 troops. The buildings, like the defences, have not been significantly altered since the fort was first built. They provide an excellent example of dignified, no-nonsense Georgian architecture. Emergency barracks, designed to be proof against plunging mortar fire, were also built under the ramparts.

The fort has remained in use as a barracks, depot and training centre until recent times. After it was clear that there was no further threat from the Highlands the fort's role was reversed and it was redesigned to house batteries to protect the coast during the Napoleonic Wars and later in the 19th century. In the sense that it never had to fire a shot in action it was a highly successful fort.

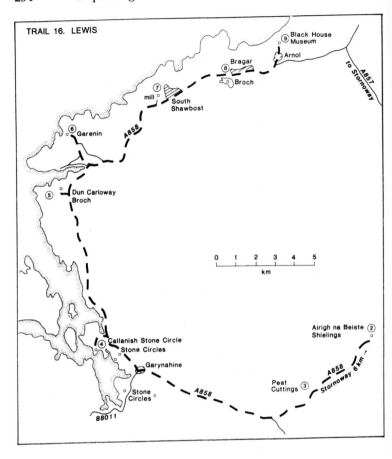

TRAIL 16. LEWIS

SIXTEEN

Lewis: A Crofting Landscape

Ordnance Survey 1:50,000 sheet 8; 1:25,000 sheets NB 33/43, 13/23, 14/24, 34/44

This trail involves a drive of 55km.

Introduction: The Environment of the Outer Hebrides

The Outer Hebrides preserve a highly distinctive culture and economy which distinguishes them from the rest of Britain, but the individuality of this area also lies in its physical landscape. In order to understand the traditional farming economy of this area and the crofting system which replaced it, the character of the natural environment and the constraints which it imposes on human activity must be appreciated. Lewis is mainly composed of ancient metamorphic rocks such as gneiss which have been eroded and sculptured by the action of ice sheets. Over much of Lewis the rocks form a low rolling plateau which has been scraped bare by ice sheets spreading from the mainland. At its most extreme, glacial erosion has produced a landscape which is sometimes known as 'knock and lochan' topography, a bleak landscape of small lakes and rocky outcrops. Because of the impermeable nature of the gneiss, the level surface of much of the interior and the relatively high rainfall, climatic conditions for most of the last 4000 years have favoured the accumulation of peat. The dominant features of the interior of Lewis are bare rock, peat and water. Settlement is confined to the coastal fringe of the island, particularly the west coast where there are some small pockets of machair land, shell sands which provide high-quality pasture and light soils for cultivation. These limited areas of light, easily-worked land in a sea of peat have proved attractive to settlers from prehistoric times. Elsewhere much of the improved land has been laboriously reclaimed from under the peat surface; the buried soils, when properly drained and manured, are moderately fertile.

The Origins of Crofting in Lewis

Crofting in the Outer Hebrides, as elsewhere in western and northern Scotland, is not an ancient agricultural and social system: the crofting township is contemporary with the steam engine and the textile mill. In some ways industrialisation in the south actually helped to produce the crofting landscape. In common terminology a croft is a smallholding anywhere in the Higlands or their fringes. The legal definition is more restricted, referring to a rented smallholding within the 'crofting counties' of the north-western Highlands whose occupation is protected by a series of Acts of Parliament. A high proportion of crofts are under five acres and are too small to provide a livelihood for their occupants unless agriculture is combined with an additional occupation. Crofting landscapes were created in the early 19th century as a result of a combination of economic and social forces. With the coming of more peaceful conditions after the failure of the 1745 rebellion, the north-west Highlands and Islands became more closely linked with the economy of the rest of Britain. Highland landowners reorganised their estates to try and maximise their cash incomes. In the Outer Hebrides at the end of the 18th century a profitable way of doing this was to let small portions of land out to tenants who made the greater part of their income from fishing and especially from kelp burning. Kelp, or seaweed, was collected from the rocks below tide level and was burnt using local peat. The ash provided chemicals which were required in the making of soap and glass. Kelp production boomed during the Napoleonic Wars when Britain was cut off from foreign supplies of chemicals. Although the landlords creamed off most of the profits, the success of the kelp industry was one of the influences behind a population rise in Lewis and the rest of the Outer Hebrides. The build-up of population encouraged further subdivision of the cultivated land into smallholdings. After about 1820, with the return of normal trading conditions, foreign competition caused a slump in kelp prices. Fishing also failed to generate the profits which had been hoped for. Mackenzie of Seaforth, the owner of Lewis, turned to commercial sheep farming as the most profitable option left to him, as many mainland proprietors had already done (Trail 17). In other parts of the north-west Highlands the introduction of commercial sheep farming had caused landowners to clear their small tenants out of the interior glens to make way for large sheep farms, moving their people to new, often previously uncultivated, land on the coast to make a living as best they could by combining farming and fishing. Wholesale clearances of the type which occurred in Sutherland did not happen in Lewis. Seaforth, for one thing, did not have the resources to carry out such a thoroughgoing reorganisation. Another drawback was that only the hilly country in southern Lewis was really suitable for sheep; the interior of the northern part of the island was too wet and boggy. In creating some large sheep farms in the south Seaforth did force many tenants out, some of whom migrated to townships on the west coast. Most of the settlements in western Lewis were not newly created, though: they were the old farming townships, swelled by population growth and re-organised on more efficient lines by the estate which replaced the scattered and fragmented plots of arable land by regular strip holdings—the modern crofts whose pattern of plot boundaries appears so striking on the 1:25,000 map. In the southern Highlands crofts are often single holdings, and even on the north-west mainland the groups of crofts, or townships, are often small: no more than a dozen units. Because of the initially high levels of population in Lewis, supported by kelp, by employment in the herring fishery later in the 19th century, and by the weaving of Harris Tweed in modern times, the townships remained large with 30 or even 50 crofts grouped together. Most crofts on the west coast of Lewis have less then five acres under cultivation with oats, potatoes, hay or improved pasture. The townships share common pastures on which each crofter can graze a stipulated number of animals. Beyond these are the peaty moorlands which, apart from supplying fuel, provide an additional reserve of low-quality grazing.

1. Stornoway (4232)

Stornoway is the only town in the Outer Hebrides. It developed around one of the best harbours in the area. Although it was made a burgh of barony by royal charter in 1607 as part of an ill-conceived scheme to settle a group of traders from Fife who were to develop commerce in the islands and thereby civilise the barbarous natives, Stornoway really began to flourish later in the century when Dutch herring fleets began to use the harbour. A castle belonging to the Seaforths stood on the promontory which protects the inner harbour. At a later date Cromwell garrisoned a small fort, probably also on the promontory, but no traces of either remain today. The town spread from the peninsula along the shores of the harbour during the 18th century, but its real period of prosperity came during the second half of the 19th century when it was one of the main bases for the west-coast herring fleet. The centre of Stornoway is largely a Victorian town with little trace of its earlier history. Lewis Castle, among the woods on the opposite side of the harbour, is Victorian Gothic, built by Sir James Matheson, who bought Lewis from the Seaforths in 1844. It later belonged to Lord Leverhulme who gifted it to the town. It now houses a technical college.

Follow the A859 out of Stornoway and after about 1 km turn left on to the A858

2. Airigh na Beiste: A Shieling Site (368342)

Park your car at 363338 where the old Pentland Road across the island leaves the modern A858.

Throughout the Highlands in the old pre-improvement economy it was customary to send most of the livestock, particularly cattle, away from the settlement and its cultivated lands during the summer period. The animals were taken to shielings, summer hill or moorland pastures, often several miles distant, and were kept there between June and August. This allowed the animals to be kept away from the cultivated land while the crops were growing; this was especially important as the arable land was not normally fenced internally and it was easy for livestock to stray into growing crops. Sending the animals away reduced pressure on the rough pasture adjacent to the settlement and utilised the resource of the upland pastures during the few weeks of high summer when their grazings were at their richest. During this period a part of the community, mostly women and children, stayed with the cattle living in temporary shieling huts which in Lewis could be up to six miles away from the main settlement. A common practice was for some of the men and boys from a community to go up to the shielings first to repair the huts, cut peat and pull heather for bedding. The women and children then followed with the cattle. The animals were grazed on the pastures around the shielings and were often folded next to the huts at night. The women and children made butter and cheese which was taken back to the main settlement, and the cattle were brought back to graze on the common pastures near the settlement before being taken inside for the winter. Shieling systems like these were found throughout the upland areas of the British Isles in earlier times, and there are close parallels with systems of transhumance which are still practised today in parts of the Alps and Scandinavia.

In Lewis the shieling system survived longer than anywhere else in Scotland. This was partly due to the fact that the shieling areas in the peaty moorlands which form the centre of the island were unsuitable for commercial sheep farming and were not appropriated by landlords during the earlier 19th century. Pressure on the limited areas of common pasture surrounding the crofting townships and the general poverty of the crofters made it as important to utilise these distant grazings during the 19th century as it had been in earlier times. The practice of going to the shielings continued well into the present century, and there are still plenty of people alive today who remember staying in shieling huts when they were children. Because of the widespread, late survival of this custom Lewis is one of the best places in Scotland for exploring groups of shieling huts although these can be found widely throughout the Highlands. The 1:25,000 Ordnance Survey map marks a large number of shieling sites: shielings were a communal resource belonging to specific townships so that the huts usually occur in clusters. Some of them require walks of several miles over rough country but they can still be rewarding to visit. The oldest huts are round, constructed of drystone which was often built up in a corbelled fashion to make a cell like a beehive, which was then clad with turf with a hole in the top for smoke to escape from. Some of these huts may date from as recently as the 18th century, some may be much earlier. Although this type of hut was not being built by the 19th century, some examples are known to have been used into the 1880s. Admittedly cramped, they did not require valuable roof timbers and they withstood winter gales more effectively than huts with normal roofs. 19th-century huts are normally rectangular or square in plan, and the ones which were used into the present century often have gables with chimneys, like miniature cottages.

They were all built of drystone and roofed with turf and heather; the more recent huts still have most of their walls standing.

The shielings at Airigh na Beiste have the advantage of being visible from the main road and are accessible by a short walk across the intervening shallow marshy valley (wellingtons recommended). The huts are rectangular with rounded corners, of rough drystone work with traces of turf on top of the walls in some places. They are more primitive in construction and design than the most modern shieling huts which were in use during the early part of this century, and probably date from some time in the 19th century.

Where a shieling site has been used over a long period the most recent huts stand on green mounds which have been formed from the accumulated remains of previous structures. This can be seen at these shielings. Excavations of such mounds on sites elsewhere have revealed the foundations of several superimposed huts although the stone has normally been re-used. The soil around the shielings has also been altered. This has been due partly to the cutting of peat for fuel, and of turf for hut construction; at Airigh na Beiste you can trace the old peat bank above the settlement. The folding of the cattle near the huts at night also enriched the soil. Because of this, shieling sites often stand out at a distance as green areas among the darker tones of heather-covered peat.

As the soil immediately next to the huts was improved by the folding of livestock, people often exploited this by taking a quick crop of oats from the fertilised ground. In time this might lead to a shieling site becoming permanently colonised as an outlying farmstead of the original settlement, new shieling grounds being established further into the hills. The permanent colonisation of shielings in this manner was one of the most important ways in which the margins of settlement were expanded from medieval times onwards. In the Southern Uplands this is shown by the number of modern farms whose names end in '-shiels' or '-shield'. In the Highlands the same process is indicated by places whose names end in '-ary' (from the Gaelic 'airigh' meaning shieling) or, in areas affected by the Norse settlement, '-set' and '-setter' (from the Old Norse 'setr'). At Airigh na Beiste this process has also occurred, but not on a permanent basis. The substantial cottage built with mortared stone contrasts with the rougher drystone work of the shieling huts. The cottage undoubtedly postdates the last period of use of the shielings and was probably built sometime during the later 19th century to house a shepherd. Traces of ridge and furrow ploughing (Trail 5) can be seen under the heather adjacent to the huts, indicating that the land has been cultivated; this activity was not necessarily contemporary with the occupation of the cottage, though.

3. Peat Cutting (3330)

Along the higher parts of the A858 from Stornoway to Achmore you can see many small modern huts with adjacent peat stacks. The huts are, in a sense, descendants of shieling huts and are used by inhabitants of Stornoway who come out here during the summer evenings to cut peat for the winter. Peat is still cut as the normal fuel for crofters throughout Lewis, and peat stacks can be seen outside almost every cottage.

4. Callanish: Stone Circle (213330)

The stone circle at Callanish has been described as a northern counterpart to Stonehenge. Certainly the two monuments have many similarities: both are associated with other remains in the immediate neighbourhood, both are complex in their structure,

Stone circle, Callanish

while their function is enigmatic and open to various interpretations. Callanish definitely wins the prize for the most evocative site; while the circle itself is impressive, its setting with the hills of Harris to the south and the island-dotted waters of Loch Roag immediately around it helps to create a powerful atmosphere.

Stone circles occur in many parts of Scotland and elsewhere in western Britain. Their distribution, period of use and function seem to have overlapped with those of the henge monuments of southern and eastern Britain. The character of the monuments suggests that they had some religious or ceremonial significance, but its precise nature has been hotly debated. Within the last 25 years various theories have been advanced suggesting that this and other stone circles were used as astronomical observatories, alignments of stones within the circle, and from the circle to distant landmarks, indicating the positions of the rising and setting of the sun at the solstices and also cycles of the moon and the positions of major planets and stars. Work by Professor Alexander Thom on the geometry of stone circles and the alignments of their stones was originally inspired by a visit to Callanish. Thom has suggested that the slightly off-circular shape of this and many other stone circles (the Callanish circle is a slightly flattened one) was due not to clumsiness but to the use of a sophisticated geometry. Thom claims to have identified five major alighments at Callanish. One of these lines up the setting of the full moon at its most southerly point at midsummer with a notch on Clisham, a mountain to the south. The dating of circles like these is difficult, but radiocarbon dates from other sites suggest that they were in use between around 2,500 and 1,500 B.C.

The occurrence of this and other stone circles down the west coast of Lewis indicates that the area was quite densely settled in prehistoric times. The environment as seen today might not seem conducive to this, but it should be remembered that at the period when the circles were built the climate was probably drier and there was less peat and more woodland in the landscape. The scale of change in the landscape, as the result of the onset of wetter conditions after use of the circle ceased, can be grasped when one appreciates that the stones were almost buried in peat and were only dug out during the middle of the last century.

The Callanish circle focuses on a central pillar some 5m high and 1m wide. Around it is a ring of 13 stones, many of them over

3m in height, forming a circle 11m in diameter. Much of the eastern part of the circle is occupied by a chambered cairn: the central pillar forms part of its kerb. Radiating outwards from the circle are avenues of stones. There is a double one 8m wide and 8m long to the north. It may originally have had 20 stones on each side; only 10 remain on the west side and 9 on the east. A single row of stones runs south from the circle, while others radiate to the east and west.

There are remains of six smaller stone circles around the head of Loch Roag, and while none is as complex or impressive as the main one at Callanish, some of them are well worth a visit. Two of them are close to Callanish at 222326 (a setting of tall slabs 20m in diameter surrounding a small cairn) and 225327 (two concentric circles of upright slabs up to 2m high). Another circle is at 230305 off the B8011 road south of Garynahine.

5. Dun Carloway Broch (190413)

Dun Carloway is one of the best surviving examples of a peculiarly Scottish type of perhistoric defensive structure, a broch. The famous broch on the small island of Mousa in Shetland, which is often shown in illustrations, has its walls standing all round to a height of 13m, but although much of the stonework at Dun Carloway has been robbed, its walls still reach a height of 10m on one side, and it is far more accessible than the one on Mousa. Over 500 brochs are known, mostly in the Western and Northern Isles and adjacent mainland areas. They appear to have been developed from around 100 B.C. and remained in use for two or three centuries. The similarity of their construction throughout the area in which they occur may indicate that they spread relatively quickly: one suggestion is that many of them were built by a single group of itinerant architects who produced them to a standard pattern as status symbols for local chieftains. One current view is that they developed originally in Skye from simpler galleried structures and reached the peak of their development in Orkney and Shetland.

Brochs were tall defensive towers: they were in a sense a late Iron Age equivalent of the medieval tower house (see Trail 1) and may have had similar functions. They consist of a massive circular drystone wall enclosing a small courtyard. The walls of Dun

Broch, Dun Carloway

Carloway are 3m thick and the courtyard is only 7m across. The walls are hollow, consisting of an inner and outer face bonded together by courses of horizontal lintel stones. The gaps between these sets of lintels form galleries within the walls, some of which may have been used for storage. Their main function, however, was structural: they lightened the wall and made it possible to build to a far greater height. A staircase ran up inside the wall, giving access to the wall head from which the defenders may have been able to drop missiles on attackers. The inner walls often contained openings which provided light for the staircase and galleries and further lightened the structure. Because of the way in which Dun Carloway has been robbed on one side it is easy to see the internal structure. The central courtyard appears to have been floored over with a timber platform: you can see the supports for the edges of this on the inside wall face. The space beneath may have served as a refuge for cattle. In some brochs there is evidence of a further floor above, and it is presumed that the structure was roofed in some way. Some examples in the Northern Isles had elaborate outer defences, but these are rare around Hebridean brochs; the rocky knoll on which Dun Carloway stands provided an additional obstacle to attackers.

The purpose of the brochs is not entirely clear: undoubtedly they were defences, but for whom and against whom? A good deal has been made of their special character, yet even in terms of their construction this can be overstated. They are clearly related in design to the type of stone forts known as duns, which are most common in the south-western Highlands but whose distribution overlaps with that of the brochs (some duns also occur on the west coast of Lewis). Brochs and duns can be considered as adaptations—in an environment with a smaller, more scattered population and abundant stone—of earth and timber defensive structures like hillforts which occur in eastern and southern Scotland. It is believed that brochs initially served as temporary refuges for local communities against aggressors; they are usually built close to the best arable land. Their coastal location has led some archaeologists to suggest that they may have been a defence against long-distance slave-raiding by sea, possibly encouraged by the expansion of the Roman Empire. Whether sea raiders or local feuding prompted the construction of the brochs, by about 200 A.D. more peaceful conditions allowed the dismantling of some and their conversion to more peaceful uses, though some at least were still imposing enough to be re-used as forts during the Norse settlement some 800 or 900 years after they were originally built. Excavations at Dun Carloway have revealed pottery which indicates that the broch was re-occupied sometime between the 5th and 8th centuries A.D.

Immediately below the rocky knoll on which Dun Carloway stands you can see the remains of a traditional Hebridean black house. This example, which was inhabited into the 1930s and possibly later, judging from old photographs, is a good example of the 'unimproved' style of black house with an integral byre and attached barn, similar to the restored example at Arnol (see below).

If you look at the modern cottages situated around the broch you will note that many of them have adjacent weaving sheds at the rear. On a calm day the noise of the looms at work is one of the few sounds of human activity. The weaving of Harris Tweed is the most important craft activity to be combined with agriculture in the modern crofting system.

Take the second turning on your left off the A858 immediately after the bridge at Carloway. Follow this minor road uphill and then down to a bay to the north.

6. Garenin: Black Houses (205442)

Garenin was one of the last clusters of inhabited black houses in Lewis. The houses were abandoned in the early 1970s when their inhabitants were moved to modern council houses nearby. Unfortunately this fine group of traditional houses was not preserved and they fell into decay rapidly once the thatch had deteriorated and frost had penetrated the cores of the thick walls. The buildings were still part-roofed in 1980 but have deteriorated further since then. Details of the construction and layout of the traditional Lewis black house are described below.

Around Garenin, and indeed almost everywhere you go in the Outer Hebrides, you will see patterns of steep-sided ridges with rounded or flattish tops up to 3m or so wide, separated by deep channels. These ridges are known as lazy beds and were produced for cultivation by spade or foot plough (*cas chrom*). They are a kind of adaptation of ridge and furrow ploughing (Trail 5) to hand cultivation and a peaty soil. They improved drainage by raising

Black House, Garenin, 1974

the crop above the level of the water table and provided a deep, well-manured soil. Cultivation by spade rather than by plough was traditional in the Outer Hebrides before the development of the crofting system. High yields could be obtained from small plots of land which were carefully dug by hand, with heavy inputs of manure and seaweed. When population built up in the later 18th and early 19th centuries and holdings were progressively subdivided, the amount of potentially cultivable land held by each crofter was too small, and their resources too limited, for plough cultivation to be viable. Ploughs were often useless for cultivating the raw peaty soils on which many of the new townships had been established. The one resource which the crofters did possess was labour, and lazy beds represent a backbreaking attempt to wring a living from a difficult environment. The outer parts of the beds were made of turf dug from the adjoining trenches. Seaweed and other manure mixed with earth was then piled in the centre. Lazy beds were used for cereals, but in the 19th century potatoes became the principal crop. They are still cultivated around many townships, though the amalgamation of crofts and improved drainage often make plough cultivation possible today. The huge areas of abandoned lazy beds now grazed by sheep testify to the former high population levels of many townships and the struggle to provide a bare subsistence for their inhabitants before large-scale emigration occurred.

7. Shawbost: Horizontal Water Mill (24464)

The local school has restored a traditional horizontal water mill at Shawbost. This type of mill was common throughout the Western and Northern Isles into the 19th century, and their remains can often be found by small streams. This was the last working mill of its kind on Lewis and continued in use into the 1930s. The mill itself was tiny and required minimal expenditure and effort in construction. The style of building is similar to that of the larger black houses. The head of water needed was also small so that almost any stream could be harnessed for power. The water came in through the mill lade to drive not a vertical wheel but a set of horizontal wooden paddles (hence the name) in a lower chamber. The upper one contained the millstones which were scarcely bigger than a quern or hand mill. This type of mill was well

Horizontal water mill, Shawbost

adapted to an economy in which the quantity of grain produced by each holding was small and to an environment where streams were too tiny to drive a vertical wheel. The horizontal water mill is thought by some to have originated in the Mediterranean during the first century B.C. and to have spread to western Britain four or five centuries later. It is known from Ireland and the Isle of Man, but it is not clear if it was characteristic only of Atlantic areas or whether it once occurred in Lowland Britain at an early date and was later replaced by large mills with vertical water wheels.

8. Bragar: Broch and Crofting Township (285474)

At 285474 in Loch an Duna on a low tongue of land which is almost cut off to form an island is another broch. Much less well preserved than Dun Carloway, the walls nevertheless remain to a height of 4m. They are 3.5m thick and enclose a courtyard 9m in diameter.

Bragar is typical of the larger crofting townships of western Lewis. Whether they were new creations to accommodate tenants displaced from the south, re-sited ones as at Arnol (see below) or merely the old farming townships reorganised on a more regular basis by the estate, they all have a similar form. The lotted lands of the crofts are usually laid out in long strips running back from the road on one or both sides. The crofters' houses and outbuildings might be placed anywhere on the narrow plot. These two elements combine to create the appearance of the townships today: a multiplicity of boundaries demarcating the strips, a patchwork of small-scale land use within the strips, and a dense scatter of buildings which are too close to be isolated cottages but at the same time are too dispersed to give the impression of a coherent village. With improved transport and increasing contact with the outside world there has been a tendency for newer houses to be located closer to the road; the remains of the older ones can often be seen behind them.

9. Arnol: The Black House Museum (311493)

The Outer Hebridean Black House is one the most distinctive types of traditional peasant dwellings in Western Europe. Adapted to a harsh environment and to the needs of the crofting economy, its materials—stone, peat, turf, heather and straw thatch—embody the landscape of Lewis in microcosm. The name 'black house' (*tigh dubh*) in Gaelic reflects not so much their smoky interiors as the contrast which their dark stone exteriors made with the bright,

Black House converted to outbuilding, Arnol

whitewashed cottages which began to replace them from the later 19th century.

The basic constructional features of a traditional black house include a massive low wall consisting of two outer layers of dry stone and an inner core of peat or earth to seal out draughts. The walls may be 2m thick at the base, tapering to about 1m at the top. The roof is supported by fairly flimsy timbers: there was a chronic shortage of timber solid enough for roofing in Lewis during the 19th century and earlier. Roof timbers were often fastened together from bits of driftwood and even then might form the most valuable part of a house, often being removed by a tenant if he went to another holding. The roof, which was thatched with straw or sometimes heather over turf, was weighted down with stones which were attached to heather ropes. At the hipped ends of the building these ropes were fixed to sticks protruding through the thatch. In present-day examples wooden boards, nylon ropes and wire netting may be used to help secure the thatch. Instead of overhanging the outer edge of the walls to form eaves, the roof came down to the inner edge of the core. This caused water running off the thatch to drain down through the earth core of the wall, sometimes making the interior damp; in the 19th century these houses were notorious as breeding grounds for tuberculosis. The reason for the roof being designed in this way was probably to reduce the chance of a strong gust of wind getting under the thatch and lifting it off. This was especially likely given the flimsy nature of the roof timbers. The whole design of the house is streamlined to reduce wind resistance: all the corners are rounded.

Traditional black houses had only one or two small windows opening in the thatch and a single low doorway, making them very dark inside. The hearth was located in the centre of the living part of the house, the smoke escaping through a gap in the thatch. When the roofing was renewed, often annually, the thatch, impregnated with soot, was valued as fertiliser for the arable land. The internal layout was that of a 'long house': the house and the byre for the cattle were accommodated in a single long range and there was only one entrance used by both men and beasts. The cattle were kept inside over the winter, and the byre end of the house was located downhill to prevent the accumulated manure from flooding into the living portion of the house. Humans and animals alike benefited from the central peat fire and kept each other warm. Before the later 19th century there were no partitions between the living quarters and the byre, merely a downhill step. It was believed that 'letting the coo see the fire' kept the animals in better condition. In spring, when the cattle were turned out on to the new grass, a portion of the byre wall was removed and the accumulated manure was shovelled out. The barn was also adjacent and, though roofed separately, could be entered from the living quarters. A development of this simple plan was to enlarge the house by converting the byre end into living quarters and building a new byre on the opposite side to the barn. The house at Dun Carloway had this plan and you can see a number of other ruined examples in Arnol. Because of its antiquated appearance the design of the black house might seem to be an ancient one: an origin in Viking times has often been proposed. However, excavation of a site at Udal in South Uist which has a long sequence of continuous occupation shows that the classic 19th-century black house was quite sophisticated compared with its predecessors. The substantial wall with its peat core was not necessarily a standard feature in earlier times: 18th-century visitors to the island described houses built with walls of peat with only an internal stone lining. This, and the constant re-use of stone for later buildings, helps to explain why remains of pre-19th century houses are scarce.

Traditional black houses like this were in use well into the present century. The museum at Arnol was lived in until the 1960s. Almost all the ruined black houses which you can see in townships like Arnol and Bragar were in use as dwellings during the 1930s; new black houses were actually being built as late as this. Even more common were modified black houses like those at Garenin where a gable was built at one end with a chimney and a fireplace replacing the central hearth, and larger windows being inserted. Both kinds of house went increasingly out of use as dwellings after the Second World War, being replaced by modern dormer cottages. Some black houses continued to be inhabited into the early 1970s — those at Garenin, for instance — but by 1980 there were only three inhabited examples on the whole of the west coast of Lewis. The roofless ruins of the old houses can be seen behind their replacements: Arnol has large numbers of them. In areas where traditional vernacular building styles are abandoned for more modern ones there is a standard downward progression of the old houses through uses which require less and less maintenance, producing a structure which is less and less weatherproof until it ends up as a roofless shell. In many cases the black houses were converted to outbuildings and are still in use as byres, storehouses for fodder and potatoes, and in some cases as garages. They have rarely been converted into weaving sheds because of their lack of light. When they become derelict and roofless the buildings may be used as sheep pens or end up as rubbish dumps. Where such houses are still actively maintained, corrugated iron or asbestos may be preferred to thatch which requires constant repair, though some thatched roofs are still being regularly renewed. Demolition of black houses has been encouraged by the availability of grants for erecting new outbuildings. Within a few years it is probable that the museum at Arnol will be the only surviving example.

The township of Arnol was originally sited further to the north on the coast along the beach around 303494. You can still see traces of the small round-cornered stone houses of the early community, perhaps dating from the late 18th century, along with their fields. Pottery finds indicate that this site was occupied from prehistoric times. The village was resited further inland during the 19th century due to growing population and a shortage of arable land and fuel in the immediate vicinity. This was a common pattern for townships in western Lewis; much the same change occurred at Shawbost. The stream draining from Loch na Muilne (the loch of the mill) to the north-east of the latter settlement had a string of small horizontal water mills along its course. The remains of the last mill to be used by the township early in the present century can be seen at 324486 on the east bank of the River Ereray just north of where the main road crosses it.

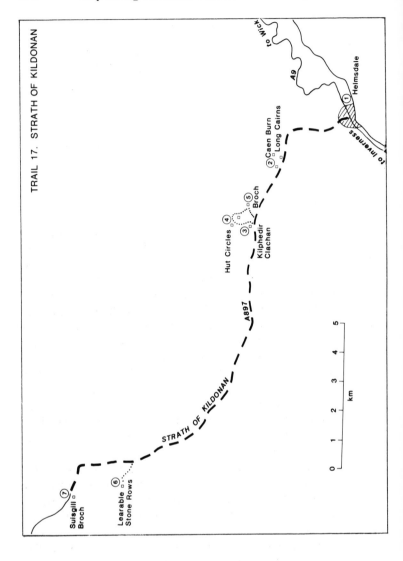

TRAIL 17. STRATH OF KILDONAN

SEVENTEEN

The Strath of Kildonan: Settlement and Clearance in a Highland Glen

Ordnance Survey 1:50,000 sheet 17; 1:25,000 sheets NC 81/91, 82/92, ND01

This trail involves a drive of 20km with two short walks.

Introduction

The Strath of Kildonan may seem a bleak, empty valley today, yet the area has a long history of human settlement and has at times supported a remarkably high population. Along the valley sides you can find remains of settlements and other features which date from early prehistoric times to the 19th century. Elements from so many periods have been preserved here because the economy has always been an essentially pastoral one with cultivation being confined to small plots; features from early times may have become overgrown, even buried in the peat, but apart from some stone-robbing many of them have been little disturbed. This is particularly the case with the hut circles and associated features, most of them probably dating from the last few centuries B.C., which occur on the slopes above the Strath, providing an excellent opportunity for looking at the links between settlement at this period and the physical landscape.

More poignant than the prehistoric remains because, being much more recent, the context of their abandonment is known in detail, are the ruins of the farming townships which are scattered along the floor and lower slopes of the valley. These are the hamlets or 'clachans' which were cleared of their population by the management of the Sutherland estates in the early years of the 19th century to make way for commercial sheep farms. Highland history has few more emotive terms than 'the Clearances', but the background to them, and the changes which were involved, are often misunderstood or oversimplified.

In the Strath of Kildonan it is possible to study two entire fossil landscapes comprising large numbers of settlements and their associated agricultural features. The prehistoric one on the valley sides and the early 19th-century one on the valley floor are separated by some 2,000 years, but they developed within the constraints of farming economies which seem to have had a good deal in common and, as a result, they exhibit some interesting similarities.

The Sutherland Clearances

The story of the Highland Clearances has often been presented by popular writers in black and white terms. The eviction of large numbers of peasant smallholders to make way for commercial sheep farming in the later 18th and early 19th centuries has been held up as an example of oppression, greed and inhumanity on the part of Highland landowners who had lost their military prestige and power with the measures taken by the government after the failure of the 1745 rebellion, and who turned to the ruthless economic exploitation of their estates instead. The clearances which occurred on the Sutherland estates, including the Strath of Kildonan, in the early years of the 19th century have become especially notorious for their insensitivity. The seemingly callous, almost brutal way in which some tenants and their families were turned out of their homes led to the famous trial of Patrick Sellar, the estate factor or manager. But the real story was more complicated.

An important background factor which is often overlooked is the rapid rise of population in the northern and western Highlands in the later 18th century. This was encouraged by more settled conditions after 1746 and was sustained by the spread of the potato which allowed more people to be supported at a bare subsistence level from the limited areas of fertile land which characterised the more rugged parts of the Highlands. In the southern and eastern Highlands population growth was tempered by migration to the Lowlands and was sustained by additional sources of income to peasant farming. In the north and west, however, the effect was to push an already impoverished population, living in an environment with limited potential, to the brink of disaster. Bad weather in 1782 brought a failed cereal harvest and blighted the potato crop, leading to a major famine. Relief was organised by landowners and the government, but too late to prevent many from dying of hunger. In Kildonan the estate supplied grain to the population, but at a high price which put them in debt for years after. The population of the valley was already outstripping its resources, leading to emigration, before the introduction of commercial sheep farming.

Large-scale sheep farming was already well established in more southerly parts of the Highlands when the Countess of Sutherland and her husband, Lord Stafford, decided that it was the only possible means of raising the low income of the estate. The small tenants practised a mixed economy with a few cattle and sheep, and small plots of cereals and potatoes. They did not have the capital to invest in large flocks of expensive imported Border sheep, and this kind of farming was only viable commercially when done on a large scale. Nor was it possible for the traditional and new farming systems to co-exist: the sheep needed all the land from the tenants' hill grazings for summer pasture down to the more fertile bottom land in the valleys for wintering.

The plan prepared for the Countess and her husband was for interior glens like the Strath of Kildonan to be turned over to large sheep runs. The tenants in these areas were to be moved down to the coast and resettled. It was hoped that they would be able to combine crofting with fishing and industrial employment such as textile manufacture. While the estate management clearly wanted to use the opportunity to remove from the estate some tenants whom they considered troublesome, large-scale eviction was not contemplated. It was hoped that the resettled tenants would be able to improve their circumstances and be more prosperous than before; it was even considered that the measures might increase the number of inhabitants on the estate.

The problems that arose were partly due to a gap between theory and practice. The process of moving the tenants at the end of their leases was badly managed, so that on more than one occasion their new allotments and houses were not ready for them when they were required to quit their existing holdings. The Countess and even the estate factors seemed to have little appreciation of the attachment of the tenants to their homes, or of the upset and dislocation which their forced removal would cause. In Kildonan the first clearances were undertaken in 1806–7. When they proved to be harder to accomplish than expected, new men were brought in from outside to speed up the process. William Young and Patrick Sellar, agricultural experts from Moray, forced through the next round of clearances in 1812 and 1813, pushing the inhabitants of Kildonan close to open revolt. But the tenants were placated remarkably easily and in 1814 came the large-scale clearances in neighbouring Strathnaver in which Patrick Sellar was alleged to have burnt several families out of their homes and thereby caused the deaths of some elderly people. He was tried and acquitted, but his hot-headed actions, coupled with Young's gross mismanagement of estate finances, led to their being replaced by James Loch, a lawyer, who was more efficient and more understanding of the people's feelings. In the large-scale clearance of the Strath of Kildonan in 1819–20 he made every effort to move the tenants and their families as humanely as possible.

The effects of the clearances on the interior glens can be summarised briefly. In 1811 the parish of Kildonan had 1574 inhabitants. By 1831 this had fallen to 257, less than a sixth of its former level. The Countess sank immense sums of money into replanning the estate, including the construction of a new community at Helmsdale for the people moved out of the Strath of Kildonan. Under Young's direction a good deal of money was squandered or ill-directed. Unfortunately the Sutherland clearances occurred at a time when all the activities into which it was hoped that the tenants could move—fishing and textiles, for instance—were going through a slump. As a result, many people left the estate immediately—some for Caithness and Ross, others for North America—and many more left after a fruitless struggle to establish themselves on the coast. This had not been the intention of the estate management, but their inability to plan realistically—something which has been a characteristic of the Highlands in more recent times—led to massive thinning of the population.

1. Helmsdale (0215)

Helmsdale is a classic example of a potential centre of economic growth and employment which failed to match up to over-optimistic expectations due to bad planning, bad timing and a lack of appreciation of the severe limitations of the resources of the Highlands, along with a poor understanding of the attitudes of the Highland population. The Highlands are littered with places like Helmsdale representing well-intentioned but impractical attempts to diversify the local economy by providing industrial jobs in order to check the drift of population from the area.

The grid plan of Helmsdale marks it out as a planned settlement, and in this sense it is comparable to the planned estate villages of the Lowlands. However, it was designed as something rather grander than an estate village. The settlement was planned to employ a substantial proportion of the population which was moved out of the Strath of Kildonan; it was even hoped that it might attract people out of the hills before the clearance were set in motion. The Countess of Sutherland spent some £14,000 in five years in trying to create a modern fishing port from scratch. The famous engineer John Rennie was employed to design the harbour, and the estate subsidised the building of a fish-curing plant as well as providing other facilities designed to entice Lowland firms to set up in the town and generate employment. Initially it was hoped that woollen, cotton and leather manufacturing industries would be established as well as fishing. But despite the large sums which were spent on the town the estate management and the Sutherland family did not give enough consideration to the problems of how peasant farmers, without any capital or skill at fishing, were going to establish themselves in this new setting. For a while Helmsdale seemed to be a boom town: in 1819 it had over 2,000 inhabitants frantically trying to adapt to their new circumstances. A certain amount of employment in fishing was maintained for some decades, but all the other industrial ventures slumped or failed to take off at all. In the end most of the inhabitants ended up depending on their small crofts and augmenting their incomes with casual labour and other seasonal activities: very much the kind of livelihood they had before their removal and quite the reverse of what the estate management had intended for them.

Drive up the Strath of Kildonan, following the A897.

2. Caen Burn: Neolithic Long Cairns (912177)

On the lower slopes of the spur between the mouth of the Caen Burn and the River Helmsdale a short way above the road are the remains of a long cairn, a Neolithic burial monument, and one of the earliest man-made landscape features in the area. It is over 50m long, 14m across at its widest, and over 2m high at its east end. Other examples occur further up the valley of the Caen Burn, on the west side at 013180 and on the east bank at 015182, but they have been much more severely robbed for stone and are badly ruined.

3. Kilphedir: The pre-Clearance Clachan (989187)

The early 19th-century clearances have left the ruins of innumerable farming settlements scattered throughout this valley, and indeed throughout the Highlands as a whole. In their layout, and even in the structure and plan of their houses and associated buildings, these townships preserve a form of settlement which goes back at least to medieval times. The 1:25,000 (though not the 1:50,000) Ordnance Survey map marks these deserted clachans in some detail along with their surrounding enclosures. It is fascinating to explore them because it is rare anywhere else in Britain to be able to walk around the remains of an entire deserted community where the walls still stand almost intact. If you park near the bridge which crosses the Kilphedir Burn at 989186, there are two of these clachans, or hamlets, close to the road on the hillside above you, one on either side of the burn. At Kilphedir, on the west of the burn, you can see the classic features of these settlements. The farm houses are characteristically long and are divided by internal stone walls into two or three units. Originally one end of the buildings would have housed the inhabitants and the other the livestock, like the traditional Lewis black houses (Trail 16). The cattle would normally have lived in the downslope end of the buildings. Between these long rectangular houses are smaller squareish buildings; some would have been barns and outbuildings, others the homes of cottagers and labourers who did not own any livestock. You can also see the remains of a round structure, a corn-drying kiln which was essential in an area of high rainfall in which the harvest was often gathered in wet. Around the houses are the remains of enclosures, some of which might have been potato plots, others livestock pens. The stones of older houses were re-used in later buildings, but despite this you can see the foundations of what seem to be an earlier generation of buildings on the site. The arable lands of the community lay downhill from the settlement, and you can make out the traces of lazy beds (Trail 16) and cultivation ridges. On the opposite side of the burn are the remains of the clachan of Chorick which seems to have been a slightly larger settlement.

The walk to the next site involves a round trip of about 2km over grass and heather moorland; stout footwear is recommended. If you do not wish to do this walk, continue the trail at No.6.

4. Kilphedir: Hut Circles (991194)

The Ordnance Survey maps of this valley are liberally sprinkled with the name 'hut circles'. These are probably the commonest prehistoric monuments in this area. They occur on the valley sides, rarely on the valley floors, at altitudes of up to 320m on ground which is generally peat-covered moorland. The remains usually occur in small, loose clusters of up to half a dozen. In appearance they consist of low circular banks, overgrown by vegetation, from about 5 to 12m in diameter. They are generally considered to have been the foundations of circular houses, and this has been established by excavation in some cases. Where these hut foundations have been built on a slope, they commonly stand on artificial platforms which have been created by cutting back into the hillside and piling the material downslope. Most of these clusters of hut circles are associated with other landscape features: low piles of stones, or cairns (often marked on the older maps as 'tumuli'). They appear to have been constructed by the clearance of stones from small plots of agricultural land rather than for burial purposes. Sometimes, too, low stone banks can be found near the huts; these are either the boundaries of cultivated plots or are simply linear clearance banks.

Although the hut circles on either side of the Kilphedir Burn are no different from those elsewhere in the Strath of Kildonan, they are of particular interest as some of them have been excavated, and so more is known about this group of hut circles than any of the others in the valley. Walk up the west side of the Kilphedir Burn above the little gorge which contains the stream to 991194. The walk is less than 1km over open moorland.

If you look back towards the road you can see that you are standing on a shelf or plateau with higher ground above forming an embayment in the hillside. This sheltered area has been attrac-

Hut circle, Kilphedir

tive for settlement over a long period. Below you, close to the road, are the remains of the early 19th-century township which may well stand on the site of medieval predecessors. Across the valley at the same level are the impressive remains of a broch. Scattered over the plateau around you and on the other side of the burn are the remains of a number of hut circles with associated cairns and banks. You may not be able to pick them out at once, but when you have spotted one you will know what to look for and you will soon spot others. The excavated site lies on the west side of the glen at 991194. Five hut circles are scattered around an area of about 100× 60m which has been roughly cleared of stones. The stones have been piled into a number of cairns and some rough banks and alignments. The huts which stand on artificial platforms are the easiest to identify. Two of them are 11–12m in diameter and two of the others are smaller. The excavation revealed the holes in the floor of the hut which had carried timber posts supporting the roof. The placing of these suggested that the roof had rested on only a low stone wall with an inner circle of posts. Despite the large size of the hut much of the space close to the walls must have been of limited use due to the low level of the roof.

The fifth hut is quite distinct in construction from the others, having a much more massive wall up to 3m thick and an entrance passage nearly 5m long. This hut seemed to be more closely related than the others to the boulder banks. The thick walls of the hut were composed of earth and stone and were kept in place by large boulders around the outside. The wall is thought to have stood over 1.5m above the level of the hut floor, providing much more usable floorspace close to the walls than in the first type. Within the hut there had either been a cell built into the thickness of the wall, or the entrance to a souterrain, an underground storage chamber (Trail 12). Elsewhere around the Strath of Kildonan you can find the same pattern of small groups of the first type of hut and single examples of the more massive second type. The excavator believed that the second type of hut represented rebuilding in a different style on the site of one of the first type. Charcoal within the huts provided dates of occupation of around 500 B.C. for the first type and 130 B.C. for the second. This was interpreted as indicating two phases of occupation of this and other sites in the area, the first type of huts being associated with the cairns, the second with the linear banks, suggesting slight differences in cultivation practices.

The large numbers of hut circles in the area could imply a substantial population in Iron Age times, greater than at the time of the clearances in the early 19th century if they had all been occupied at the same time. But this is unlikely; it is more probable that the huts were associated with some kind of shifting cultivation and that after a few years, when the fertility of the small plots, cultivated with a hoe or digging stick rather than a plough, fell off a new settlement would have been established elsewhere. Thus, a relatively small population could have created the visible remains over a few generations. The positioning of the huts might seem bleak and exposed but the peat cover seems to have formed after the huts had been built and abandoned. It is likely that the main valley was still quite heavily wooded when the huts were in use. It may be that the technology of these settlers was too primitive to allow successful cultivation of the heavier valley bottom soils; there was nothing in the finds from the huts to suggest that they had anything other than a Stone Age level of technology, and they may have selected these semi-upland sites on lighter soils for preference. Alternatively they may have been forced to move up out of the valley because of population pressure. We have seen with the cairns at Caen Burn that some pre-Iron Age remains do occur quite

K

low down in the valley, and it is possible that the settlement sites of these earlier peoples have been destroyed by later building in this more intensively used area.

Cross the Kildonan Burn to its eastern side. At 992191 you should be able to find another similar group of hut circles, one of them with the remains of a souterrain inside, and the associated cairns and linear stone banks. What you have within this valley is an entire agricultural landscape which has been buried and protected by the growth of a thin layer of peat. Had the peat been any thicker, or had the hut foundations been constructed of turf rather than stone, very little would remain on the surface today to show this former phase of occupation. In other parts of Scotland, deeper peat may hide entire landscapes like the one which is partially exposed here.

5. Kilphedir Broch (994189)

There are a number of brochs in the strath; many of them occur in embayments like this one, with remains of hut circles round about them. The relationship between the huts and the brochs is not clear, but the date for the later, more massive hut at Kilphedir, c130 B.C., is close to the earliest known phase of broch construction and, as only one date for the occupation of these huts is available so far, it is possible that there was more overlap between the two. The brochs are generally considered to have acted as communal refuges for scattered local communities against raiding, in this case possibly against attack from the sea. Certainly the massive walling and long entrance passages of the later huts show an ability to build in stone which fits in well with the construction of the brochs.

Brochs have been discussed in detail in Trail 16. While the example at Kilphedir has not survived as well as ones like Dun Carloway in Lewis, it is still an impressive structure. It stands on a knoll on the highest part of the plateau area commanding a wide view up and down the main valley. It has an internal diameter of just under 11m with an entrance in the north-west side, away from the valley. The walls are still some 2–3m high but the whole structure is badly ruined. One of the most striking features is the massive ditch which encircles the base of the hillock on which the broch stands. It is about 7m wide and 3m deep with the remains of a thick rampart on the inner side.

Return to your car and continue up the valley.

6. Learable: The Stone Rows (893235)

The walk to this site involves a return trip of under 2km. If you do not wish to do the walk, continue the trail at No.7.

Leave your car near 901233 and cross the river by the footbridge. A path leads under the railway line and through the woods to open ground. Climb the spur of the hillside above, past a deserted early 19th-century clachan at 896236. The stone rows are on a flatter area of the spur above you. The best landmark to aim for is the prominent standing stone which has a cross cut into its west face; whether it was erected as an early-Christian marker or whether it is earlier and the cross was cut to counteract its pagan symbolism is uncertain. Around the stone, especially to the south, are a number of cairns. These are more substantial features than the small clearance cairns associated with the hut circles, and one of them to the west of the standing stone has been excavated and was found to contain a burial chamber with the remains of a cremation and some jet beads. Other cairns lie at a similar distance from the standing stone to the south-east and south-west. Further to the south-west are several lines of stone rows. The stones are mostly under 1m high but are spaced out fairly regularly to make a striking pattern. Another set of them can be seen north-west of the standing stone. There is no clear indication of their purpose, but by analogy with more impressive megalithic monuments else-where they may have had some kind of an unspecified ritual function; this is always a good explanation for a prehistoric feature whose function is not immediately obvious! It is by no means certain that the cairns, the stone rows and the standing stone were contemporary. They may indicate that the site was used over quite a long period, but it is likely that most of the monuments are of pre-Iron Age date.

Return to your car and continue up the valley.

7. Suisgill Broch (888253)

This broch is similar to the one at Kilphedir in many respects but, although it is in an even more ruined condition, it has the advantage of being in full view of the road and is more immediately accessible. It stands beside the Helmsdale River on a low but steeply sloping mound. The eastern and western sides of the mound have been fortified by means of a ditch and an internal wall with an entrance to the south. The ditch is up to 10m wide and 3m deep. The broch has clearly been used as a stone quarry over a long period and is badly ruined.

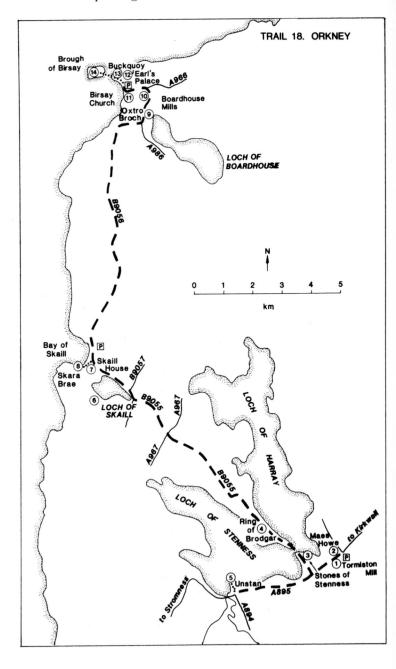

EIGHTEEN

Orkney: Prehistoric and Norse Settlement

Ordnance Survey 1:50,000 sheet 6; 1:25,000 sheets HY 21/31, 22/32

This trail involves a drive of 30km with some short walks.

Introduction

Orkney is probably richer in visible remains of past settlement and other human activities than any other part of Scotland of comparable size. The long and very dense occupation of this island group is due largely to its distinctive geology. While the Western Isles and Shetland are composed of hard metamorphic rocks which often form rugged landscapes and do not break down readily to form a rich soil, Orkney is formed from sandstones which produce light, easily-worked, well-drained soils which are comparatively rich in lime where the sandstone is calcareous. The landscape of Orkney, except for the western coasts where there is some spectacular cliff scenery, is neither rocky nor dramatic. Lowlands dotted with lochs are broken up by low, rolling hills. The inherent fertility of the soils has allowed Orkney to support a large population for its size at various periods, and today the prosperity of its agriculture contrasts with other areas of northern Scotland. The well-bedded sandstones have also proved to be an ideal building material. In places the flagstones can be split thinly enough to be used for roofing, or set upright for walling. The thicker slabs were well adapted for drystone wall construction, producing some of the most sophisticated prehistoric architecture in Britain. Although Orkney was forested during the early part of the post-glacial period, the woodland cover was soon removed by man and a deteriorating, more maritime climate with windier and wetter conditions, which set in at the end of the Bronze Age, did not encourage any woodland to regenerate. Consequently, lack of timber and the presence of such easily-worked stone led to many articles being made in stone which were fashioned from timber elsewhere. The stone furniture from the houses at Skara Brae has survived, almost uniquely, as a result. The drowned coastline with its many sheltered bays also helped to make the islands attractive to seafaring peoples, from the immigrants who built the great chambered tombs to the Vikings who came first to raid and then to settle. The mild winter climate of Orkney is comparable with south-eastern England or the head of the Adriatic, and though the summer is comparatively cool, with an ever-present wind, this is compensated for by the long hours of daylight.

Within such a short space it is impossible to do full justice to the complexity of the Orkney landscape, but the trail concentrates on two of its most important formative periods: the Neolithic and Bronze Ages on one hand and the Norse settlement on the other.

1. Tormiston Mill (319125)

Park in the car park beside the mill.

The two peninsulas which are linked together by the Bridge of Brodgar contain one of the most impressive groups of prehistoric monuments in Britain, comparable in scale and significance, as well as in the period of their construction, with the groups of monuments centred on Stonehenge and Avebury.

The mill emphasises the importance of grain production in Orkney before the present century. As early as the 17th century Orkney was exporting grain to Edinburgh and abroad while, nearer at hand, much grain was sent to Shetland which could never produce enough for its own needs. Tormiston Mill, which has been restored, dates from the prosperous mid-19th century when Orkney's agriculture was radically improved. The mill is a substantial three-storey building, complete with a kiln for drying the corn, and a 4.5m diameter water wheel. Large mills of this type with vertical water wheels replaced the smaller horizontal or 'click' mills, similar to those in the Outer Hebrides (Trail 16) which had been the normal type of mill in Orkney from medieval times.

2. Maes Howe Chambered Tomb (319128)

Maes Howe lies a little way north Tormiston Mill and can be reached by a short walk up a side road which leaves the A965 just east of the mill.

Maes Howe is maintained by the Department of the Environment, and a key to it can be obtained at the nearby farm. It has been described as the finest prehistoric chambered-tomb in North-Western Europe, and it is certainly an impressive piece of architecture. Radiocarbon dates for organic matter which accumulated in the ditch surrounding the cairn soon after it was dug suggests that the monument dates from c2,900–2,500 B.C., towards the end of the Neolithic Period, representing the culmination of a tradition of building going back over 1000 years. Archaeologists classify it as a 'passage grave', but this is only a variety of a more general type of collective burial tomb which occurs widely throughout the British Isles and elsewhere in Atlantic Europe. It is thought that such tombs were used for ceremonial purposes and for interring the remains of an elite social group, an aristocracy or more probably a priesthood, over a long period of time. Archaeologists have debated the origins of this group and their tombs. One widely-held view is that these collective tombs originated in Iberia around the mid-5th millennium B.C. and were constructed for a priesthood belonging to a religion the beliefs of which enabled them to dominate a simple agricultural society and mobilise its labour in the construction of these large monuments. This elite spread out, establishing itself among the peasant farming communities of North-Western Europe. It is not clear whether they originated in Iberia or whether they developed there after migrating from the eastern Mediterranean. One theory is that this religious revolution may have come from the Middle East where societies dominated by priesthoods had developed at a sufficiently early date to have spread to the Western Mediterranean by the time the earliest known tombs were being built in Iberia. As these elite groups spread through northern Spain and Portugal, Western France and the British Isles, their tradition of collective burials in large tombs developed different characteristics in different areas, perhaps in response to local conditions. Despite this they still formed a remarkably uniform cultural province. In southern and eastern England burial in timber mortuary structures under earthen long barrows was usual. In western England and around the Clyde estuary in Arran and Argyll, with outliers as far north as Caithness, tombs took the form of elongated cairns surrounding rectangular chambers with numerous side galleries. In the Western and Northern Isles and adjacent mainland areas passage graves were normal;

these were cairns, often round, with long passages leading to central chambers. In Orkney the passage graves developed in two different ways. In one type the chamber became longer and longer and was divided into compartments or stalls by vertical slabs. The nearby cairn at Onstan is an example of this type (see below). The other type of chamber was cruciform in plan, the cairns becoming larger and more complex, culminating in Maes Howe. Superficially it might seem surprising to find such an impressive monument in what might appear to have been a remote backwater in prehistory, but pottery and other finds from the Orkney tombs show that their builders had wide contacts with other similar groups via the Atlantic seaways of Western Europe.

The burial chamber of Maes Howe is covered by a mound of stones and earth 35m in diameter and 7m high. The mound stands on a platform surrounded by a ditch which is 15m wide and up to 2m deep. The material from the ditch was used to construct the mound. From the entrance a passage 16m long leads to the main chamber which is 4.5m square. Originally the four massive stone buttresses in the corners of the chamber supported a cleverly designed corbelled roof but the upper part of this was destroyed by Viking and later robbers and has been replaced by a modern one. You can see how well the builders used the qualities of the local stone, and so skilful is their work that they may have been professional engineers, like the later broch builders (Trail 16). Three side chambers lead off from the main one above floor level. They could be sealed with the massive stones which lie on the floor of the main chamber. No finds of any significance have been recovered here; the tomb was so prominent that it proved an irresistible attraction to later treasure hunters. Norsemen broke into it on several occasions, and you can see the runic inscriptions left by some of them. One inscription records that crusaders broke into the tomb: probably members of Earl Rognvald's expedition who wintered here in 1150–1. Other inscriptions wistfully record that the great treasure which they assumed the tomb must have contained had been removed by earlier visitors. The Norsemen have also left some fine carvings as well as this early example of graffiti.

Return to your car and drive west along the A965 for 1 km, then turn right on to the B9055.

3. The Standing Stones of Stennes (307125)

As you approach the main group of standing stones, note the
Barnhouse Stone (312122), an outlier 50m north of Barnhouse
farm which may be associated with the main monument. At first
glance the Stones of Stenness are a small group of standing stones,
but in fact they form part of a henge monument, a ceremonial
enclosure surrounded by an outer bank and inner ditch. The bank
and ditch have been almost obliterated by later cultivation and are
only faintly visible. The single entrance to the henge was on the
north-west side.

Henges are similar in date to stone circles such as the one at
Callanish (Trail 16). Their distribution concentrates on eastern,
lowland Britain while stone circles are more common in the
highland north and west. Here, and at the Ring of Brodgar (see
below), the henge contains a stone circle, as do the large, complex
ones at Stonehenge and Avebury. The henges and stone circles are
later in date than chambered tombs like Maes Howe, spanning the
period c2,500–1,500 B.C., but the periods of their construction did
overlap. Radiocarbon dates from charcoal under the stones at
Stenness and from animal bones in the ditch suggest that it was
built around 2,300 B.C., some centuries after Maes Howe but when
the tomb may still have been in use. While chambered tombs have a
wide distribution in north-west Europe, stone circles and henges
mainly occur in the British Isles and Western France. It has been
suggested that they were built by the successors of the same priest
groups who had the chambered tombs constructed, possibly under
the influence of a religious revival which may have involved a sun
and moon cult.

The Stones of Stenness have been badly knocked about in the
past. Only four are standing from what may have been a circle of
twelve. The henge is about 60m in diameter within the ditch which
is cut through solid rock and may have taken some 50,000 man-
hours to excavate. The four standing stones are impressively high:
up to 5m. In 1814 a local farmer tried to demolish them, toppling
one and breaking up another before public outcry stopped him. In
1906 the Office of Works re-erected the fallen stone and built a
dolmen with three uprights and a capstone in the centre. The
western upright seems to have been brought from another site. The
capstone was pushed over in 1972, leaving archaeologists to puzzle

over the original layout of the remaining stones which seem to be more or less in their original positions. Excavation in 1973 and 1974 showed that this was not the only feature within the circle of the henge; another setting of four recumbent stones was discovered but their function remains obscure.

Beyond the Stones of Stenness at 307127 is the Watch Stone, another outlier and the largest stone in the area, some 6m high. 50m north of the henge stood another stone, the Stone of Odin, which was pierced by a hole. Promises made by lovers while holding hands through this stone were considered to be sacred. Unfortunately the stone was demolished and broken up by the farmer who vandalised the henge.

4. The Ring of Brodgar (295134)

Like the stone circle at Callanish (Trail 16), the Ring of Brodgar (or Brogar), the largest henge in Scotland, while impressive in itself, gains immeasurably in atmosphere from its magnificent setting on a promontory between two lochs. Unlike the Stones of Stenness, the rock-cut ditch is still deep and well marked. Originally it was up to 3m deep and 9m across with two opposite entrances in the north-west and south-east sides. The circle may originally have contained 60 stones but some have been toppled. It is 113m in diameter and the stones, though smaller than at Stenness, are over 3m high in many cases. A substantial body of evidence has accumulated in recent years which suggests that the ceremonies associated with henges and stone circles included astronomical observations of the sun and moon and that the alignments of stones were often carefully calculated to allow the prediction of key events in the solar and lunar cycles. At the Ring of Brodgar some of the mounds surrounding the henge may have been linked to alignments of stones within the circle which lined up with topographical markers on the distant cliffs of Hoy to identify critical phases on the moon's cycle.

50m east of the Ring, on a low circular platform, is the Comet Stone. The edge of the platform on which it stands abuts the faint remains of an old dyke of a type known in Orkney as a 'gairsty' dyke. These are common in Orkney, representing land divisions which go back to very early times. The word 'gairsty' derives from Old Norse, but in some areas these features are called 'treb' dykes, a

Ring of Brodgar

word which may be Celtic, pre-dating the Norse settlement. So these dykes may represent a Pictish system of land division taken over as a going concern by the Norse. In places the dykes occur below the peat, suggesting that their origins may lie even further back in prehistoric times. Orkney must have had a substantial population when monuments like the Ring of Brodgar were built: the effort of cutting the ditch of the henge has been estimated at 80,000 man-hours let alone the labour of transporting and erecting the stones. It is possible that land divisions from this time formed the basis of the later Pictish and Norse systems and that some of these dykes are contemporary with the henges. At a larger scale the parishes of the Mainland of Orkney, which follow natural topographic features, may be older than their Norse names suggest.

Return to the road junction with the A965 at Barnhouse, turn right and follow the A965 west for just under 2km. Immediately before you reach the junction with the A964 park your car and walk along a track which follows the edge of a promontory extending into the Loch of Stenness.

5. Onstan (or Unstan): A Stalled Cairn (283117)

On the promontory is an example of the other type of chambered cairn found in Orkney. This is a stalled cairn, whose long rectangular chamber was divided into segments by vertical stone slabs protruding from the walls. The chamber is 15m long, leading off from a 6m-long entrance passage, and is divided into five sets of stalls. Other stones projecting from the side walls suggest that the stalls may have been divided horizontally into smaller compartments, presumably as a kind of charnel house to hold bones.

The tip of the peninsula (283118) has been fortified by two lines of ramparts and ditches enclosing an area of 1.5 acres. Early groups of Viking raiders are known to have started wintering in Orkney by fortifying headlands of this sort, a process which they termed 'nessnam'—literally 'ness (promontory) taking'. More recently, however, it has been appreciated that such promontory forts are similar in character to the outworks surrounding many brochs in Orkney and Shetland, and to groups of forts outside the Northern Isles in areas like Caithness, Forfarshire, Berwickshire, Galloway and the Isle of Man. They are now thought to belong to the early Iron Age rather than the Viking period.

Return to your car. Retrace your route back to the Ring of Brodgar and follow the B9055 on past the Loch of Skaill to the coast. Stop at the car park on the right-hand side of the Bay of Skaill.

Between the Loch of Stenness and the Bay of Skaill you pass through typical Orkney farming country. The farmsteads and field patterns are too regular to suggest any great antiquity. Agriculture and the rural landscape were thoroughly modernised during the 19th century. The pattern of square, regular fields enclosed by drystone walls and many of the solid-looking farmsteads date from this time. They replaced a landscape which was not unlike that of much of the Scottish Lowlands in which farms were clustered together in small hamlets surrounded by open arable fields and common pastures. The fragmented farms with their lands scattered and intermingled in innumerable strips and parcels were consolidated and new steadings built in the middle of compact, reorganised holdings. Many farms were amalgamated to create larger units. The commons were divided between the various estates, and much rough pasture was ploughed up to create new farms. Orkney farms were often small by the standards of the Lowlands but they were much larger than the crofts of the West Highlands, large enough to be viable and prosperous. The small holding size was partly the legacy of the Norse system of landholding known as odal tenure. This was a freehold tenure without feudal obligations. Odallers' rights extended from the lowest stone on the seashore to the highest stone on the hill, giving each farm a share of seaweed for fertilising the arable land, and access to the hill pastures. Odal tenure involved the division of land between all surviving heirs on the death of the odaller, and this tended to keep holdings small and fragmented. After Scotland annexed Orkney, odal tenure was phased out and replaced by ordinary leasehold, but it continued to survive in some areas like the parish of Harray, east of the Loch of Harray. Here the fields are smaller and less regular than in Sandwick, the parish through which you are driving.

6. Place Names and the Settlement of Orkney

The Norse settlement of Orkney was so dense that modern Orkney place names derive overwhelmingly from Old Norse or the later Orcadian dialect which incorporated many Norse words. Very few of the earlier Celtic names have survived. Place names help to show how the Norse colonisation of Orkney occurred, allowing us to distinguish early centres of influence and power from places which were marginal and were only settled at a later date. These different phases of settlement can be seen around the Bay of Skaill and between here and the final part of the trail at Birsay. Try picking out the appropriate settlement names on the map and comparing them with their situation in the landscape.

Certain types of name characterised the earliest settlements from the late 8th and 9th centuries. The name 'skaill' which is attached to the bay and the impressive house on its southern side derives from the Old Norse 'skali' originally referring to the large timber hall of an important chieftain. All Orkney skaill names for which there is early documentary evidence were the most important farms of their districts. Another early place-name element was 'bu' from a word meaning 'farmstead' or 'estate'. This name also became attached to the principal house of an area so that Skaill House was originally the 'bu of Skaill'. In its earliest form 'bu' was used to describe the fortified promontory camps of early raiding parties. A third early settlement name element is 'by', another Old Norse term for a farmstead.

Around these early, important settlements groups of dependent farms were established by the followers of the original leader. The Bu of Skaill had some twenty dependent farms. Many places from this phase of settlement have names ending in 'garth' (enclosure), 'land' and 'bister' (farm). Modern farms with these names are usually sited fairly centrally within their parishes on good-quality land and were probably established before the end of the 9th century.

A slightly later type of name ends in 'ston' (a dwelling place or farm). These places are thought to have been established at the time of the creation of the Earldom of Orkney, after the first main phases of settlement. On the Mainland of Orkney these 'ston' names are scattered in a belt of country inland between the two centres of the earldom at Birsay and Orphir. They are thought to relate to land which was granted by the first earls to their followers at a time when all the coastal sites were already occupied. Can you locate any of these 'ston' names on the map?

Names ending in 'quoy' are even later: from the 10th century onwards. In later Orkney dialect a quoy was simply an enclosure, but originally it meant a farm carved out of the waste on the margins of settlement. Even today the quoy farms are characteristically small and often lie high against the moorland edge.

You can see something of this sequence round the Bay of Skaill. The original settlement, which became a very large farm, is at the head of the bay. The earliest dependent settlements are located at the far end of the Loch of Skaill because most of the lowland between the loch and the sea was part of the Bu. These farms mostly have 'garth' names. On the higher ground south-west of the loch is an area known as Southerquoy, on a steep north-facing slope which would only have been attractive once the better ground below was already settled. Further north around Marwick you can see the same pattern. The skaill is on low ground at the head of the bay, and a line of farms with quoy names runs along the slopes of Marwick head above the bay.

7. Skaill House (234186)

Skaill House has a complicated plan with three parallel blocks joined by a range at right angles forming an E-shape with another block enclosing a courtyard on the east side. The central block with its crowstepped gables is the oldest part of the house, dating from the 17th century. The rest of the house is 18th and 19th century in date. The home farm attached to Skaill House extends to some 900 acres and is one of the largest in Orkney, reflecting the importance of Skaill as an estate centre in earlier times.

8. Skara Brae: A Neolithic Settlement (231187)

A short distance beyond Skaill House, close to the high water mark, stands the famous settlement of Skara Brae. The site was discovered in 1850 after a storm had blown away the sand which had buried it. Early excavations led archaeologists to believe that it was comparatively recent in date—around 500 B.C—but recent radiocarbon dates place it around 3,100 B.C. for the first phase of occupation, roughly contemporary with the building of Maes Howe, and about 2,500 B.C. for the remains which can be seen today: almost contemporary with the henges at the Loch of Stenness. The settlement was thus occupied for a long period but only traces of the earliest dwellings have survived below the houses which are visible now. The site consists of nine closely-grouped stone houses laid out on either side of a passageway roofed with stone slabs which allowed people to move from hut to hut under cover. The entire settlement became buried by a midden of domestic rubbish thrown out by the occupants. The debris accumulated to the height of the tops of the walls and covered the passageways so that from a distance only the roofs of the huts would have stuck up above it. If this sounds insanitary, at least it protected the settlement from the elements. One hut, at the western end on the far side of a small paved courtyard, seems to have been a kitchen-cum-workshop; flakes of flint and chert on the floor indicated tool-making, piles of clay suggested pottery-turning, and round heat-cracked stones, warmed in a fire and used as pot boilers to heat liquids, hinted at communal cooking. In other huts the remains of stone furniture can be seen: dressers, seats, hearths, clay-lined pits possibly for preserving shellfish, cupboards and rectangular

Interior of Neolithic house, Skara Brae

arrangements of slabs which may have been beds. None of these would have survived had they been made of timber, as would have been normal in most places. The settlement seems to have been abandoned in a hurry, perhaps during a storm. In the doorway of one hut a cluster of stone beads was found with others scattered down the passageway, suggesting that one of the inhabitants had broken a necklace while making a hasty exit. The settlement was then buried by sand, although there was some intermittent re-occupation of the site before it was finally overwhelmed.

Skara Brae is unique in the quality of its preservation, though smaller sites with similar types of huts have also been found at Rinyo in Rousay and Knap of Howar on Papa Westray. This uniqueness makes the site difficult to explain. Was it typical of the kind of settlement inhabited by Neolithic peasants, save that it was built in stone rather than turf and timber? This was the interpretation of Professor V.G. Childe, the original excavator in the 1930s, who envisaged the inhabitants living a simple existence herding sheep and cattle and collecting shellfish. On the other hand some of the finds of pottery and stone ceremonial objects indicated contact with communities over a wide area. Dr. Euan MacKie has pointed out that the quality of the construction and furnishings of the huts is quite high, even by the standards of much later times.

He has re-interpreted Skara Brae as the home of one of the groups of priests associated with the chambered tombs and the henge monuments (although the settlement is rather far from the main group at Stenness). This would explain the communal kitchen and also one of the huts which could be barred from the outside; MacKie suggested that this might have been a cell for meditation. Certainly the diet of the inhabitants, as reconstructed from the bones in the midden, was very different from that of other (admittedly later) sites where the amount of game consumed was substantial. At Skara Brae the bones were almost entirely of domestic animals, which MacKie believed represented tribute from the surrounding farming communities. Until more Neolithic sites are discovered and excavated either interpretation may be valid, but this does show how the same evidence can be interpreted in contrasting ways by different people. We must also beware of comparing too closely with our own the lifestyles of people who lived in the past, particularly the distant past. By our standards even the wealthiest of prehistoric and medieval people would have led a squalid, insanitary and dangerous life.

Return to your car and follow the B9056 north to its junction with the A967 at the Loch of Boardhouse. Turn left and stop.

9. Oxtro Broch (254268)

Orkney has a dense concentration of brochs (see Trail 16). The most complete example is at Gurness on the Mainland opposite Rousay, but Oxtro is more typical of the many ruined brochs which have been heavily robbed for later building. It was cleared of turf in the 19th century, exposing its structure, and you can make out the 4m-thick wall and the central courtyard within. The mound marked 'Saebar Howe' on the map at 245270 is probably another broch but it has not been explored.

10. Boardhouse Mills (255275)

Birsay was always considered to be the most fertile part of the Mainland because shell sand from the bay provided an ideal fertiliser. The district produced oats and bere (a hardy form of barley), and the Point of Buckquoy forming the northern edge of the bay derives its name from 'bere-quoy' (an enclosure for barley). This impressive group of mills, which is open to the public, emphasises the importance of cereal cultivation in Orkney in the past. The large three-storey mill dates from 1873 and was powered by a 4.5m-diameter water wheel. The other two mills date from the late 18th and early 19th centuries.

Turn left at the junction with the A966. Follow the A966 to the sea and turn right. There is a car park at 248281).

11. Birsay Parish Church (247277)

Most of Orkney's parish churches are fairly recent, having been built after the Reformation to replace the earlier chapels which were usually close to the bu of the district. Birsay church dates from 1644 though it incorporates additions and alterations from the 18th and 19th centuries. A 13th-century window in the south wall hints at an earlier structure. Recent research has indicated that there was a bishop's palace, in use in the 16th century, close to this site, some remains of which could still be seen in the 18th century. There was also a medieval church of some size, the foundations of which lay just to the east of the present building. This seems to have been larger than any other medieval church in Orkney apart from St. Magnus' Cathedral in Kirkwall and is likely to have been the site of the Christchurch established in the 11th century of Earl Thorfinn as the seat of the bishopric of Orkney.

12. Birsay: The Earl's Palace (249278)

The earldom of Orkney was established by King Harald Fairhair of Norway who granted it to Rognvald of More, one of his principal followers. After 1468, when Orkney was incorporated into the rest of Scotland, the earldom continued to survive until James V annexed it to the crown. In 1564 Mary, Queen of Scots, granted the crown lands in Orkney to her half-brother, Robert Stewart, an illegitimate son of James V. In 1581 Robert Stewart became Earl of Orkney but he had already, around 1574, begun the building of this imposing palace. It was laid out around three sides of a rectangular courtyard which was open to the north. Twenty or thirty years later this side was closed in by an additional range of buildings. The palace is badly ruined and its internal layout is not always clear, but its scale emphasises the power of the Stewart Earls of Orkney who were tyrants within their territory, almost beyond the control of the crown. If Robert was a notorious oppressor of the ordinary Orkney folk, his son Patrick was even worse. It was Patrick who built the architecturally more sophisticated palace at Kirkwall in 1607. His misdeeds eventually caught up with him and he was imprisoned in 1609. After inciting his son Robert to try to recover Orkney by force he was executed in 1615.

13. Buckquoy (243282)

This site was excavated by Dr. Anna Ritchie in 1970–1. It provided evidence of the link between Pictish and Norse settlement in Orkney. Three successive Pictish houses from the 7th and 8th centuries were discovered. The two earliest ones consisted of central chambers surrounded by a series of small rounded cells: five in the earliest house, three in the later one. The third Pictish house was more sophisticated and impressive. It comprised a large oval chamber with a smaller circular one attached, producing a figure-of-eight appearance. The main hall of the building had a central hearth, and the area round the walls was divided into sections by drystone pillars. The design was moving towards that of a rectangular Norse house, though it is uncertain whether this indicates direct Norse influence. Similar figure-of-eight houses have been found in Caithness and North Uist. This house was abandoned, apparently peacefully, and was partly overlain by a sequence of three rectangular Norse buildings at right angles to the final Pictish house. These Norse structures probably all related to the earliest phase of settlement in the 9th century because some time after they were abandoned a pagan burial, with finds dated to the third quarter of the 10th century, was inserted into the overgrown mound of the last building. Most of the finds from the Norse houses were of local origin, suggesting that there had been a relatively peaceful admixture of Pict and Norseman and that the Norse settlement of Orkney had not entirely been one of pillage and plunder.

14. Brough of Birsay (239825)

This classic site has a complex sequence of remains spanning six centuries of occupation in Pictish and especially Norse times: The remains form three clusters: first, the church of St. Peter, its cemetery and associated buildings; second, the complex of Norse buildings between the church and the cliff; and third, the scatter of individual buildings on the slope above the church.

The island is cut off from the mainland for three hours before and after high tide. It is essential to check the time of high water before crossing the causeway to make sure you are not marooned. The island has low cliffs to the west but slopes gently towards the mainland, and the settlement remains are scattered across the eastern end.

The earliest features which have been discovered are a Pictish cemetery with a curving wall, underlying the rectangular Norse cemetery. The wall can be seen in the south-east corner of the Norse cemetery and outside its east wall. This was probably an early-Christian monastic site dating from a 6th-century mission by followers of St. Kentigern. There are indications of a building which may have been a church under the south wall of the nave of the Norse church which is the main visible structure here. The remains of Pictish graves can be seen as slabs sunk into the ground marking the position of stone coffins. The later Norse graves are more upstanding and mostly lie south and east of the church.

It was originally believed that St. Peter's church dated from around 1050, having been built by Earl Thorfinn, after his pilgrimage to Rome, as the seat of the bishopric of Orkney. More recently it has been re-assessed as an early 12th-century building, and it is now thought that Thorfinn's Christchurch was on the adjacent mainland. The church on the Brough has a rectangular nave and square chancel with an apse end. A tower at the western end was planned but never finished. In the centre of the nave a grave was discovered. It was once thought that the skeleton inside was that of Earl Thorfinn himself, but the re-location of his church on the Mainland rather than on the Brough makes this less likely.

Immediately north of the church is a range of buildings which has been interpreted as a bishop's palace, a monastic cloister, or a large farmstead. The later phases of these buildings may date from the 15th century. The bishopric of Orkney, centred on the Brough, was established early in the 12th century. The layout of the buildings resembles that of the bishop's residence at Gardar in Greenland, but the function of these buildings remains uncertain.

West of the church and its associated buildings, on the edge of the cliff, is a complex of buildings which have been interpreted as an early hall with turf walls and an outer facing of stone, possibly belonging to Earl Sigurd, who was killed at the Battle of Clontarf in 1014. On top of it is a series of buildings including a stone-walled hall which was probably the palace of Earl Thorfinn, contemporary with the church. It is hard to make out the layout of individual buildings because so many phases are superimposed: structures from the 12th century overlie Earl Thorfinn's 11th-century palace. At the cliff edge a paved ramp or slipway may have been used for drawing up boats.

Above the church on the hillside there is a scatter of buildings only some of which have been excavated. They seem to have been farmsteads, some relating to the earliest phase of Norse settlement in the 9th and 10th centuries, some of them later in date.

The trail ends here, but if you have more time to spend in Orkney you may wish to explore the many interesting sites which we have not had space to cover. Kirkwall in particular is an interesting place to spend a day.

Some Suggested Reading

The physical landscape

J.B. Whittow. *Geology and scenery in Scotland*. London 1977

Archaeology

E.W. MacKie. *Scotland: an archaeological guide*. London 1975
E.W. MacKie. *The megalith builders*. London 1977
G. & A. Ritchie. *Scotland: archaeology and early history*. London 1985

Historical Background

T.C. Smout. *A history of the Scottish people 1560-1830*. London 1972
D. Turnock. *The historical geography of Scotland since 1707*. London 1982
G. Whittington & I.D. Whyte (eds.). *An historical geography of Scotland*. London 1983

Place Names

W.F.H. Nicolaisen *Scottish place names*. London 1976

The Countryside

R.A. Dodgshon. *Land and society in early Scotland*. Oxford 1981
A. Fenton. *Scottish country life*. Edinburgh 1976
R. Muir. *The Shell guide to reading the Celtic landscapes*. London 1985
M.L. Parry & T.R. Slater (eds.). *The making of the Scottish countryside*. London 1980

Buildings

S. Cruden. *Scottish abbeys.* Edinburgh 1960
S. Cruden. *The Scottish castle.* London 1981
J.G. Dunbar. *The historic architecture of Scotland.* London 1978
R. Fawcett. *Scottish medieval churches.* Edinburgh 1985
A. Fenton & B. Walker. *The rural architecture of Scotland.* Edinburgh 1981
R.J. Naismith. *Buildings of the Scottish countryside.* London 1985
N. Tranter. *The fortified house in Scotland.* Edinburgh 1962-70

Industrial Archaeology

J.R. Hume. *The industrial archaeology of Scotland. I. The Lowlands and Borders.* London 1976
J.R. Hume. *The industrial archaeology of Scotland. II. The Highlands and Islands.* London 1977

The Towns

C. McWilliam. *Scottish townscape.* London 1975
I.H. Adams. *The making of urban Scotland.* London 1978

Index